Exploring Caves

Exploring Caves:

A Guide to the Underground Wilderness

DAVID R. McCLURG

Stackpole Books

Exploring Caves: A Guide to the Underground Wilderness

Copyright © 1980 by David R. McClurg

Published by
STACKPOLE BOOKS
Cameron and Kelker Streets
P.O. Box 1831
Harrisburg, Pa. 17105

Published simultaneously in Don Mills, Ontario, Canada by Thomas Nelson & Sons, Ltd.

Photos by David R. McClurg

Printed in the U.S.A.

Library of Congress Cataloging in Publication Data

McClurg, David R
    Exploring caves.

    Bibliography: p.
    Includes index.
    1. Caving. 2. Caving—Equipment and supplies.
I. Title.
GV200.62.M3 1980   796.5'25   80-14524
ISBN 0-8117-2083-7 (pbk.)

Contents

Preface

This book describes the equipment and techniques needed to explore caves safely and responsibly. It explains how to go caving without injuring yourself or damaging the cave's fragile contents. Both beginning and advanced techniques are included.

A word of caution: No book by itself can teach you caving. To learn properly, practice and experience in the actual underground environment with a group of experienced explorers is essential. Caving is strenuous and requires good physical conditioning.

Above all, never go caving alone. It's far too dangerous, even for experienced cavers.

My wife and I are active cavers with over twenty years experience in horizontal and vertical caves. Rather than surveying all techniques, we have concentrated on the equipment and methods that we and other active cavers have proven effective in regular field use.

When my earlier book, *Amateur's Guide to Caves and Caving*, was written (in the early 1970s), caving was in a state of transition. Many specialized types of equipment—ascenders, rappel racks, caving ropes—were just emerging, as were the techniques for their proper use. Since then, things have pretty much settled down.

What has changed is the degree of interest in caving. Some observers predict that caving is on the brink of a population explosion like that experienced by climbing and backpacking in the 1960s and 1970s. If that comes about, it is my hope that this new book will play a part in directing new cavers toward safe and environmentally responsible caving.

Acknowledgements

The knot drawings in chapter 8 are by Bruce Rogers of Palo Alto, California. The battery charger circuit in chapter 7 is by John Tinsley of Menlo Park, California. The information about heat cutters for ropes was provided by John de Boer of Concord, California.

I would like to thank the National Speleological Society and the following persons for comments, suggestions, and answers to questions: Robert Addis, John de Boer, Evelyn Bradshaw, John Cooper, Rane Curl, James Dawson, Mike Dyas, David Des Marais, Ian Ellis, William Harter, Steve Hudson, Stephen Knutson, Charlie and Jo Larson, George Moore, Neal Morris, Donna Mroczkowski, J.R. Newell, Thomas Rea, Douglas Rhodes, Bruce Rogers, Ray Smutek, Robert Stitt, Robert Thrun, John Tinsley, and Eugene Vehslage. Perhaps because my earlier book was one of the first widely distributed books on American caving techniques, it received a good deal of comment. Much of this has been extremely helpful in preparing this new book. My apologies to the many others far too numerous to list who also contributed to the preparation of this book.

Finally, I want to thank my constant caving companion, my wife Janet, and our children Rachel, Dai, and Molly, who are pictured in many of the illustrations.

1

Exploring the Underground Wilderness

Cave exploring is not thrill seeking or defying danger for danger's sake. It is probing the unknown—going into an underground wilderness where few have ventured before.

In the silent darkness, none of us could see the yawning mouth of the pit. Nevertheless, we knew it was there, just a few feet down the abrupt slope. A slip on this mud-greased roller coaster and you would hit the lake 110 feet below in less than 3½ seconds. And a few minutes later, as the surface became placid once more, the lake's 70-foot depth would almost certainly claim its first victim.

"Are you ready?"

"Yes."

"Then go ahead."

As I checked my rappel rigging, my eye followed the course of the 7/16-inch, rock-climbing rope snaking its way over the carabiner brake bars that would allow me to glide on down safely. I glanced at my two companions. One sat perched in a small nest-like rock enclosure, the other clung to a knob at the

Fig. 1–1. Rappelling (roped descent) in a Yugoslavian cave.

edge of the slope. Both were securely tied into a safety line. Their job was to guide personnel and equipment down the slope into the pit. The 48-degree temperature and near 100 percent humidity had chilled them and they were glad for a little activity.

It was quiet and dark. Time seemed to have stopped. Even our breathing was soft and measured.

Then it happened.

A small rock under my left foot, previously tested and thought to be lodged securely in the soft mud, skidded sickeningly down toward the pit. I skidded right after it.

At a time like this, the proper signal according to our mountaineering friends is "Falling." However, my voice, along with the rest of me, was temporarily paralyzed. A long second later, the safety line around my chest tightened and the belayer 45 feet above at the cave entrance stopped my fall.

My two companions automatically checked their own tie-in slings and their safety line.

"What the hell happened?" shouted a voice from above.

"Just a slip on the mud slope," I answered. "Nothing to worry about."

And indeed, it wasn't anything to worry about because we had adhered to our own inflexible rule: Never work on a muddy slope without a belay.

In today's caving world, most of us forgo a safety line when rappelling in a cave. Even though unbelayed rappelling is now generally considered safe, our rule governing that muddy slope took precedence and turned what could have been a serious accident into little more than a nasty scare.

With the crisis past, I descended into the cool darkness without incident. Only the whisper of the rope as it slid over and under the brake bars accompanied me down to a safe landing at the edge of the lake 110 feet below.

That incident occurred several years ago. It taught me rather forcefully that good technique, proper training, and experienced companions are the foundations on which safe and sane caving is constructed.

Since then my interest and love of caving has been paralleled by a deep sense of responsibility to teach safe caving and to help new cavers develop an awareness of conservation.

What is it like in a cave? Caves are not all like Mammoth Cave or Carlsbad Caverns with huge rooms, smooth trails, and tunnels large enough for a subway train to speed through. The fact is, many caves are small, wet, and short. They have walking passages, crawlways, streams, narrow fissures, lakes, canyons, muddy slopes, arches, waterfalls, pits, and domes. You walk on floors covered with jagged rocks and stones, crawl through mud, climb on sharp rock and breakdown slabs, slosh through running streams, scramble up and down slippery slopes, negotiate tricky pits, or experience any combination of these in succession.

Caving Hazards

Besides slippery slopes and deep pits, what other hazards do cavers run into? How about getting lost? It would seem that losing your way in the labyrinth of interconnecting passages that make up many caves would be pretty easy. Surprisingly, it is not. It turns out that cavers seldom get lost, although most of us will admit to being momentarily confused at times. Normally at least one fellow caver has been paying enough attention, so you are seldom lost for long.

No seasoned caver ever caves alone. Two, or preferably three, other experienced explorers are a minimum. Put another way, beginners should seek out an organized group before they go rushing off to a cave.

My first maxim in training beginning cavers is that going caving alone is very dangerous. Nothing will get you into trouble quicker than entering a cave alone with a flashlight and a ball of string: the flashlight to see with, and the ball of string to lead you back out.

As you'll soon realize, the string is worthless because it's only a few hundred feet long and anyone would have a hard time getting lost in a cave that short. As for light, one flashlight—in fact only one of any kind of light—just isn't enough. Always take three sources of light. A spare flashlight plus candles and matches would meet the bare minimum, but spare batteries will put you a notch up on the safety scale and improve your chances of surviving a mishap. So will two or three companions similarly equipped.

Getting stuck is probably the next most horrifying situation noncavers worry about. Actually, this can be a real problem depending on your physical dimensions. It is very seldom, though, that people get really stuck to the point where they can't get out without help. Still, claustrophobia is one thing that plagues even experienced cavers from time to time. The fear of walls closing in on you can become a very powerful and real thing. Fortunately most squeezes are blessedly short.

Fig. 1–2. Not all caves have entrances big enough to walk into. Here, a caver squeezes through an 11-inch high opening.

(See chapter 10 for some specific recommendations on getting through tight places.)

Then there are water and mud. Getting covered with mud is bad enough, but getting soaked with water carries with it the possibility of hypothermia. Flooding is also an extreme danger. Beware of caves with active streams when the weather threatens.

Caving is not for everyone. If you suffer from claustrophobia or acrophobia, or if you believe that cleanliness in all things at all times is next to godliness, then maybe the tight crawls, dark pits, and muddy wetness will deter you. If so, don't despair. Get your underground kicks from visiting commercial caves. That's what cavers do when they want to see some of the most beautiful caves of all.

A word about courtesy when visiting a commercial or show cave. Do the owner a favor and don't stray off the tour route. It can be just as dangerous caving alone in a show cave as in a wild one. Save those exploring instincts for caving with an organized group in a wild cave. And, if you're an experienced caver, don't ask a lot of questions or tease the guides. Just pretend you're a tourist and enjoy the scenery.

Why is it that people go caving at all? What brings them to subject themselves to agonies which would cause an Inquisition torturer to rub his hands in glee?

In my case, the first impulse that carried me into wild or noncommercial caves was simply a desire to probe the unknown, to see something not too many other people had seen. I knew it could be beautiful underground from having been in commercial caves, but that didn't propel me, at least not at first.

Call it a sense of adventure if you like, but I draw the line at labeling cave exploration as thrill seeking. Most cavers derive satisfaction from acknowledging danger and devising ways to overcome it. But skirting along the cutting edge of danger is not the objective—seeking the unknown is.

I could perhaps explain it best by telling you that one of the most frequent activities on any cave trip is checking for leads to new passages. When doing this, the question cavers ask is, "Does it go?" Translated into plain English, this means true cavers never want the cave to end. We always hope that around the next twist in the crawlway will be a new passage that will go for a few hundred yards at least, if not a half mile or more, and carry us into the caves beyond where no one has trod before.

2

Conservation

Misuse of the fragile underground wilderness can destroy irreplaceable works of natural beauty that took millions of years to create.

Conservation is a lot more than a convenient list of dos and don'ts. It is a state of mind—a belief that some natural features of this earth are worth saving because they help us know more about ourselves and broaden our increasingly narrow view of nature.

Caves are especially fragile. Underground beauty that took millions of years to develop can be destroyed in seconds by the thoughtless or accidental acts of cavers and noncavers alike. Please keep this in mind. Every beginning caver must be ready to join with others in observing the simple conservation practices needed to save caves. If you are not willing to make this personal commitment, it would probably be better for you to forget about cave exploration. There is no doubt that the caves of the world, limited as they are in number, will not be able to handle the increased traffic of new cavers unless these

Fig. 2–1. The magic and mystery of underground exploration are experienced by a caver standing at the threshold of this heavily decorated chamber.

cavers are fully committed to preserving the underground wilderness.

In caving, we have added a twist to the familiar slogan of other conservationists.

Take nothing but pictures.

Leave nothing but footprints (but only on established trails).

Kill nothing but time.

Conservation Precepts

Inside a cave, the rules of conservation are simple. Don't *leave* anything and don't *take* anything. This means don't leave behind candy wrappers, tin cans, spent carbide, or dead batteries. Instead, take them home and throw them in your own garbage can. Also, don't take your carbide or batteries out of the cave only to dump them outside on a farmer's land. Animals have died from this thoughtless act.

Don't remove any speleothems or cave formations, such as stalactites or stalagmites. It doesn't matter if they are already broken off. If you want a record of a particular formation, take a picture of it. Even broken speleothems can tell a story that a geologist can interpret. The same goes for leaves, tree branches, and other organic materials. Natural cave debris is actually a vital link in the ecological chain.

The entrance area just outside a cave is often a common dumping ground for broken speleothems that somehow didn't seem as pretty in the daylight as they did in the cave. It's the same with stream pebbles. Their glistening underwater beauty disappears when they dry out in the sun.

Remember, if you break a formation, you're destroying it forever. To a speleologist, a vandalized cave is like a museum in which a madman has broken all the display cases, scattered the contents all over the floor, and even ruined the walls with names and obscenities.

When you come to a fragile area be careful, particularly on the way out when you are tired. If any damage could occur, try to choose an alternate route. Stay on established trails and be careful not to bump into walls or ceiling since many speleothems are accidentally destroyed in this way.

Don't collect animal or plant life in caves except under the specific direction of a scientist. He or she will provide the proper containers and outline the correct methods of handling so the sample will have value. If you find something you think would be of interest, tell a speleologist about it first. A specimen may already be on record, and taking another could upset the delicate life chain in the cave unnecessarily. As a safety note, never handle a bat, especially one found lying on the floor. It could be sick.

Several years ago, it was common to smoke arrows on the walls of caves with carbide lamps indicating the way out of junction rooms or confusing places. No responsible caver marks a cave wall any more with arrows, names, or anything else. In complex mazes bring along Scotchlite arrows or other brightly colored trail markers that can be removed upon departure.

Cave conservation is a must, for if cavers who visit the caves the most don't preserve them, then no one else will. Those delicate soda straws and elf-like gypsum flowers, those blind fish, insect-devouring bats, and pure white salamanders will become as extinct as the pterodactyl.

Conservation Project: A Cave Cleanup. An excellent project is to clean up a local cave. Select one that has had a lot of local traffic and has been pretty badly trashed up. You may be surprised to learn that if people find a cave clean when they

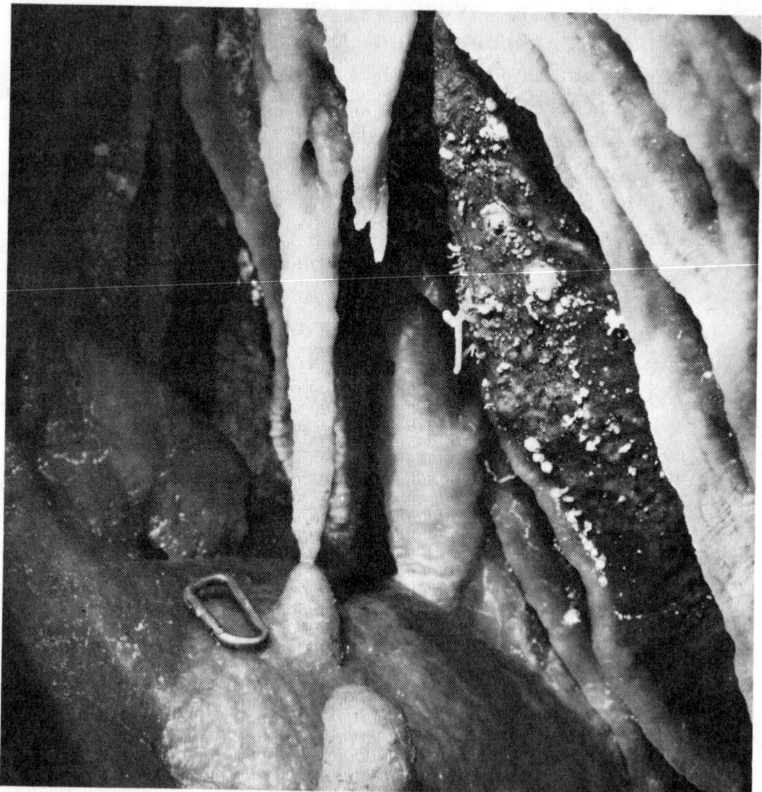

Fig. 2–2. Fragile beauty that took millions of years to create can be destroyed in seconds.

visit it (or a park or whatever) they are much more inclined to leave it clean when they leave. However, if it's already a mess, they assume that nobody cares, so they tend to toss their trash on the ground too.

We recently conducted a cleanup of a well-visited local cave as a lesson in cave conservation. Armed with heavy-duty plastic bags, garden trowels (to fish out broken glass), and a couple of small shovels, eighteen of us descended on this cave. Three hours later we had collected 179 pounds of trash! A lot of the weight was broken beer bottles, but I believe we found just about every other kind of trash, too. When we were done, it actually looked almost beautiful again, particularly the entrance room which had suffered the most.

We also cleaned a few speleothems, but in that category we take off our hard hats to cavers in the southwest for the fine restoration job they did in Fort Stanton Cave, New Mexico. The description in the *NSS News* (Rhodes 1976) not only makes rewarding reading but also contains some excellent tips on how to do it.

They recommend nylon bristle scrub brushes, a garden sprayer (well-flushed to remove any residual insecticides), and hydrochloric acid (in a weak 5 to 10 percent solution) in a spray bottle. Lye and paint remover are not advised because they are harmful to the cave environment. Hydrochloric acid is reasonably safe if handled with care and will remove about 75 percent of cave graffiti. Plain water can also be effective all by itself, especially if under pressure as in a garden sprayer.

Before embarking on a cleanup involving the use of chemicals, it would be wise to consider the impact on the cave environment. To be safe, consult with a biologist to be sure no harm will be done to cave animals. Also, before removing all cave graffiti, evaluate the historical significance of names and dates from earlier periods.

3

Cave Safety

The danger in caves is very real, but proper equipment, training, experienced companions, and a good safety attitude can reduce the risks.

Caving can be dangerous, there is no doubt about that. But it is also true that caving is only as dangerous as you make it. A properly trained and equipped caver is usually safer underground than a careless or tired driver on the highway.

Caving requires teamwork. This is another way of saying that the first rule of safe caving is *don't cave alone*. A relatively minor accident when in the company of an experienced group, such as a twisted ankle, a failing light, or a fall into a stream, could be much more serious to a solo caver. There is no doubt the potential risk of injury is very high when you enter a cave alone, especially for the neophyte who only has a flashlight.

Danger is always present in caves, just as it is in rock climbing, sailing, scuba diving, or hang gliding. To some, this aspect of caving is one of its main attractions. But no one courts danger deliberately. Rather, by good technique, training, and equipment, danger can be overcome. It is this fact that provides deep satisfaction to many cavers.

Choosing the Safer Alternative. Just as you automatically choose the alternative action that helps conserve caves, so must you always select the alternative that is the safer one when possible. This kind of awareness and attitude about safety translates into three basic rules: always take three sources of light, cave with companions, and leave word as to where you're going.

Ask yourself when confronted with a decision: Which is the safer alternative? In many cases the stakes are infinite because a human life is involved. So, always think first, then choose the safer way to do it.

Four Cavers Minimum. What is the minimum number for a safe cave trip? Many once considered three experienced cavers as the minimum, but four is safer. In case of an accident, four cavers are needed so that one can stay with the injured caver (assuming only one was injured), while the other two go for help. Remember, when help is needed, the same never-cave-alone rule should still apply. Furthermore, two can usually deliver a more complete and coherent description of the accident than one can.

Leaving Word. When going off on a cave trip, always tell a responsible person about your plans. Include the name and location of the cave, what parts you plan to visit, and when you expect to come out. Allow an hour or two leeway on the exit time. It never hurts to come out early, but somehow when a caving party meets its rescuers determinedly slugging their way in on a mission of pure mercy, the would-be saviors never see the humor of the situation.

A good person to leave word with is the cave owner or caretaker at the time their permission is sought. If no one is home, leave a note (if standing permission to enter the cave has been granted). It's a good idea to tell someone back home too, like your family or a fellow caver. No matter who it is, be explicit about plans (and any likely changes in plans due to weather or other contingencies). In this way, rescuers, if any are needed, can find the group with a minimum of time and effort.

Lost? Getting lost in caves is a much rarer occurrence than you might think, but nearly every caver (or at least every honest one) will admit to having been "momentarily confused" once or twice in complex cave systems. The best way to keep track of the route is to turn around regularly and see what the passage looks like coming the other way. Sounds simple, but it works (see chapter 4).

Entering a New Cave. When you are with a group that is the first to enter a recently discovered cave or section of an older cave, remember that the thrill of discovery can have its dark side, too. Passages previously unvisited may have some unstable rocks or small boulders wedged between larger breakdown that can be knocked loose. Floyd Collins (a solo caver, by the way) was trapped by a 50-pound rock that he dislodged while exploring a new cave and died of hypothermia before he could be rescued (Miller 1942). So, in new areas, go slowly and quietly. Watch out, too, for floors of thin calcite under which the dirt or gravel has been washed away. They may be false floors many feet above the real floor level.

Remember also the responsibility of conservation. Choose routes carefully in new caves to cause as little damage as possible.

Hard Hats and Lights. No experienced caver ever goes underground without a good quality, impact-resistant hard hat equipped with a chin strap and light. (Both elastic and nonelastic chin straps are in use today. See chapter 7 for details.)

Three sources of light and spares are needed. Commonly these are a carbide or electric lamp on the helmet, a flashlight, candles and matches in a waterproof container, and a chemical lightstick light. Candles used to be the almost universal third source of light. But they are not very good unless you're sitting and resting. They get blown out too easily and are hard to carry when lit.

Some cavers carry three carbide lamps, or an electric head-lamp and two flashlights. The magic number is at least three. With whatever type of main light, always carry spares for twice the expected stay—extra carbide, water, and spare parts, or extra batteries and bulbs.

Underground Dangers

Mines. Never explore mines alone or with an experienced group. They can be extremely dangerous. Whereas caves were formed hundreds of thousands of years ago and have been subjected to countless earthquakes and similar forces, mines are only tens or at most hundreds of years old. Falling timbers, bad air (insufficient oxygen), passage collapse—these are a few of the ways to get yourself injured in a mine.

Cave Air. Unlike mines, where oxygen deficient air is common, it is estimated that less than 1 percent of caves have bad air (Breisch 1975). This is because air circulation is usually better in caves since many of them breathe on a regular cycle. But bad air can be encountered in small passages where the oxygen gets depleted by the cavers, or in cases where there are large quantities of decaying vegetation, pollution from nearby gasoline or chemical storage tanks, or thermal springs with high concentrations of carbon dioxide or hydrogen sulfide.

If anyone in the group seems to be unaccountably short of breath in a cave, the best thing to do is to leave that area fast. The effects of bad air are swift and deadly. Contrary to popular opinion, neither a carbide lamp nor a candle provides a good test. They will continue to burn after the danger point to humans is reached.

Underground Fires. Never light a fire underground. If hot food is desired, take along a Sterno kit or a small backpacking stove. Be sure to use it in a well-ventilated area. Large fires might ignite bat guano, which is flammable and explosive. One case is recorded of a fatal explosion and fire in a Texas cave. Besides, a fire uses up the air supply, produces deadly carbon monoxide, and pollutes the cave. Also, be careful of tumbleweed, dry brush, and leaves in the entrance, which can be easily ignited. Be cautious with the spent carbide in your pack, too. It may still be giving off some acetylene and, if you put it into a tightly sealed container, it has been known to explode (*American Caving Accidents*, 1971).

Cave Flooding. Stream passages in caves will often flood during the rainy season. This is a real danger in some parts of the country and the risk cannot be taken lightly. As a precaution, check the weather forecast before going caving. In particular, don't go into a cave with an active stream running in the entrance, or with a steep sinkhole entrance, if the skies are dark, or if it has rained a lot in the past few hours or days. Even though it may seem to be clearing up, the flood water may just be reaching the cave or passages you want to enter. Be especially wary about entering a stream passage with leaves and branches caught on rocks and ledges high up on the wall above your head. These undoubtedly indicate recent flooding.

When there is such a passage, be alert for any changes in air movement, rising stream or lake levels, increased noise from a stream, a sudden increase in the foam at the base of a waterfall, or increased debris and mud in the water. If any of these warning signs are observed, you need to act quickly. If you are just entering the area with water hazards and there are no streams or low-lying water passages on the way back to the entrance, the best choice may be to head out of the cave. If, however, the entrance has an active stream flowing into it or if there are other water hazards between you and the entrance, it's usually much safer to climb up into an upper passage above the stream level and wait it out. The water will likely recede in a matter of hours, so try to get comfortable and conserve your light and energy.

Old Ladders and Ropes. One word of caution which shouldn't be forgotten. Don't rely on old wooden ladders or natural-fiber ropes (manila, hemp, or sisal) found in a cave. The high humidity of caves is destructive to these materials. Bolts and other mechanical aids installed as anchors for technical climbing (see chapter 12) should be treated with caution unless you know their history. Even then, they should be

Fig. 3–1. Wading in cave streams is often required, and presents special hazards. In caves with active streams, be especially cautious during the rainy season. For safety in wet caves, woolen underclothing or a complete wet suit may be required to combat the dangers of hypothermia.

tested before use. As a corollary, you should generally avoid installing any permanent or semi-permanent ladders or rigging yourself. Leaving these kinds of fixtures in a cave invites accidents and liability problems. As a matter of fact, the National Speleological Society now encourages the removal of old vertical equipment.

Disease Hazards

Bats and Rabies. Bats, though often misunderstood and feared, are for the most part harmless creatures who are valuable friends to humankind. Some species consume gigantic quantities of insects, for example. Part of the general fear of bats stems from occasional reports of rabies-infected bats in various parts of North America. In this context, it is certainly worth noting that the state of California found in a 1977 study that only a small fraction (less than .5 percent) of seemingly normal bats were infected. This is a figure similar to that seen in recent studies of wild foxes and skunks (*California Bat Rabies Control Policy*, 1977).

Therefore, the chances of the average citizen being bitten by a sick bat are pretty small. Cavers, however, increase the risk since they regularly invade the bat's natural habitat. Also, rabies is a frightening disease because it is deadly and incurable once the symptoms have begun. Furthermore, even though you should never handle any bat, especially one lying on the floor since it could be sick, direct contact with a rabid animal is not necessary to contract rabies (Constantine 1967). It is possible to develop the disease from breathing the virus-laden air in those rare caves with extremely dense bat populations, an atmosphere heavily saturated with ammonia from the guano, poor air circulation, and high temperatures. However, in a normal cave, the occasional collision of bat and caver in a narrow passage or crawlway poses no real threat.

Preexposure Immunization. If you plan to visit caves that contain extensive bat colonies or large bat guano deposits, make local inquiries first with public health officials and cavers. In case rabid bats have been reported, you would do well to consider preexposure immunization (Reddell 1974).

A new type of duck embryo vaccine for preexposure immunization is now available from Ely Lilly and Company. Called Rabies Vaccine, USP, it is administered under supervision of a doctor in a series of three or four preexposure shots over a four month period. Side effects are minimal. To confirm protection, the presence of virus-neutralizing antibodies is checked by a titer test after the innoculations are completed. If the antibody level is not high enough a booster is administered. Protection lasts from one to two years and is easily confirmed by a titer test. More or less permanent immunity can be achieved by regular booster injections.

After immunization, only a single booster is usually required if you are exposed to rabies. Without this preexposure immunity, if you are absolutely certain you have been exposed, you must receive treatment immediately. There is a serum that can be administered with some hope of success, but only if the symptoms (which appear in five to ten days) haven't already begun. The problem is that the side effects of the serum on the nervous system are pretty severe even though it may save your life.

Clearly, if you plan to visit caves where rabies infection is possible, this simple new preexposure procedure is the only way to go. Our family, several members of our caving club, and many other cavers have taken the preexposure immunization shots with no problems at all.

Histoplasmosis. Histoplasmosis—a disease resembling mild pulmonary tuberculosis, though sometimes fatal—can be contracted from fungi found in the dust of caves in several parts of the country. If you are sensitive to lung disorders, make local inquiry for details.

Accidents and First Aid

Cave accidents, fortunately, are usually of a minor nature. The most common ones are sprained ankles, pulled muscles, scratches and bruises, and some degree of exhaustion. Serious cave accidents including deaths, are usually caused by drowning, falling into pits, loose rocks, hypothermia, and fire (Breisch 1976).

In general, cave accidents involve inexperienced people. Good cavers should know their own limitations and never exceed them, realizing that putting themselves in danger puts the entire group in danger. For this reason, cavers usually learn to watch themselves as well as the others for signs of exhaustion and hypothermia.

Knowing what you can and can't do is also essential to safe caving. As a beginner, you should never be afraid to say you want a belay (safety line) or don't feel you can make a certain climb. If you're tired or don't feel well that day, you shouldn't go in at all. Or, if already in the cave, you should tell the others. Reckless or inconsiderate cavers don't endanger just themselves, they are a menace to the whole group. If you should injure yourself by a careless move or a foolhardy stunt, it's the others who will end up caring for you and carrying you out—no small task in cave passages and pits. Caving is a team activity, and this includes knowing and never exceeding your limitations.

The best safety rule is: *don't hurt yourself.* All cavers are responsible to themselves to know their limitations and to take care of themselves properly when underground.

Accidents. Drowning in caves results from two distinct situations. The first, and by far the largest by a factor of ten, is accidents during scuba diving. From 1967 to 1975, scuba diving, mostly in Florida, accounted for more than one hundred reported deaths. The other main cause of drownings in caves is by flooding. In the same period, ten deaths from flooding were reported.

Injuries from cave-ins and falling rocks have been reported fifteen times in the 1967–75 period. These almost always occur during the first trips into new caves or new sections of known caves and are usually caused by the cavers themselves.

Falling into pits remains a major cause of cave accidents. Of the six cases reported each year to the NSS, the victim was not using a rope in about two-thirds of the accidents. Losing contact during roped descent (rappelling) accounted for most of the rest. Also, Breisch reports that an unusually large number of injuries are due to the use and failure of old ladders found in caves. Accidents from fire include asphyxiation from smoke plus minor burns from carbide lamps or improperly stored carbide supplies. Bad air, as we have indicated, is relatively rare in caves and is only a minor hazard.

Hypothermia—Killer of the Unprepared. Hypothermia (the preferred medical term—also called exposure or freezing to death) is one of the most dangerous and least understood hazards of caving. In fact, it has only been in the past decade that mountaineering and outdoor medical professionals have focused their attention on it. Some coroners still do not list it as a cause of death (Martin 1976).

Hypothermia has aptly been called the killer of the unprepared (Lathrop 1972). The common elements are cold, wetness (especially against the skin), and exhaustion. Make no mistake, it can be a real killer. And the cold, wet conditions in many northern latitude and high-elevation caves are almost perfect breeding grounds. Contrary to what you might think, it doesn't take freezing or subzero cold to cause hypothermia. Temperatures of 30 to 50 degrees F (−1 to 10 degrees C) are just as bad, especially if there is cold water against the skin.

Symptoms, which may not be noticed or recognized as dangerous by the victim, are uncontrolled shivering, lack of coordination, stumbling, slurred speech, weak or irregular pulse, a feeling of numbness, and a lack of willpower.

How can you prevent hypothermia? When preparing to explore cold, wet caves, select the proper clothing. A good choice would be several layers beginning with woolen underwear. Or, if you expect to get fully immersed in water, wear a wet suit. The idea is to avoid getting wet and to keep as warm and dry as possible. Whenever there is a choice between a wet and a dry passage, stay dry, especially on the way into the cave. Water conducts heat away from the body twenty-five times better than air. Avoid becoming overly fatigued. Eat a good meal before a strenuous trip and high energy snacks during the trip. Keep a positive mental attitude. This includes recognizing the dangers involved and being prepared for them.

If you get chilled, food can restore body heat to a small extent, particularly a warm drink like hot chocolate or tea (avoid alcohol). But it's far better to eat the proper food before getting cold in the first place. Remember that a full meal of familiar, easily-digested food is essential before any cave trip. It is mandatory before a trip to a wet cave.

Medically, hypothermia is a failure of the body's temperature-regulatory mechanism caused by prolonged activity, cold, exhaustion, and wetness on the body. It is essentially a condition where the body loses heat faster than it can replace it. The result is a downward spiral in which the temperature of the body core gets progressively lower, resulting in coma, then death.

Hypothermia can result from a severe soaking after a fall in a cold stream or being trapped under a waterfall. When you get wet, the immediate effect is cooling since the water replaces the air which provided an insulating barrier. Then, since water is a much better conductor of heat than air, it tends to divert body heat away from you much more quickly. The body responds by curbing circulation to the wet area and a state of shock can follow. This is why a wet suit is necessary for really nasty caves.

However, you don't have to get fully immersed in water to be in trouble. Continued exposure to cold and wetness, as on a long cave trip, can be dangerous, too. Their debilitating effects are cumulative and are accompanied by a loss in willpower and a desire to resist.

Treatment of Hypothermia. Treatment must be immediate. Further heat loss must be stopped, and heat added slowly to rewarm the victim's body (Lathrop 1973). Some specific suggestions for treatment of hypothermia, which could apply to any serious cave accident are:

1. Move the victim out of the water. This is a must. Handle gently, as you would someone with a broken neck (Bangs 1979).

2. Replace wet clothing with dry clothing.

3. Insulate the victim from the ground.

4. Move the victim away from the path of air currents and block currents with clothing and gear.

5. Try to keep the victim awake, but be gentle and don't encourage any movement or exercise.

6. Warm the victim slowly (rather than suddenly) with your down clothes, direct skin-to-skin body contact (as with the victim and another person in a sleeping bag), carbide lamps, or whatever. This may take from 20 minutes to an hour or more. Don't forget to keep the head warm, since the head and neck account for about half of the body heat lost by radiation. A scarf around the neck or head is a good idea. Keep the victim immobile until some signs of improvement are noted. Remember, and this is vital: you must not only prevent further loss of body heat, you must actually raise the victim's temperature before recovery can begin.

7. Do not leave the victim alone.

8. Do not give hot liquids by mouth.
9. Do not give alcohol.

Alcohol and Caving. Alcohol has no place in caving, either as a beverage to slake the thirst or as a stimulant to give to an injured person. As a beverage imbibed before or during a trip, it dulls the brain, slows the reflexes, and reduces mental concentration. More seriously, and this applies especially to an injured person, it opens the peripheral blood vessels and causes the blood to be circulated more closely to the skin. The result is that heat is drawn away from the body core more rapidly. This is the very thing you are trying to prevent by covering up a hypothermia victim, wearing woolen long johns, or investing in a wet suit.

Shock and First Aid. Shock can occur not only from getting wet and chilled, it can accompany any injury, even a minor one like a cut finger. Since it is in reality the first step down the dangerous road to hypothermia, it is often said that there can be more danger from these complications than from the injury itself. This is why one of the basic tenets of first aid calls for stabilizing the victim's condition first—stop the bleeding, clear the air passages to permit breathing, and look for broken bones. Then the second thing to do is to make the patient warm and comfortable to head off shock. These apply with added emphasis in cave injuries.

First Aid Kit. A first aid kit for minor injuries should be carried by at least one member of each caving team. It should include several sizes of Band-Aids, a couple of butterfly bandages, gauze pads, adhesive tape, disinfectant or first aid cream, and aspirin. Install these in a small plastic or metal box secured with a rubber band or strip of tape. An emergency combination blanket and ground cloth, such as a Space Blanket, is also useful. Splints, tourniquets, or the more elaborate paraphernalia of advanced first aid are not especially recommended for the average caver. These are better left to the members of an experienced rescue team. It is also a good idea to have a more complete first aid kit in the car along with a blanket, plenty of spare drinking water, and food.

First Aid Training. Regular first aid classes are conducted in many communities by the Red Cross. This is an excellent way to prepare for emergencies on cave trips. Check locally for details.

Cave Rescue

Cave rescue is an extremely specialized caving technique. Beginners on a caving trip where a serious accident happens can make themselves useful by keeping as cool as possible and following the directions of the leader or more experienced cavers to the letter. When an injury occurs in a cave, it is best if two people carry the message out to get help. Two people can remember the details of the accident better than one can. Whenever possible, before leaving the injured person, write down the extent of the injuries, the exact location of the injured person in the cave, the surface location of the cave itself, and the number of people in the party. If unfamiliar with the cave, or as an aid to the rescuers, it may be a good idea to leave trail markers at passage junctions.

The other members of the party must stay with the injured person to keep his or her spirits up and minister to needs. As stated before, shock and hypothermia may become the most serious problems. Therefore, everyone should contribute clothing to insulate an injured caver from the wet floor and to cover the victim as much as is possible. If necessary, those going out of the cave can leave some of their clothing since they will usually be moving quickly enough to keep warm. Sometimes a low wall can be built of ropes, clothing, or packs to stop drafts from reaching the victim. Assuming that the victim is conscious, a warm drink of chocolate or tea will be quite a spirit lifter and will help the others, too.

A fundamental decision must be made by the leader with the consensus of those in the party as to whether or not to move an injured person. This is an important question. In some cases the danger of hypothermia in a wet cave where no extra clothing is available may be more serious than moving the person. In the case of head and spinal injuries or broken bones, the proper decision might be to stay put.

One benefit of moving accident victims out of the cave is that it tends to warm them up and gets them closer to rescuers who may already be on the way. It also gives the others in the party something to do. However, you must go slowly to be sure to avoid any further injury.

The actual techniques of rescue involve the use of litters, ropes, pulleys, and as large a number of experienced cavers as can practically help out. No attempt will be made here to describe the special techniques required. Detailed information can be found in *A Manual of Caving Techniques* and *Cave Rescue Operations* (see Bibliography).

Press Coverage of Rescues. Be especially wary of involving local news media when an accident occurs in a cave. The sensationalism of injury to an underground explorer is of great interest to the average newspaper, so much so that distortion in reporting cave accidents is sometimes a problem. For this reason, make contact only with the local civil defense, police, fire departments, or other authorized rescue groups. Be especially careful that reporters don't put words into your mouth.

If a serious full-scale rescue is required, some of the less experienced cavers may end up being the ones going out of the cave to get help. After help arrives, they will often be on the surface and can assist the total effort by avoiding unnecessary sensational conversation with outsiders and by emphasizing the need to control any crowds of sightseers that may develop. Depending on the type of cave entrance, a large group of people milling around it can be a serious danger both to the injured person and the rescuers, particularly if a pit is involved.

4

Getting Underground

Joining a club, pretrip planning, underground route-finding.

What's the best way to get started in caving? Above all, you should begin by contacting some experienced cavers, preferably an organized club, such as one of the 100-plus chapters or grottoes of the National Speleological Society.

Organized caving groups have several things to offer that are essential to any beginner: First, they know how to cave and can train new people. Second, they know where the caves are, which is worth the price of admission all by itself. Third, they know which caves require special equipment like ropes and other vertical gear and they probably own this gear already. Finally, many of them conduct organized trips that beginners can safely take part in to find out if they are interested in pursuing it further.

Caving clubs will usually welcome anyone seriously interested in caves. However, they are not in the business of running guided tours or consciousness-raising/self-discovery programs. What they do offer is fellowship and a framework for cave exploration.

The National Speleological Society. If you're at all serious about caving and cave conservation, it doesn't take long to find out that the National Speleological Society is where most of the action is.

To get information about the Society and its goals, plus the address of the nearest chapter, write to NSS, Cave Avenue, Huntsville, Alabama 35810. Since they get numerous inquiries each month, a self-addressed envelope will be much appreciated.

Other Caving Clubs. Other important groups that sponsor organized caving trips are outing clubs at local colleges, universities, sporting associations, athletic clubs, and the like. In some cases, the college groups will be student grottoes of the National Speleological Society. In other cases, they may be a section of a recreational group involved with several outdoor activities such as canoeing, mountain climbing, biking, or backpacking.

A third place to find cavers is the Sierra Club chapters around the country. Some of these may have caving activities, particularly if they have a rock climbing section. Some of them cooperate and share trips with nearby NSS groups. Information about Sierra Club chapters is available from the Sierra Club, 1050 Mills Towers, San Francisco, California 94104. Again, a self-addressed envelope is a big help.

Finally, check with cave owners and the guides at show caves. They often know of local caving clubs that have visited their caves and can refer you to them.

Pretrip Preparations

It may sound a little simpleminded, but by far the best way to find a cave is to go with someone who has been there before and knows where the entrance is. Furthermore, cavers are increasingly reluctant to give directions to newcomers unless they themselves go along to be sure that the proper safety and conservation practices are followed.

Before setting out on a trip, check with the others in the group to find out what equipment to take, what clothes to wear, and what to expect. Often you can save time and effort through a little inquiry before setting off. If a map of the cave is available, it is certainly worth studying, although relating a given passage underground to a line on a map can be quite difficult. What a map can do is to give you a good idea of the cave's main structure, routes, and different levels. With map in hand, a person who knows the cave can usually explain most of the hazards quite clearly.

Cave-Owner Relations. A visit to a cave always depends on proper landowner relations. Never enter a cave without obtaining the owner's permission. If the cave is gated, don't force the gate or break into the cave. It's illegal, and it will make the owner and the local constabulary very unforgiving.

In case the family isn't at home when you arrive and they are known to be friendly to cavers, it *may* be all right to leave them a note. But if there is any doubt, wait for them or check back later. In either case, tell them how long you plan to be in the cave, adding a few hours in case of delays. When coming out, be sure to check with them in person or by leaving a note. If for any reason they say the cave is closed, thank them and leave politely. They may have been burned by some rather thoughtless visitors. Cavers have been known to end up with buckshot in their backsides for being too persistent. Sometimes reluctant owners can be convinced to let you see their cave if you prepare and sign a written waiver holding them blameless in case of injury or accident.

Cars should be parked where the owners suggest, even if it means a somewhat longer hike. Most important—leave open gates open and closed gates closed. There is a reason for their being the way they are. The owners are sure to be annoyed, if not violent, if they have to go out and open the gate for the cows to come home or if they find the garden being eaten up by pigs or goats.

As a courtesy, cave owners should be told what you have found in their cave. With any owners you come to know well, send a photo of the cave or even of the house or barn. If you've

Fig. 4–1. Typical cave gate at the entrance to a heavily-visited California cave.

made a map of the cave, a copy is a nice gift, as is a Christmas card each year thanking them for past courtesies.

Caves on Public Land. Caves on state or federal land, as in the western United States and Canada, are not exempt from the rule about getting permission to enter. However, it's sometimes a problem finding who to ask. The NSS grotto or local caving group sometimes has this kind of information and may have set up a procedure with the right agency. It's often necessary to write ahead of time (two or three weeks) telling the ranger or supervisor what your group is and what your qualifications are for going in. Most public officials responsible for outdoor recreation are helpful, so be sure to follow their requirements for signing waivers, letting them know when the group comes out, and returning the keys, if the cave is gated.

In the U.S., the public agencies most often responsible for caves are the National Park Service, National Forest Service, and the Bureau of Land Management. On the state level, administration is usually by a recreation, conservation and wildlife, or natural resource department.

Trip Leaders. The question of trip leaders can be a tricky one because many cavers tend to be essentially anarchists at heart. With beginners, however, our experience has been that a designated trip leader assisted by a ratio of about one experienced explorer for every four or five novices is best. At a minimum, don't go with less than two experienced persons, one to lead, one to bring up the rear.

Implicit Leaders. On a trip made up entirely of seasoned cavers, an implicit leadership, usually in the person of the trip organizer, is more often the case. But he or she rarely gives any actual instructions because everybody in the group knows what is expected. In a sense, all are equally in command and share responsibility for the success of the trip. All trip members are looked on to perform the task they do best: rigging, climbing, or scientific interpretation. Then, if a situation arises where a leader is needed because of some unexpected danger or accident, a leader will emerge, almost by unspoken agreement. This leader will not necessarily be the original trip organizer. It is usually the person most experienced in that particular cave or in the particular technique required for the situation.

For example, a cave we visit regularly, Lost Soldier Cave in California, has 30- and 60-foot pits (10- and 20-meters) that require rigging with ropes for safe descent and ascent (rappelling and prusiking, see chapters 14 and 15). The person best at rigging takes on that job.

On our last trip, this was a 29-year-old woman, assisted by two men. After the rigging was set and tested, the person most skilled in rappelling went down first. Further into the cave, there are several narrow pits and fissures, loosely called chimneys. Chimneying is my particular specialty. I love any kind of climbing where I can stretch out my arms and legs and feel the security of the cave wall pressing firmly against my back. After I got down the pit, I talked the others down, pointing out the knobs, ledges, and crannies that make chimneying such a joy.

On the way out, we climbed a cable ladder for the 30-foot pitch. Here my wife went first using a self-safetying method on the rappel rope (see chapter 15). Ladder climbs (short ones, that is—not many cavers enjoy more than 30 feet or so) appeal to her. Finally, when it was time to derig, the last ones out joined together to haul the ropes up after checking to be sure everyone had climbed the drop.

Length of Trip. A typical cave trip in any kind of respectable system seems to last a minimum of six to ten hours. However, trips involving new cavers should probably be limited to three to five hours on their first encounter. After a few trips, new cavers can usually handle a longer trip without any trouble. But don't expect a raw neophyte to have the kind of experience and endurance needed for those sixteen to twenty hour marathons that many hard-charging cavers do routinely.

Size of Group. Our recommendation in chapter 3 is for a minimum of four cavers. However, we would be the last to say that you should cancel a cave trip if only two or three cavers were available, especially to an easy cave.

On the flip side, the maximum number of cavers per trip depends mostly on the nature of the cave and the number of experienced cavers in the party. Consider a cave with several bottlenecks, such as tight squeezes or tricky pits, where traffic will back up. Here a group of only four or five could cause undue delays and might even be in some danger due to hypothermia if the cave is cold and wet.

A cave without these hazards, with mostly walking passages, can accommodate a much larger number comfortably. About twelve to eighteen cavers in any one section of the cave at any one time is about the biggest party that's practical. But it's hard to give more than a guideline since every cave is different.

Order of Movement. Normally, movement in a cave is in single file, both for safety and conservation reasons. The leader or most experienced person should go first, the novices or inexperienced cavers in the middle, and the second-most experienced person at the end. Single file is more efficient because it is easier to pass messages back and forth from one to the next and maintain close contact. Refrain from any unnecessary talking or yelling so that messages can be easily heard and everyone's attention can be kept directed on carefully balanced movement. Single file causes less damage, too. Never leave the established path, especially in a heavily decorated area.

Underground Route-finding

Surprising as it may seem, very few people ever get lost in a cave, although all of us get turned around sometimes. In the early days, many cavers (including members of the National Speleological Society) carried string into a cave as Tom Sawyer did in his well-known underground adventure. However, it was soon discovered that a cave small enough for an average-sized ball of string didn't need string anyway, and a really large cave required far more string than could be easily carried, even by a group.

The trick to finding your way underground is to turn around regularly in each passage and study it carefully. This is particularly true at junction rooms from which several passages take off. Pay close attention to the passage ahead also. Look for distinctive passage shapes, speleothems, flat ceilings or floors, or other features that can be identified when finding your way back.

If the group gets lost, it is often a good idea to call a halt and take a rest. Then send one or two people back down the passage and up ahead to see if it looks familiar. Usually, this will get you reoriented quickly. If not, talk it over and see if your collective recollection doesn't solve the riddle.

Fig. 4–2. Single-file movement on a narrow trail is usually the best method of progressing through a cave both for safety and conservation.

If you ever get separated from the group and wander into unfamiliar territory, try not to panic. The worst thing to do is to go running headlong down the passage. Instead, you should sit still for a moment and collect your senses. Light a candle and turn your main light down or off completely. Give a loud yell at regular intervals to see if the others will answer. Keep it up, even if you don't get a reply. Sometimes, because of intertwining passages, others can hear you but you can't hear them. Believe it or not, you'll be found sooner than you expect, and you'll be none the worse for wear—if you stay put and don't lose your head.

Obvious signs of caver traffic in the passage are good clues. These may be footprints, survey markers, "out" arrows, Scotchlite markers, and other signs of human presence (including, regrettably, trash). But be careful that these signs don't lead into new or difficult areas off the main route rather than leading out of the cave. "Out" arrows, smoked on the wall with a carbide lamp (although not a recommended practice anymore), are still seen in some well-traveled passages and normally point out of the cave. When coming to an unfamiliar area, the trip leader (or an experienced caver) plus one other caver should check ahead for the best route. It can be very tiring and disheartening to push into a passage that pinches out in twenty or thirty yards and have to backtrack.

When confronted with a series of confusing leads, particularly in a three-dimensional maze, leave a person, candle, or Scotchlite marker at the exits of the passages traversed so they can be easily identified when returning. Also, no cavers, especially new ones, should ever leave their packs behind when checking a side passage. You can never tell when a light will fail and spares will be needed from the pack.

The correct route in a cave is not always the most obvious one. In some cases, a small hole above, below, or to the side of what seems like the main route often turns out to be the right one. Sometimes, studying the cave map carefully before the trip and making note of distinctive areas and pits can be a real help in finding the route. However, in many caves a map does not begin to make real sense until after you have made one or

Fig. 4–3. Sometimes route finding in a cave is easy because there is only one way you can go!

two trips so you can relate where you have been to the passages on the map.

Route-finding in New Caves. Discovering a new cave or a new section in a known cave is certainly one of the thrills of caving and speleology. It also carries certain responsibilities. First, take care not to disturb anything: formations, cave life, or even debris like wood and stream stones. As with any cave, photograph, don't collect. If something is found of special interest, it should be left in place and a scientist told about it. Avoid beautiful sections if they cannot be entered except by destroying some of the speleothems.

Be especially careful in selecting a route in a new cave or new section because the chances are that others will follow the same footprints. Always choose the route that will damage the cave the least.

From a safety standpoint, remember that if the passage has not had traffic before, it may have loose stones, false floors, or unstable ceilings that can be quite dangerous. Proceed quietly, cautiously, and slowly. Be especially wary of streams and pools. Because of the poor light and the clearness of undisturbed cave water, these are often far deeper than they look. As in any kind of caving, the entire group should stay together with no one rushing off haphazardly. It's best to wait and do it right. Remember, it is not necessary to explore the whole cave the first time in!

Transporting Gear

Generally speaking, all cavers should carry their own gear because it's faster and more efficient. Nevertheless, in tight passages or vertical pitches, helping others move gear is part of caving teamwork. Quite often this can be done by just handing a pack from one person to the next. If the slope or pit is too deep, then your 12-foot caver's sling (see chapter 7) can be used as a single length and knotted with a figure-of-eight loop (see chapter 8) to tie to gear for lowering. When hauling gear, remember that a string of small bundles is better than one large one because they don't hang up as easily.

5

Finding New Caves

The thrill of discovery awaits those lucky few who are willing to do some detective work, then tramp the hills and ridges on the quest.

Have you ever discovered a new cave? This is a thrill eagerly sought after by many cavers. Equally exciting is finding a new section in an existing cave or the connection between two caves. Discovering new caves is not easy, especially if you live in an area where there aren't many to start with. This chapter gives you some hints about where to start. First, you'll have to do your homework. Then you must expect to spend many hours in the field before you make a strike.

Where to Start. Caves occur primarily in limestone, gypsum, or lava. By far the largest number were created by water dissolving out limestone. Limestone (or its heat- and pressure-altered form, marble) tends to be deposited either in broad beds covering fairly large areas or in discrete, but sizable chunks, called pods or lenses. To support cavern development, the limestone must be a dense, fractured type which has had sizable quantities of water in contact with it for considerable periods of time in its geologic history.

A good way to seek out caves is to ask commercial cave owners or guides at a commercial cave if they know of any wild caves nearby. The chances are they do. They may even have explored them. Where there are known caves, either commercial or wild, the chances are there are other caves nearby.

Check also with local farmers, hunters, miners, fishermen, hikers, utility company linemen, and some of the old-timers of the area. Frequently the oldest inhabitants will have heard of some caves in their youth and can suggest where to search for them. Try the local library, historical society, newspaper office, or county recorders.

Topographic Maps. Most outdoors people are familiar with topographic maps so we won't describe them in detail here.

As an aid to finding caves, the first step should be to get all topographic maps for your local caving area. Mark on them the location of caves you already know to establish general areas to check. A good way to mark a map (or an aerial photo) is to make a pinhole at the exact location. Then, on the back where you have plenty of room, circle each hole and write down the name of the cave and other pertinent data in ink. By holding it up to the light, you can easily spot the holes.

Geologic Maps. An invaluable source of information for locating caves is geologic maps. These are contained in reports of state mineral resource agencies, the U.S. Geological Survey, and in university geology department theses. Often they are not available for purchase, but usually can be studied and portions photocopied at a library or university geology department. Be sure to bring along your own topographic maps to transfer data onto them for field use.

Geologic maps use colors or patterns to show where the different kinds of rocks that lie directly below the soil or vegetation occur. If the maps are sufficiently detailed, sedimentary rocks like limestone and igneous rocks like lava are usually pointed out with separate colors or patterns.

Geologic maps are a little imposing to the uninitiated.

Fig. 5–1. Entrance to a limestone cave tucked away among gigantic boulders in the High Sierra.

However, once you figure out which color means cave-bearing rock you can really zero in on the areas worth searching for caves. It turns out that one of the more common cave-bearing rocks is limestone of the Paleozoic age about 300 million years old. It is usually shown in blue. In the most detailed maps, limestone and marble will be separately distinguished as *ls* and *m*. Look also for other rock formations that contain some limestone but are made up primarily of other rocks.

Boundaries of rock formations are not intended to be absolutely exact on geologic maps because they are often based on interpolation from selected field data. Therefore, when you're out looking for caves in the field, search beyond the indicated boundaries to some extent and correct your personal maps as necessary.

Aerial Photos. Aerial photos can also be a big help before actually heading for the hills once you've isolated a likely limestone, gypsum, or lava area. At their best, they show you depressions (hopefully sinkholes), roads, buildings, hills, and other useful details. The only problem is, aerials are quite expensive to buy. If you're lucky, a library or geology department may have a set covering the area of interest that you can look at. You'll want to do this anyway before you buy some to be sure they have enough detail to help you. Sometimes the area will be too heavily forested to see enough details. Aerial

Fig. 5–2. Silhouetted figures in the entrance add drama to this New Mexico cave entrance.

photos can be studied with a stereoscopic tabletop viewer. The hills and depressions really jump out at you in stereo.

We have used aerial photos with great success in locating lava tubes in northern California near Mt. Shasta and Lava Beds National Monument. Although this is a heavily forested area, it has been extensively logged, so the ground cover often doesn't conceal details. Also, the lava flows themselves have few trees directly on them. Sometimes the large roof-collapse-windows of tubes can be seen quite clearly. We have been able to trace large systems on aerial photos, running nearly 20 miles in one case. These systems usually alternate as collapsed trench and underground tubes.

Limestone Entrances. With limestone, once an area is isolated as having possibilities, pick a relatively small part and concentrate on that. First, establish the local drainage, then canvass the logical sites where water flows into and out of the hills. Limestone entrances generally are of two types, solution and collapse. Solution entrances occur where the water action is. Watch for sinkholes and streams disappearing underground and for springs where water comes back out after traveling underground. These are indicators of possible cave entrances somewhere nearby. Entrances are often at the bottom of a sinkhole, near or at the bottom of a valley or gully, or a hole in the side of a valley or canyon.

Solution sinkholes are usually bowl-shaped with smooth sides. They will often be located along a line between where a stream sinks and resurges. In flat, exposed limestone plateaus, where there aren't many surface streams, sinkholes may indicate a cave passage beneath.

Collapse entrances are harder to predict. They depend more on the earlier rather than the present-day water-flow patterns of the area. Look for entrances on the side or base of steep hillside escarpments where a cave passage may have been interrupted when part of the hill slid down. Entrances may also be found in collapse sinkholes (these are very common in lava tubes). Collapse sinkholes are not generally bowl-shaped or smooth-walled like solution sinks. Instead they may be almost any shape and have steep walls. They too can be along a line between stream sink and resurgence or along a line of contact between limestone and an adjacent rock.

Limestone Outcroppings. If an area has limestone outcroppings, check for any that have air blowing between cracks or out of small openings. Air coming from caves is sometimes easier to see in the winter, because a cave in the middle latitudes is normally warmer (45 to 55 degrees F) than the surrounding air. There may even be melted snow at cave entrances.

Karst. Another good indication of caving country is an area that has a great deal of rainfall but not much evidence of water on the surface. Small brooks and streams are strangely absent. This generally means that surface water goes quickly underground and flows through channels in the limestone or gypsum. This kind of terrain is called *karst* and it is usually marked by a number of small or large sinkholes. These may not be so obvious from the surface, but when studied from above as from an airplane or a high hill, they stand out quite clearly. Should you come across a sinkhole or hill that has a small stream pouring into it with no obvious exit, a cave entrance is more than likely at the bottom of the sink or base of the hill.

Swallets. Sometimes a well-known surface stream will suddenly disappear into the ground into what is called a swallow hole or swallet. The actual size of a hole is not a very good indicator of the possible size of the cave below. It may turn out that a large swallow hole will lead into a very small passage. That's why there is so much water up above. Or a small swallow hole may be small because it is pouring water very rapidly into a large passage below. Be very careful when pursuing a lead indicated by a swallow hole. Many times the rocks are rather precariously perched on the sides of such a hole. It may take no more than the pressure from a caver's boot to cause a cave-in.

Leads Without Entrances. If you find some possible cave leads but no entrances, first discuss the matter with the landowner and get permission to proceed further. If any surface digging is required, be sure to fence the dig off in order to prevent harm to farm animals. Many caves have been discovered by digging, but the procedure has its own special hazards. If the dig is going to go any distance at all, special care must be taken to shore up the sides of the excavation to prevent collapse. If any blasting becomes necessary, the services of a licensed professional are mandatory. Many cavers object to the use of blasting because explosives are dangerous, and they damage the ecology. We suggest you think seriously about the impact of such action and consult both with local cavers and the local citizenry before blasting away.

New Areas of Known Caves. Even if a caving group is unable to discover any new caves, there's no reason for them to be discouraged. Many very large cave systems have been discovered one piece at a time. Mammoth Cave in Kentucky, for example, had been commercialized for many years before

Fig. 5–3. High elevation karst (limestone terrain) is frequently riddled with interconnecting cave entrances and sinkholes.

one of the guides pushed into a vast new area on his day off. This was later commercialized and added to the standard tour.

Then, in more recent times, years of difficult and often frustrating exploration by a group of devoted cavers culminated in a record-breaking connection: Mammoth was joined to the caves in nearby Flint Ridge to make the longest cave system in the world. Total surveyed length now stands at about 190 miles (307 kilometers). Its nearest known competitor is Hölloch Cave in Switzerland with over 84 miles (136 kilometers).

When seeking new passages inside a cave, look for areas that are obviously filled with dirt or large break-down blocks. With careful excavation, these can sometimes be penetrated to find more cave. A passage filled with mud or breakdown is usually the result of flooding or a collapse in the roof. The passage may continue on the other side. When seeking new leads, a surface survey can sometimes reveal the most likely direction of a new area. Quite often, promising leads, when correlated with surface features, will be found to end at a sharp cliff. Or a resurgence of water may be seen indicating that no more cave may be found in that particular direction. This is where a good map of the cave, coordinated to an accurate surface survey, is of great value.

Lava Tube Entrances. Lava tubes are formed when the outer surface of the lava flow begins to cool and harden but its molten interior continues inside to form a tube of its own making. Tubes are found in areas where there has been relatively recent volcanic activity, such as the western United States and Hawaii. Of the several types of lava, tubes form only in pahoehoe basalt (a Hawaiian term, pronounced pahoy-hoy). This is the ropey and relatively smooth type of lava. The other type of lava is the jagged type, with sharp points and edges, called a-a (Hawaiian for hurtful to the bare feet).

Most lava tube entrances are created when the roof of the tube collapses. Sometimes the tube is collapsed for some distance, forming a distinctive trench. In addition to naturally collapsed entrances, there are man-made ones, too. Road-building crews and loggers sometimes break into the roof of a

Fig. 5–4. Three cavers experience the thrill of discovery at an entrance created by ceiling collapse in a northern California lava tube.

tube accidentally. For this reason, many entrances are found near recently constructed roads and in logging areas.

Aerial photos and surveillance from a plane or high cinder cone will often reveal the course of pahoehoe lava flow and possible entrances. Steam plumes from lava tubes are not uncommon in winter months and can also signal an entrance.

6

Personal Caving Equipment: Clothes

Proper clothing makes the difference between a comfort-able visit to a cave and a cold, wet, miserable one.

It used to be said that all a caver needed for a trip underground was some old clothes, a hard hat, and a carbide lamp. While it's true that many cavers give the impression that they never wear anything but old clothes (and discards from a surplus store at that), their personal equipment is really chosen with great care, each piece serving a definite purpose and selected accordingly.

There isn't any semblance of a standard uniform for cavers (unless it might be muddy coveralls). All cavers tend to look a little rumpled because the rugged cave environment makes all articles of clothing, new or old, take on the patina of wear after their first use in a cave. One thing is for sure—cave mud penetrates all the way to the skin, no matter how many layers are worn. So be prepared to have one set of clothes (or more) for caving and another set of clothes for more normal activities.

Fig. 6–1. The well equipped caver. *From the top:* hard hat with chin strap, carbide lamp, coveralls (over regular shirt and pants—preferably woolen—and woolen underwear, if in cold climate), caver's sling with locking carabiner, cave pack, gloves, boots with lug soles.

To get started, all you actually need is a borrowed hard hat and light, some old clothes, and a good pair of boots. The boots should have lug soles which are also useful for hiking and rock climbing, if caving proves a washout after the first few tries. Besides the borrowed light, the first-time caver should plan to bring a flashlight and either a chemical light-stick or candles with matches in a waterproof container (for the other two sources of light). As spares, bring along extra carbide or batteries for twice the expected stay on the trip.

Clothing

Choosing the proper clothing for caving depends mostly on the type of cave trip and the temperature of the cave, but there are still some general considerations. Basically, cave clothes should keep you warm enough for periods of inactivity yet not be too bulky or tight that they restrict movement during crawling or climbing. They must also be free of floppy pockets, loops, or belts that catch on rocks or projections.

In caving, it is a dead certainty that anything that can catch will catch. I can't tell how often we've seen a caver backing out of a crawlway to unsnag clothing or pack straps, amid vile imprecations that would make a sailor blush.

Layering clothes, particularly woolens, insulates against the cold and reflects back natural body warmth. In any sport involving exertion in a cold or wet environment, several thin layers are better than one heavy one. Layering provides multiple air barriers for insulation and still allows freedom of movement. Ski clothing is a classic example—an outer windbreaker over two or more layers of wool or knitted fabrics.

Underclothing. For trips of almost any duration to the dry caves of Texas, Alabama, Arizona, and Mexico (to name a few), regular underclothes are probably best. For trips of more than two or three hours in colder caves (50 degrees F or less), we recommend woolen uppers and long johns worn over regular underwear (unless you are going to be especially active, in which case they may be too warm). Even in caves with higher temperatures, you may find woollies a blessing if you have to sit and wait very long. Wool is an excellent insulator. It also can absorb a great deal of water and still keep you warm. It may smell (some people think wet wool smells awful), but it does its job. Natural fibers, like wool, also are preferred because they do a better job of carrying perspiration away from the skin than artificial fibers do.

Heavy woolen undergarments, which can still be found in surplus stores, are best, unless you're allergic to wool. If so, the layered wool/nylon/cotton (such as the Duofold brand) or the angora or lamb's wool garments in 100 percent or in mixtures are good alternatives. Just be sure it's wool (or, second best, a synthetic material woven like wool, such as Orlon). Some cavers have had success with wool net underwear worn next to the skin for uppers. But avoid this type for the bottoms, because it's hard on the knees when crawling, unless you wear knee pads.

So-called thermal underwear, which is usually all cotton, may seem to be a good choice. In reality, thermal underwear is inferior to wool in insulating ability. Tests by mountaineering groups have shown that wet cotton clothes can be worse than no clothes at all under wet, windy conditions because of the windchill factor. It has even been recommended (Stein, J.M. 1976) that if you don't have a change of clothes with you, and you know you are going to get thoroughly soaked, it's better to take your clothes off, get wet, then put them back on again. With dry clothes, you will warm up quickly and stay warm. With wet clothes you may never get warm until you can change into something dry.

Pants and Shirt. Although blue jeans are used a lot by North American cavers, relatively loose-fitting trousers of cotton or woolen flannel or worsted give better protection and warmth. The cotton denim of blue jeans is really too thin and stiff to offer the knees much protection. Also, many jeans are too tight in the hips and legs to allow comfortable movement for the climbing and crawling common in caving.

As with the pants, a caving shirt should be relatively loose-fitting. Many people wear flat-weave cotton shirts, but in

Fig. 6–2. Cave clothing in warmer caves often omits coveralls in favor of shirt or sweatshirt and blue jeans. Other clothing is standard, including hard hat and light, gloves, knee pads, and lug-soled boots.

really cold caves a woolen shirt may be preferred for warmth. Be sure any shirt has long enough tails to stay tucked in when bending over, reaching up, or twisting.

Over the pants and shirt, many cavers in the northern latitudes wear a suit of coveralls (called a boilersuit in Britain). Coveralls, as the name implies, cover everything and keep other clothes in place. This is more essential than might be imagined when squeezing through a tight vertical slot or horizontal crawlway. When shopping for coveralls, try to find ones made of heavy material, particularly in the seat. It turns out the seat is often the first thing to go. One important point:

don't load the pockets of either your coveralls or pants with anything hard. Crawling on a tin of spare parts or a pocketknife can be quite painful.

If you expect to be sitting a lot during rigging, surveying, or photographic trips, a good insulation for the seat of your pants is $\frac{1}{8}$-inch Ensolite (a high-density foam pad used for sleeping pads by backpackers). Cut a piece wide enough to extend from hip to hip, and long enough to go down about halfway or less to the knees. To secure it in place with a pocket, cut a piece of old sheeting or denim an inch or so larger than the Ensolite, and sew it inside the pants, slotting both it and the pad to fit down inside the legs. Leave the top of the pocket open so the pad can come out when the pants are washed. (Our thanks to Luther Perry of the San Francisco Bay chapter for this very practical idea.)

Wet Suits. For caving in very wet caves where you won't be able to stay out of water, or in very cold caves, a wet suit is a necessity. (fig. 6–3). Water, according to a leading manufacturer of wet suits, draws heat from the body twenty-five times faster than air. This makes a dunking in cold water comparable to standing naked in a cold, brisk wind.

The wet suit has become indispensable to advanced cavers all over the world for pushing wet passages in caves with streams, waterfalls, or lakes. In fact, some caves could not be explored at all without the protection of a wet suit. The wetter the cave, the better, as far as wet suits are concerned. While in the water, the wet suit is warm and comfortable. However, overheating is rapid when you leave the water and have to trek, somewhat clumsily, in dry cave for any distance.

A wet suit is usually made of $\frac{3}{16}$- or $\frac{1}{4}$-inch (5- or 6-millimeter) Neoprene foam rubber with or without a nylon lining and a nylon exterior. It fits tightly, like a glove. So much so, that dusting the inside with talcum powder may be required to help put it on. A nylon lining helps in this regard. This type is popular with cavers. A nylon exterior resists cuts and tears but is more expensive, so many cavers opt for the interior lining and protect the uncoated outside with coveralls.

How does a wet suit work? It is made up of thousands of

Fig. 6–3. Wet suit for caving is usually made of $^3/_{16}$- or ¼-inch rubber, with nylon lining on the inside. Standard caving hard hat replaces the hood. Coveralls protect the soft, unlined exterior surface. Wet suit booties serve as socks inside caving boots, in this case a larger size of surplus jungle boots was bought especially by Kathy Williams to complete her wet suit ensemble. Seat harness for vertical work is worn directly over wet suit, inside of coveralls.

tiny closed air cells which serve as an excellent insulating barrier. Any water that seeps in through the body openings or a tear is quickly warmed.

For caving, wet suits should be purchased a little looser than for diving. The ideal fit is such that it should just touch the body at all points when you lift your arms over your head. Some cavers prefer the 3/16-inch thickness (5-millimeter) as the best compromise between warmth and flexibility. If you expect to spend long periods of time in icy water, the 1/4-inch material may be better. Thinner (1/8-inch) suits designed for rafters give somewhat better freedom of movement, but are too fragile and cold for cave use.

Since a wet suit tends to be worn for a much longer period when caving than when scuba diving, the two-piece version, especially if it has a nylon lining, is more comfortable as well as far easier to put on. Occasionally, cavers will wear the top or bottom half alone in partially wet caves where the conditions are simply grim but not devastatingly cold. Booties complete the outfit. They neatly replace the two pairs of caving socks and are easily slipped into boots if first inserted into small plastic bags. Boots, such as the versatile Vietnam jungle boots with water drainage holes, should be two sizes larger to fit over wet suit booties. This footwear is also good without the rest of the wet suit if a lot of wading is to be done.

A major advantage of wet suits is their ease of repair when torn or ripped. Just cut a patch from a scrap and cement it back on. This also allows you to add extra layers of padding at the knees, elbows, seat, or wherever extra comfort or extra wear protection is desired.

In contrast to wet suits, the dry suits popular in Britain twenty years ago are of thin rubber construction, not cellular like wet suits. They are designed to be sealed at the ankles, wrists, and neck to keep water out. They tend to tear quite easily and are not considered suitable for caving purposes.

A Lesson in Keeping Dry. I remember well an occasion when I accidentally plunged into a pool of water and emerged seconds later fortunately only barely damp. It was an advanced training trip to a wet, miserable cave with mud thick enough to pull the boots right off your feet.

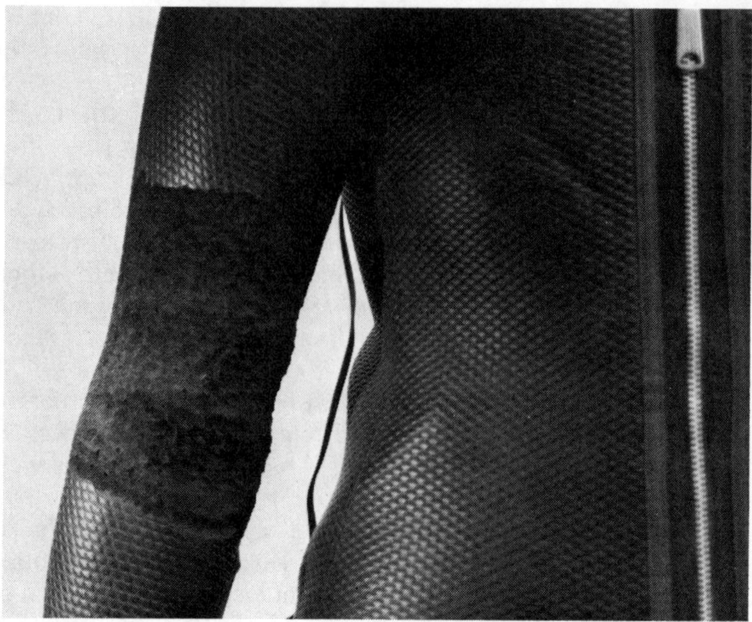

Fig. 6–4. Outer layer of rubber at the inside of the elbow has been snipped away to reduce chafing and allow greater freedom of movement. This can also be done at the back of the knee and front of the ankle.

We had just wallowed through a particularly mushy section and had climbed up on some breakdown near the small pool. Our next move was to step across this pond to another piece of breakdown on the other side. The step across was only about three feet horizontally at a level of about three or four feet above the surface of the water.

I had made this move many times. So, when one of our eager trainees hesitated, I naturally came forward to play hero and show her and the others how to do it. Firmly planting my foot on a slippery knife-edge hold, I leaned forward, one hand braced above me on the rather low ceiling. I had two good points of support, and was reaching my other hand across to the top of a block on the other side to get a third. The entire climbing fraternity knows you need three points of contact when rock climbing. I knew that as soon as I had my hand on the opposite hold I could lean forward and shift my weight so my body would be at about a 45 degree angle. Then, all I'd have to do would be straighten up, put my foot on that neat foothold over there, and swing on over. My audience waited expectantly as I tensed to make the move.

Unfortunately, that neat foothold was greased with mud. It also wasn't horizontal, as advertised. In fact, it was tilted at a very steep angle.

In one smooth, well-coordinated motion, my foot came off and I slid directly down into the water. Everyone, including me, was too surprised to say anything. It was about four- to five-feet deep (as proven by my instant depth-sounding method), so my shoulders and head didn't go under. Since I was standing almost upright when I plunged in, my feet went right to the bottom. I instinctively flexed my knees, pushed off, and shot back up like a cork. Frantically, as I rose majestically from the depths, I grabbed the top of the slab in front of me and hung on for dear life. My feet thrashed around for a second or two and finally found a foothold that allowed me to scramble up to a flat spot.

Total time in the water? Probably less than two seconds. Degree of wetness? Luckily, negligible. I had a small notebook in the outside pocket of my coveralls. It wasn't even moist. Since my head and shoulders didn't go under, no water ran down my neck. My coveralls had some water on the surface, but they weren't especially wet.

All in all, it was quite a show for the trainees and a sobering brush with extreme danger for me.

When they recovered from their surprise, one said, "What do you call that move, coach?"

For a long time, it was known as McClurg's Breathless Plunge. It probably still would be except that the cave was closed for conservation reasons a year or so later.

Socks and Gloves. For the feet, two pairs of wool socks are recommended, one light and one heavy, although some cavers prefer both to be heavy. Again, wool is preferable to cotton because it will keep you warm even when wet. If you are allergic to wool next to the skin, use cotton or Orlon for the lighter pair. To help keep the feet dry when shallow stream sloshing will be encountered, small plastic garbage bags worn inside the boots work well. They should be big enough to cover the socks and extend up above the top of the boot. They are not good for dry caves, however, because the feet will sweat too much. For deeper streams, wet suit booties worn in two-sizes-too-large Vietnam jungle boots are much favored by northeastern cavers, according to Bob Addis.

For the hands, gloves are really essential for almost any type of caving. The gloves we like best are leather-faced cloth gloves with gauntlets that extend up high enough to cover the gap between wrist and hand and help keep water and mud from slopping inside. They tend to be a little warmer than plain cotton gloves. Cotton gloves have the virtue of being very inexpensive and can be easily discarded if they don't recover after washing. Leather gloves, such as the thin gloves much in favor with sports car drivers, are also good because they give a nice close feel when climbing and scrambling underground. Unfortunately, they are expensive and require a great deal more care to keep them soft and pliable. Another recommended type are the heavy, rubberized plastic gloves sold for gardening. They are very durable and will usually outlast several pairs of the other materials. They are a bit clumsy, but they will outwear cotton or leather.

A note about nails—finger and toe, that is. Be sure finger and toenails are clipped on the short side before caving. A caver's hands get so muddy that long fingernails become reservoirs for what seems like acres of dirt. Besides, long fingernails get in the way and are easily broken. Long toenails are also a bother since they can be forced against the toe of the boot, which may be irritating or painful.

Boots

The best footwear for caving is lug-soled boots. These are readily available in nearly any backpacking, sports, or department store. Lug-soled army jungle boots (also called Vietnam boots) are a low-cost alternative. (Genuine surplus jungle boots are definitely superior to the Korean copies.) One of the most common (and best) lug soles is made by Vibram, although there are several similar brands on the market now. Vibram soles grip well on both wet and dry limestone, but may slip on some muddy surfaces. If a great deal of mud is encountered, stomp the foot sharply to remove mud from between the lugs before attempting any climbing or traversing involving small footholds.

Many cavers are reluctant to buy an expensive pair of hiking or rock climbing boots for caving because the wet, muddy environment is so punishing. With proper care, however, a good pair of boots can be made to last a long time.

Boots come in two heights, ankle high and over the ankle. Some choose the ankle-high type (five to six inches high), because they permit somewhat better flexibility for climbing, traversing, and scrambling. The higher or over-the-ankle type offers greater ankle support, but some claim they are too confining. With either style, the toe should be hard enough to protect the toes and allow pushing off with the foot in tight crawls.

Avoid tennis shoes, other types of soft shoes, or oxfords. Low shoes are often left behind in the mud accompanied by a strange sucking sound as you try to step forward. They also offer little ankle support or protection, and the soles are not strong enough to support ascending slings. Smooth soles are also to be avoided, particularly crepe soles which usually will slip on any wet surface. Similarly, nailed climbing boots are unsuitable, though they may seem to make sense for muddy rock. The problem is they can easily damage ladders, cave formations, and climbing ropes.

Generally, a pair of cave boots will weigh somewhere between 2½ and 5½ pounds. Avoid the very lightweight rock-climbing boots without heels. A heel is needed both for comfort and to hook onto the rungs of cable ladders. Boots come with either a medium or narrow welt (the layer between the sole and upper part of the boot). If your caving will involve mostly walking and scrambling but not much technical rock climbing, the medium welt of hiking shoes is probably better. It is wider and supports the weight more evenly. For climbing, a narrow welt is preferred because you can feel the holds better and put your weight on extremely narrow ledges much more successfully.

Buying Boots. When buying a pair of boots, be sure to put on both boots and walk around the store to see how they feel. Wear the same two pairs of woolen socks that will be worn underground. Watch particularly for excessive snugness at the instep and be sure that the lacing of the boot holds the foot well back into the boot. With the laces tied normally, bang the toe of the boot on the floor. If you can feel your toes, the boot is probably too small. To check for proper length, tighten the laces snugly with your heel pushed tightly against the back. Then do two or three deep knee bends. If you can feel either heel raise up more than ⅛ inch, try a different pair. As for lacing, the types that use holes rather than clips are better because clips can hang up in a tight spot or on a cable ladder.

The overall fit of caving boots should be somewhere between the very tight fit needed for rock climbing and the loose fit needed for hiking. In general, it would be better if they were loose rather than tight, because of possible circulation problems in a cold cave.

Although Vibram soles are best for caving, they will not last forever. One of their advantages is that they can be replaced at about half the cost of new boots at many local shoe repair shops. If you have chosen narrow welt boots, be sure the cobbler understands that the final sole needs to be trimmed very close (either completely flush or even slightly undercut) to the sides of the boot.

Boot Care. New boots should be waterproofed with a commercial preparation like Sno-Seal for chrome-tanned boots, or an oil such as neat's-foot oil or Huberd's Shoe Grease for oil-tanned boots. Check the store or the manufacturer's literature to find which tanning process was used. If in doubt, a silicon-wax-type like Sno-Seal can be used for either (Kemsley 1977). Exposed welt or stitching can be sealed with Welt Seal or Leath-R-Seal (REI 1978).

To care for wet caving boots, stand them upright on the soles and dry them slowly, stuffing them first with paper to hold the shape. Don't dry them in front of a fire or heater because the leather may crack. When dry, it is surprisingly easy to brush off loose mud. For really stubborn mud, wash the outside with warm water before drying. Don't let mud stay on your boots any longer than necessary.

When dry, treat the leather again with a silicon wax or oil sealer to restore the waterproofing. To protect the toes of your boots, particularly older ones or the Vietnam type, a protective coating can be added. We have had some luck with one or more coatings or Pliobond contact cement. But you really can't get a thick enough coat, because the upper layers don't adhere to the lower ones too well.

Fig. 6–5. Garbage bag, lightweight and compact, can serve as an emergency poncho.

A better solution is Flexane 80 S.F. (J. Baz-Dresch 1978). This is an industrial, urethane compound with high tensile strength, good tear resistance, plus superior elongation and elasticity characteristics. It comes in a putty form which adheres well and is easy to trowel into a 1/16-inch layer. It's best if the surface has been roughened a bit, so if the boots are new, sandpapering is called for.

One drawback to Flexane is that the smallest quantity you can buy is one pound (enough for six pairs). Once it's been opened, it can't be resealed and stored. So, the obvious solution is to have a Flexane party and trowel up a toe storm. For the name of the nearest distributor contact Devcon Corporation, Danvers, MA 01923, 617/777–1100.

For repairs to torn or worn out boots, try Boot Patch. We have rejuvenated several pairs of boots with this product. It's easy to use and really seems to work. The manufacturer is Kiwi Polish Co., Pottstown, PA 19464.

Garbage Bag Glad Rags. For emergency purposes or for those wet, cold, miserable caves where you expect to have to sit and wait, Davison (1977) has this recommendation. Carry a trash bag in your pack, and when you need protection, cut a hole in the bottom for your head and wear it like a poncho (fig. 6–5). If you need to have your arms free (to belay, for example) you can cut armholes in the two corners. It will keep your body warmth contained and fend off those cave winds that can cut right through you. If it's really cold, bring your carbide lamp inside this plastic tent to serve as a mini furnace. Be careful, though, that you don't burn yourself or the bag. A convenient size for this purpose, is the Glad Disposer trash bags, 2½ by 3 feet (93 by 90 centimeter) by 1½ mil thick for average-sized people.

A change of clothing back at the entrance of the cave or at the car is also recommended.

7

Personal Equipment: Caving Gear

Proper caving gear is just as important as clothing for a safe, comfortable cave trip.

Hard Hats

A hard hat (fig. 7–1), also called a helmet, protects you in three ways. Primarily, it keeps you from banging your head on rocks and overhangs. Second, it protects you in case of a fall. This is the time when a chin strap, preferably a nonstretching strap is vital because it keeps the hat on your head even if you do a somersault. Finally, a helmet helps fend off falling rocks. These are almost certain to cause serious injury if you don't have a hard hat on. Even a small stone, not to mention a rock or boulder, can reach lethal speed in a cave.

Types of Hats. So, now that you know you have to have a hard hat, what's the best kind? Although there is as yet no general agreement on this, the hats designed for rock climbers seem clearly superior to the more common construction type.

In the past, most cavers settled for either the plastic, metal, or fiberglass hard hats used by the construction and mining industries. These are still in widespread use, although some mining helmets tend to be too flat on top and don't deflect fixed or falling objects as well as rounded tops. These may be all right for starting out, but the serious caver needs a better hard hat. The best hard hats are those designed for climbing, including the MSR, Joe Brown, Ultimate, and Premier, among others. These are made of high-impact materials like polycarbonate Lexan, polyethylene, and fiberglass. Many cavers recommend the MSR helmet. Its features (which make up a good checklist for any helmet) include a Lexan shell with excellent side-to-side rigidity, a crushable styrene foam liner, no inside knobs or buttons, and a nonelastic chin and nape strap attached at four points.

Fig. 7–1. Modern caving helmet made of fiberglass with four-point nonelastic chin strap. Other high-impact materials used for caving and mountain climbing helmets are polyethylene and polycarbonate Lexan, among others. Electric headlamp is powered by five surplus Ni-Cad batteries housed in a canvas belt pack. In the foreground is a spare battery. A small leather strap at the rear of the helmet routes the electric cable out of the way.

Some of the newer hats are modified specifically for caving, such as the Speleoshoppe caving helmets. For example, they have a narrower brim in front than a construction model, making it much easier to see in a crawlway. Also, one version curves down in the back to offer greater protection to the head and neck from falling rocks or from an injury during a fall.

Suspension. Equally important as the impact-resistant shell is the interior webbing, or suspension. This should be an approved miner or safety suspension of durable nylon or plastic material in which all the inner edges of the suspension are rounded. Some of the climbing hats also have a crushable layer of foam plastic between the liner and shell at the top or sides for added protection.

Chin Straps. A caver's hard hat always has a chin strap. It never takes more than one trip back down a slope to retrieve a dropped hat to convince a caver that a chin strap is necessary. But a chin strap also has a more important safety function in keeping your hat on your head where it can protect you in case of a fall.

The preferred type of chin strap is nonelastic with four points of suspension. Until recently we would have unequivocably recommended this type, because elastic straps will not reliably keep your hat on your head during a fall. However, a nonelastic strap appears to have caused a choking fatality in West Virginia (*NSS News*, February 1979). For that reason, we suggest a Velcro quick-release arrangement. About two inches of overlapped Velcro will do the trick. Alternatively, instead of tightening a nonelastic strap snugly under the chin, leave it slightly loose—not so loose that the helmet will fly off in a spill, but enough so you can pull it off in an emergency.

A word of warning. If you are tempted to bolt anything to your helmet, try short rivets or epoxy. Bolt heads or nuts extending inside the helmet could puncture your skull in a fall.

On the front of a caver's hat is a lamp bracket. The most common type accepts the flat spade bracket of the carbide or electric lamp. Some older ones will also accept the wire bale found on earlier model carbide lamps. Check the bracket to be sure no screws are protruding into the interior space. If you buy a hat without a bracket, be sure to observe the precautions about protruding nuts or bolts when you install it. The MSR people recommend using sheet-rubber washers under the bolt heads and not tightening the nuts too much. MSR also warns against painting their helmets because it might weaken the shell material. This precaution is probably best heeded with any kind of plastic helmet.

Head Lamps

Carbide versus Electric

Carbide and electric lights are the two most common types of caving lamp. Although carbide lamps used to be cheaper, the price of each is now twelve to fifteen dollars. It wasn't too long ago that the brass carbide lamp reigned supreme as the primary source of light. It still does in some areas. However, an informal survey we have taken indicates that in the past few years the electric lamp has increased in popularity to a point where it now commands the loyalty of about 15 to 20 percent of organized cavers.

Some feel that electric lamps are more reliable and less finicky to operate than carbide lamps. However, for long trips, carbide lamps have an advantage because spare carbide is lighter in weight and takes up less space than spare batteries for the same duration of light. Most batteries will last a minimum of about eight hours (alkaline) to twelve hours (lead acid) before needing recharging or replacement. Carbide for twenty to twenty-four hours of light can be carried in a regular-size (8-fluid-ounce) baby bottle and weighs 13 ounces. Water for this amount of time would total about 20 ounces (including bottle) for a total of about 2 pounds (1 kilogram). Alkaline batteries for twenty to twenty-four hours (three sets of four, conservatively) will weigh about 3½ pounds (1½ kilograms) and will take up a lot more room. Lead acid would weigh even more: 3½ pounds each for two twelve-hour batteries, and would take up even more room.

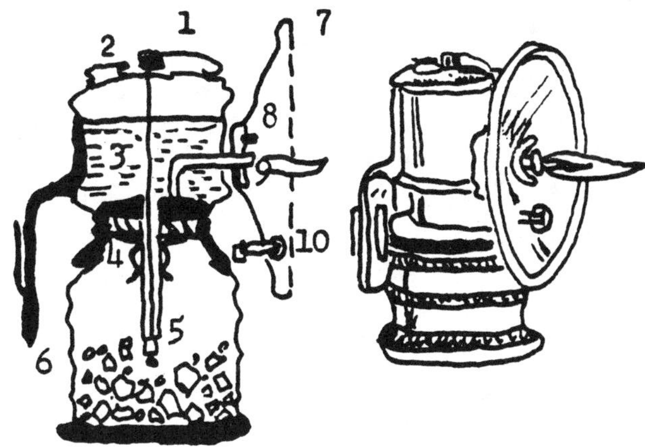

Carbide Lamp.

1. WATER VALVE
2. WATER FILLER CAP
3. WATER
4. FELT AND RETAINING SPRING
5. WATER OUTLET
6. BOTTOM WITH CARBIDE
7. REFLECTOR
8. REFLECTOR NUT
9. TIP
10. FLINT AND STRIKER

Fig. 7–2. Carbide lamp.

Another advantage of carbide lamps is their open flame. Sometimes this is useful in a cave for fusing rope ends, providing warmth, cooking, or heating water. A major disadvantage of a carbide lamp is that it blows out quite easily in windy passages and is completely useless when climbing in a waterfall. Its flame can also damage climbing ropes when you're climbing, though experienced cavers don't seem to have too much problem with this.

In the late 1960s the last American manufacturer of carbide lamps, Justrite, discontinued its excellent brass lamp and replaced it with what turned out to be an unsuccessful plastic model. The plastic lamp is still being marketed. Justrite also remains a major supplier of electric helmet lamps. Spare parts for their carbide lamps, however, can still be obtained. Fortunately, a fine British lamp, the Premier, is available in this country. Several of its parts (except the tip, and occasionally the bottoms) are interchangeable with the Justrite. Incidentally, Bob Addis advises that some older Premier bottoms will not fit the newer lamps and vice versa. Always check this and the general operation of your lamp before going underground. A worthwhile modification to a Premier carbide lamp is to replace the stock aluminum reflector with a parabolic reflector. It increases light output significantly and allows you to turn the lamp down thereby extending carbide life.

Carbide Lamps

How They Work. Carbide lamps are quite simple in principle. They use small lumps—from $1/16$ to $1/4$ inch (2 to 6 millimeters)—of calcium carbide, onto which drops of water from a separate water compartment are released to produce acetylene gas. This gas is directed up a tube to a tip with a small hole where it mixes with air and can be ignited with a spark, match, or the flame of another carbide lamp. To keep small particles of carbide from clogging the gas tube, a circular piece of felt or foam rubber just under the mouth of the gas tube acts as a filter.

Charge a carbide lamp by filling the bottom about one-half to two-thirds full (this is about 1½ ounces or 43 grams) of carbide. Then fill the top with water (typical capacity is 1½ fluid ounces or 45 milliliters) and adjust the flow by moving the water lever on the top one or two clicks. To check for proper water flow, watch for a steady stream of droplets before reassembling the lamp.

After screwing the parts back together snugly, gas should be coming from the tip. This can be detected easily by holding the lamp close to the face and feeling or smelling the flow. Next, place your hand over the entire reflector assembly to entrap a quantity of acetylene gas. Wait five or six seconds, then draw the hand sharply across the striker wheel on the reflector with the heel of the hand. This operation takes a little practice but it's really quite easy once you get the hang of it. If the gas has ignited, a loud pop will be heard, which can be deafening in small rooms or passages.

When using the lamp underground, an economical flame size is ½ inch to 1½ inches. Some prefer the greater light output of a longer flame at the expense of less time per charge.

Troubleshooting. If the lamp doesn't ignite, there can be several causes, each of which is quite simple to remedy. First of all, be sure that a stream of acetylene is issuing from the tip. If not, the chances are that the tip is clogged. This can be easily corrected with a tip reamer or cleaner. Check, too, to be sure that the bottom is tightly screwed into the top. If it isn't, acetylene gas may be leaking out this way rather than traveling through the tube to the tip. This can be detected by taking the lamp off your helmet and holding an open flame from another carbide lamp near the bottom to see if it will burst into flame. (The flame can be blown out very quickly, but hold the lamp away from your clothing.) If so, the remedy is usually a simple tightening of the bottom. If this doesn't work, try turning the gasket upside down or wetting it before reassembling.

Felts. Although the Premier lamp is generally superior to the Justrite, its felt filtering system is inferior. Many cavers have replaced the Premier felt and holder with the larger Justrite types to improve reliability and keep the gas tube clearer of carbide particles. Another good practice suggested by Mike Dyas and others, is to use plastic foam in place of felt, cut to the same circular size from ¼-inch (6-millimeter) foam. This will not clog up or harden, and can be easily cleaned by rinsing in water and wringing out.

When using the lamp, be careful to keep the felt or foam dry. If it gets wet, the lamp will sputter and become very balky and disagreeable. The flame will alternately drop down to nothing, then suddenly shoot out to 6 inches or more. It may go out completely or begin to whistle shrilly. If any of these things happen, check the filter and replace it if it is wet with one from your lamp spares. If none is available, try wringing it out (this works better with the foam type) or drying it gently with the flame of another lamp or candle. In an emergency, you can also operate the lamp without a filter, but be sure to clean the gas tube as soon as you can.

Recharging. One charge of carbide will usually last two to three hours. During this period, it may be necessary to increase the setting of the water lever to increase or decrease the light. When doing this, keep in mind that it takes at least five or six seconds for the lamp to respond to a change in water. Also, be careful not to get too much water in the bottom, because this will produce flooding, a very messy situation, usually indicating that the carbide is spent or nearly so. After about two to three hours, the lamp will run down and the flame will become lower and lower. Be sure to blow out the flame before it gets so low that it clogs the tip with carbon. If this has happened, a wire tip cleaner can be used to remove the carbon.

At this point, it's time to reload the carbide. One of the easiest ways to handle recharging is to have two or three separate lamp bottoms, each complete with a gasket and top. (These weigh about 4 ounces or 115 grams each, including the carbide.) Simply exchange the old one for the new one. When doing this, don't tighten the top on the old (spent) bottom too snugly. This is a safety precaution because there is usually a little life left in the carbide and acetylene generation is still going on.

Many cavers don't like to carry spare bottoms because of the added bulk (particularly on a really long trip) and expense. The more common method is to carry along a plastic bag or bottle and empty the spent carbide into it. Again, be careful not to tighten the used carbide container too tightly.

Extra carbide is carried in a nonbreakable, waterproof container, such as a plastic baby bottle. Never use a glass bottle. The larger plastic bottle (8 fluid ounces or ¼ liter) holds about 11 ounces of carbide, enough for about eight typical 1½-ounce charges or twenty to twenty-four hours of light. The smaller bottle (4 fluid ounces or ⅛ liter) cuts these figures in half and would be suitable for a smaller cave. Also, don't use the 2-pound cans that carbide comes in—the lid comes off too easily. Water is carried in a small plastic bottle, sometimes another baby bottle, but more often a larger pint or 500 milliliter size, if this is to be used for drinking water too. A bottle with a squirt-top, like those for dishwashing detergent, is handy. But be sure to clean it thoroughly to get rid of all traces of the detergent. Otherwise you may turn your lamp into a bubble machine.

When tapping the lamp bottom on a rock to loosen the carbide prior to emptying it into a plastic bag, be careful not to strike the threads on top of the lamp bottom. Tapping the threads can bend them and cause a leaky joint between the top and the bottom. If it's necessary to loosen up the carbide in the bottom, use a blunt tool like a stick or tap it on the bottom— not the top edge.

After recharging, check the water supply. It is probable that the water will already have been replenished during the first charge and the top will still be about half-full. This is because, at least in our experience, the water tends to run out more quickly (or spill out in crawls) than the carbide.

Be very careful when blowing away spent carbide from lamp parts or from the bottom. Chemically, it's no longer calcium carbide, but has changed to calcium hydroxide. This is very harmful to the eyes, particularly if it's rubbed in. Those who get a good eyeful of used carbide should see a doctor immediately.

Never leave used carbide, whether buried or not, in a cave. Always carry it out along with your other trash. Similarly, don't dump spent carbide around the cave entrance or any-where on the owner's property. It's very messy and can be dangerous to plants and animals, particularly if dumped into a stream.

Cleaning. Some cavers seem to have nothing but trouble with their carbide lamps. Yet others have lamps that work perfectly for years. The secret is nothing more than maintain-ing a clean lamp.

You should clean your lamp carefully, ideally after each trip. Occasionally take out the tip to be sure there is no accumulation of small carbide particles in the gas tube. Simi-larly, check the condition of the flint, felt, and felt-retaining clip, and replace them if necessary. Polish the reflector, using soap and water, or toothpaste, a mild abrasive. Avoid harsh abrasive cleaners.

Usually felts will dry out and become brittle after several hours of caving and should be discarded. If you're using the foam type, they can be rinsed out and reused. Clean out lamp bottoms after each trip, scrubbing them with water and a toothbrush if necessary. Be sure they are dry before reassembling or filling with carbide.

A good general cleaner for the entire lamp and reflector is a commercial product, available in grocery or hardware stores, called Lime-Away. It's especially recommended for carbide-encrusted bottoms, felts, and gas tubes. If you give your lamp the Lime-Away treatment after every thirty or forty hours of use, it will reward you with reliable service for years. Lime-Away is potent stuff and will etch tile, porcelain, and some metals, so be careful. Lime-Away is manufactured by Economics Laboratory, Inc., St. Paul, MN 55102. Vinegar in a weak solution with water is also used by some cavers.

Real Life Lamp Failure. I remember a time when my lamp wouldn't work at all. We were 120 feet down in a muddy fissure cave in the California Mother Lode country at the end of a long summer day. Two of us were the last to come out. At the surface, the others were impatiently waiting because the restaurant in town was due to close within the hour. But my lamp simply wouldn't stay lit.

There was nothing to do for it but to sit down in the mud, light a candle, and take the blasted lamp completely apart.

It had been an especially heavy caving season, and I probably had let lamp maintenance slide. Now I was paying the price. After several minutes of fumbling and dropping parts in the mud, we discovered that the felt was plugged nearly solid and so was the gas tube above. Fortunately, I had a tip reamer and by judicious poking got the tube cleared. Putting in a new felt solved *that* problem. Finally, with a whirl of the spark wheel, the flame sprang back to life. Now it was time to haul out of there.

We squirmed up the 40-foot by-pass chimney, paused to derig a 30-foot ladder (preferred by some of our larger members to avoid the snug bypass chimney), climbed up through a tall, narrow fissure, scrambled up a 20-foot flowstone slope, and inched along to the top of a treacherous mud slope. Once there, I quickly clipped into the belay line for the 20-foot entrance ladder.

"Ready to climb," I said to a startled belayer.

"Where the hell did you come from?" said he.

It seems we had set some kind of speed record: 13 minutes flat for the 100 vertical feet from mud crawl to mud slope. Normally, it took about a half an hour, but we had to make up for the agonizing minutes spent fixing the lamp.

Oh, yes—we all made it to the restaurant in time for dinner!

Spares. As a postscript to the story of my lamp failure: it had a happy ending because I had spares in a waterproof container. Spare parts in a watertight container are essential on each trip. Besides extra carbide, your spare-parts kit should include a tip reamer (either the single-needle type or the flexible-wire type), one or two tips, gaskets, felts, felt retainer clips, flints, plus a complete striker-wheel assembly. No lamp can be depended on without a kit of spares. A good container for your spares is the small (4-ounce) size plastic baby bottle. A plastic bag sealed with a rubber band is a less successful alternative. Empty 35mm film cans are also widely used for this purpose.

Electric Lamps

Electric head lamps have become more popular in recent years because of their reliability, simpler operation, and lighter weight on the helmet. An electric lamp head weighs about 4½ ounces (125 grams). A carbide lamp, fully charged with water and carbide, weighs about 11 ounces (300 grams). They also have this major advantage: you can swivel them downward to light up the area directly in front of your feet.

An electric lamp consists of a lamp assembly and a separate battery pack. This battery pack is connected to the lamp with either a fixed or detachable cord. It is usually positioned on the belt or hip or can be carried in a separate shoulder or waist pack. Some cavers mount the cord inside the coveralls to avoid a snagging the battery cable. A hung-up battery cable can be a real problem in a tight cave where it may be hard to back up and free the cable from a protuberance. Using a cord that's detachable at both ends helps alleviate this but is more complex, hence potentially less reliable.

A big plus with electric lamps is that you can operate them with bulbs of different light outputs: average, bright, or energy-saving dim, and thus different current drains. This means that when the batteries get low during a long trip, you can switch to a lower output bulb and extend the life of the battery. Incidentally, when resting in a cave, most cavers using electric lamps switch off their lamps to get a ride off the carbide caver and thus conserve battery life. Typically, the life of a set of alkaline batteries can be increased about 50 percent (from eight to twelve hours) by turning off your lamp whenever safe and possible.

The most common brands of lamps are the Justrite, Ray-O-Vac, Wonder, and Koehler. A clear choice among the lower cost models is Justrite, which has an excellent lamp head, complete with a clip for a spare bulb. It comes with a utilitarian plastic battery case that can be modified rather easily to improve its reliability. It uses four D cells. Alkaline or nickel cadmium are best.

The Ray-O-Vac is more widely distributed in sporting goods, discount, and department stores. It is cheaper but not rugged enough to hold up in caves. It uses a 6-volt lantern battery. The Wonder is a French import with the flat 4.5-volt battery common in European flashlights. Battery life is about 5 to 7 hours. Batteries are available in some bike stores. It is not as well made as the Justrite, and is not really intended for rugged use. The battery pack has its own bulb and reflector (it functions as a flat, European-style flashlight). This is disconnected when the head lamp is plugged in. While the design is ingenious, and makes the lamp possibly useful as a back-up caving light and a primary camping lamp, the nonstandard battery and its relatively short life make it impractical for use as a first source of light.

Justrite Lamp Modifications. There are some simpler modifications that can be made to a standard Justrite head lamp. A lens of honeycomb construction can replace the clear glass supplied with the lamp. This diffuses the beam and makes it more suitable for general illumination.

A second modification is made with pieces of cardboard in the stock battery pack. A long piece between the batteries will wedge them in tighter. Smaller pieces behind the spring metal contacts will keep them pressed tight against the battery. RTV (silicone sealant by GE) potting compound can also be used to fill in behind the upper contacts to assure a flexible yet firm pressure against the batteries. While you're at it, clean the contacts with a pencil eraser. Finally, you may want to install mud-proof, screw-on connectors either at the lamp end or the battery pack end (or both), to relieve the problem of snagged cables. Quarter-turn BNC electronic signal connectors are good for this purpose (Strudwick 1972).

Koehler Wheat Lamps. One of the best all-around electric lamps seen in caves is the Koehler Wheat Lamp. Koehler rigs are extremely rugged, having been developed for continuous-duty operation in mines. They use rechargeable lead-acid cells. Automatic chargers for AC or car battery are available. Koehler lamps have a single dual-filament bulb: one normal, the other bright. Bulb life is 335 hours (275 hours for the normal filament, 60 hours for the bright) compared to only 15 to 100 hours for regular bulbs. Koehler batteries are specified to be rechargeable 500 times, which translates into 6000 hours of battery use.

Caution: Battery electrolyte (potassium hydroxide) used in vented lead-acid and nickel-cadmium batteries will damage nylon ropes and slings. You must be very careful to keep vented-type batteries away from ropes in caves or in storage. Be especially careful not to throw your lamp and batteries into the trunk of a car with your ropes. Sealed lamp batteries can leak too, so make it a practice to keep all batteries away from climbing gear.

Koehler batteries are a heavy-duty, lead-acid-type which must be vented during recharging. This is accomplished through two vent holes which are designed to be spillproof in normal (presumably mining) usage. However, since spillproof is not 100 percent leakproof, it is best to cover these holes with rubber or plastic electrical tape when caving (they come this way from the manufacturer). During recharging this tape should be removed, but in case you forget, the battery will still vent itself and won't explode.

Davison (1978) recommends installing #8 by ½-inch long stainless steel, self-tapping, hex-head screws. This will indeed make the battery vents 100 percent leakproof. However, if you choose this option, you must be aware of the danger from explosion. It would be prudent to put a sign on your lamp charger: *Danger: To prevent explosion, remove screws before recharging.*

Alkaline Batteries Batteries are of two basic types: primary or dry cells, which are not rechargeable, and secondary or wet cells, which are rechargeable. The best type of dry cells for use in caves is alkaline cells. They are somewhat heavier than the standard zinc carbon, but last anywhere from five to ten times as long. They will give a very usable but gradually diminishing light for eight to sixteen hours or more, depending on the bulb. Remember, battery life can be extended as much as 50 percent if your lamp is turned off whenever possible to allow the batteries to self-regenerate.

Alkaline cells in the D size are rated at 10 ampere/hours, but it is best to expect a 20 percent efficiency loss for any battery to account for shelf-life losses or aging (Strudwick 1972). That means that four alkaline D cells matched up with a #425 bulb (0.5 ampere), should deliver about sixteen hours of light. To be safe, we recommend you plan on eight to twelve hours maximum in calculating the spares to carry.

Another advantage of alkaline over zinc carbon is longer shelf life: three years as against one year. To extend the shelf life of any type of dry cell, store it in a freezer. Even a refrigerator at under about 40 degrees F (5 degrees C) will help. Allow a couple of hours for recovery before putting them to use.

Mercury cells, widely used for transistor and other low current drain applications, are not practical for caving use because they're too sensitive to cold and lose their voltage when the temperature drops.

Nickel-Cadmium Cells. Many cavers who are seriously interested in using electric lamps often end up either with the Koehler lamp or some type of do-it-yourself system with nickel-cadmium cells. With proper recharging, nickel-cadmium cells can be used indefinitely. Common sizes are four- or six-ampere-hour-capacity which will last eight to twelve hours on the average with a half-ampere bulb. Ni-Cad cells, as they are commonly referred to, have a high initial cost, but in only one heavy caving season they will pay for themselves, as compared to the expense of one-shot alkaline flashlight batteries. Before recharging, it's best to discharge Ni-Cads completely as they seem to respond better when this is done. Storing them when completely discharged apparently does not damage them. The discharge characteristics of the Ni-Cad cells are such that they maintain almost their full rated output until they are just about ready to quit. On the other hand, they give little warning that they are nearing discharge. This is not true of alkaline, lead-acid, or zinc-carbon cells where the power steadily decreases until it is exhausted.

Many cavers have found vented Ni-Cad cells at surplus stores in various parts of the country at $.75 to $1.00 per pound. At that price, they're a good buy, but be sure that they will charge and recharge before installing them in a permanent cave pack. As long as they are not completely dried out, they can usually be rejuvenated.

To check them, refill the cells with electrolyte as needed and recharge. If they hold a charge, great. If not, you haven't lost much. The electrolyte is made up of one-third potassium hydroxide (in pellet form, J. T. Baker Cat. No. 15-3140) and two-thirds water. Be careful with this. It's irritating and poisonous.

Vented Ni-Cads come in several sizes, but those about ¾ by 3 by 6 inches (18 by 75 by 150 millimeters) are convenient. They have a nominal capacity of four ampere-hours and a voltage rating of 1.2 volts. With a ½-ampere bulb, typical life will be about eight hours. With a ¼-ampere bulb, fifteen or sixteen hours. Occasionally check the electrolyte level, but don't overfill. The level may appear low, but it will rise during the charging cycle.

Because the cells are relatively small, a good working voltage can be obtained by using several connected in series to give from 5 to 12 volts, depending on the types of bulbs available (see fig. 7–3) and how much weight and bulk you want to carry. A group of four Ni-Cad cells (a nominal 5 volts) will fit nicely in a square 50-caliber plastic ammunition case still available in some surplus stores. Other combinations are possible depending on the availability of suitable containers in the local area. Rather than assembling the batteries into a single container, some cavers separate them so they don't snag so easily in crawlways and chimneys. One possible location for carrying them is inside the pouches on a 50-millimeter ammunition belt. This can be easily removed if necessary and dragged or pushed through a crawl. Another possibility is to tape them in pairs on the ankles or legs with the connecting wires running under the knee pads, pants, and shirt.

No matter where you carry them, protect the cells against shock and dampness by sealing the top of the cells (leaving only the vents clear for the filler tubes) with a generous coating of RTV compound sold in electronics stores.

Sealed Ni-Cad cells in the standard D size are also available with a 4 ampere-hour capacity. These can very nicely replace alkaline batteries in a standard Justrite battery pack. They are a good compromise for those who want the economy of a rechargeable cell without the hassle of building a do-it-yourself system.

Battery Chargers. To get the best value from Ni-Cads, many cavers buy or build their own chargers. Desirable features include ability to work off either a 110-volt line or a 12-volt car battery, good regulation, and an adjustable output to handle different capacity batteries.

Suggested circuits with parts lists are shown in figure 7–4 and 7–6, along with a charging guide (fig. 7–5) and a table of commonly available bulbs (fig. 7–3). Eveready has a ready-made charger, Model ACC-100, with five current settings that will charge from one to ten NiCad batteries. This is a good choice for those who don't want to build their own.

ELECTRIC LAMP DATA

Number	Volts	Amps	Candlepower	Avg. Lamp Life	Base	Remarks
PR-2	2.38	.50	0.80	15 hr	flange	2 D cells
PR-3	3.6	.50	1.5	NA	flange	3C or 3D cells
PR-4	2.33	.27	0.40	10 hr	flange	2AA or 2C cells
PR-6	2.47	.30	0.45	30 hr	flange	2AA or 2D cells
PR-9	2.7	.15	0.25	45 hr	flange	emergency use
PR-12	5.95	.50	2.9	NA	flange	lantern battery
PR-13	4.75	.50	2.0	NA	flange	lantern battery
PR-17	5.0	0.3	NA	NA	flange	lantern battery
395X	2.0	.06	NA	1000 hr	flange	emergency use
425	5.0	.50	2.3	15 hr	screw	for 5-volt
27	4.9	.30	1.4	30 hr	screw	system or
502	5.1	.15	0.6	100 hr	screw	4 cells
1913	4.0	.06	0.06	1000 hr	screw	emergency use
605	6.15	.50	3.4	15 hr	screw	for 6-volt
31	6.15	.30	2.0	15 hr	screw	system or
40	6.3	.15	0.52	3000 hr	screw	5 cells

Fig. 7–3. Electric lamp data (adapted from R. Strudwick, 1972 NSS Convention presentation).

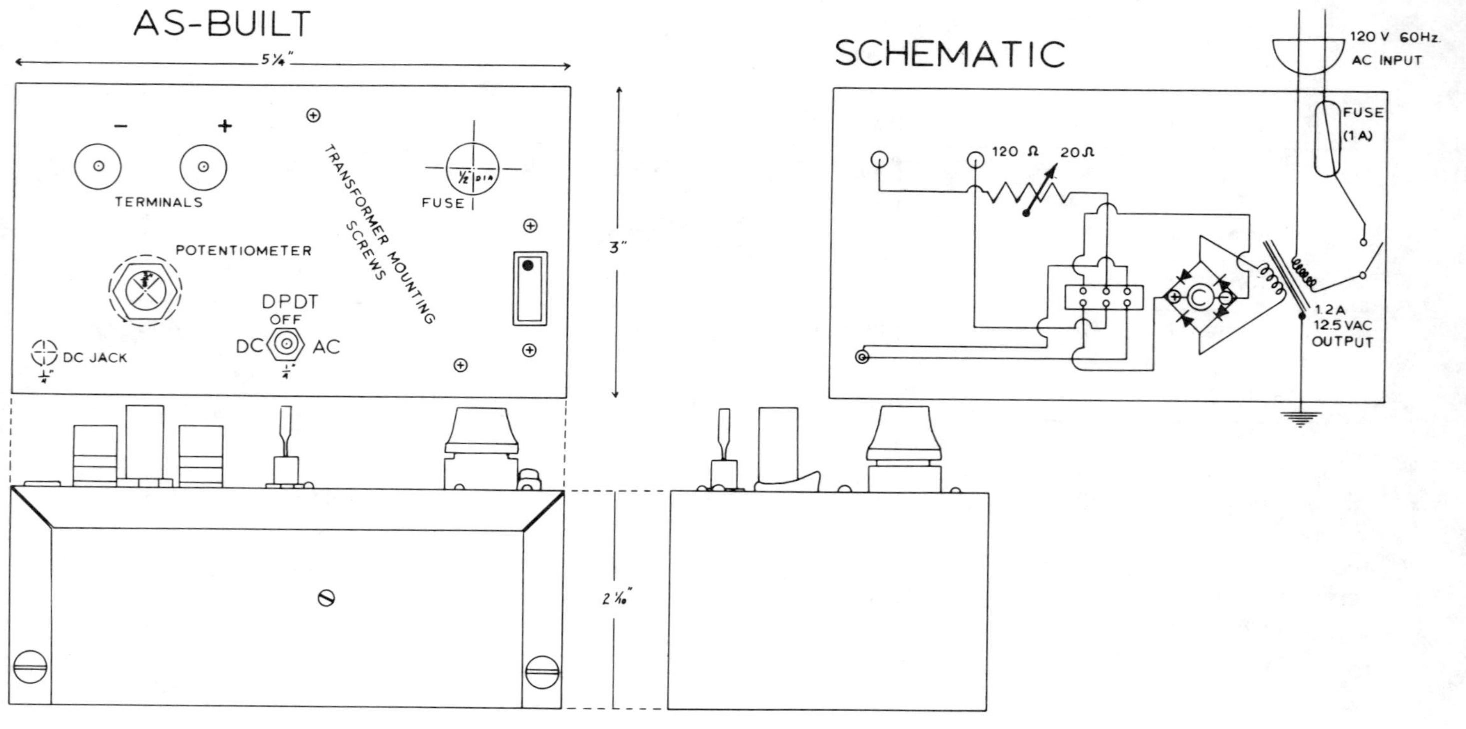

VARIABLE-RATE CHARGER FOR NICKEL-CADMIUM BATTERY

Fig. 7−4. Variable rate charger for nickel-cadmium batteries. (*Courtesy John Tinsley*)

VENTED 6 A-H		VENTED 4 A-H		0.5 A-H (AA Cell)	
Amp	Time (Hr)	Amp	Time (Hr)	Amp	Time (Hr)
1.0	8.2	1.0	5.6	(Sealed Cell)	
0.9	9.2	0.9	6.2	Higher Rates	
0.8	10.3	0.8	7.0	of Recharge	
0.7	12.0	0.7	8.0	Not Recommended	
0.6	14.0	0.6	9.3	.06	11.6
0.5	16.4	0.5	11.2	.05*	14.0
0.4	21.0	0.4*	14.0	.04	17.5
0.3	28.0	0.3	18.7	.03	23.3
0.2	42.0	0.2	28.0	.02	35.0
0.1	84.0	0.1	56.0	.01	70.0

*Maximum Charging Rate

Fig. 7–5. A fully discharged Ni-Cad battery should be charged to 140% of its capacity at a 14-hour rate (sealed cell) at an applied voltage at least two times the output voltage of the battery. Vented cells tolerate blitz charging currents of 3A, however 1A is the best maximum. *(Courtesy John Tinsley)*

	Radio Shack Catalog No.
1 Plug for 115 VAC Wall Outlet	
1 Transformer 12.6 V	273-1505
1 SPST Rocker Switch 6A @250VAC	275-611
1 DPDT Sub Miniature, Center-Off 3A @120VAC	275-1545
1 2 Amp Full-Wave Bridge Rectifier 50 PIV	276-1151
1 100Ω Var. Resistor (POT) 14 Watt	
2 10 Watt Power Resistors (10Ω each)	271-132
1 Set Banana Jacks (1 pr)	274-725
1 Set Banana Plugs (1 pr)	274-721
1 Panel-Mounted Fuse Holder	270-364
1 Pkg 1-A Fuses—3/Pkg	270-1273
1 ¼" Phone Jack, Open Circuit, 2 conductor	274-280
1 ¼" Rt Angle Phone Plug	274-256
1 2-Conductor Miniature Phone Plug	274-286
1 Miniature Closed Circuit Enclosed Phone Jack	274-297
1 Aluminum Box 4" × 6" × 2"	270-245
1 100 μF 35 WVDC Axial Capacitor	

Fig. 7–6. Parts list for battery charger. *(Courtesy John Tinsley)*

Back-up Lights

How many sources of light do cavers need? If you didn't answer *three* without hesitation, you haven't been paying attention. This translates into a main helmet-mounted lamp plus at least two back-up sources. We recommend three back-ups: a flashlight, a chemical light stick, and a candle with matches in a waterproof container. Some cavers take along a complete carbide lamp as a second source. It's an excellent back-up light for both electric or carbide cavers, and if you're of the latter persuasion, it gives you some additional spare parts, too. Furthermore, it is a head lamp so if you need to use it for your main source, it doesn't tie up one of your hands the way a flashlight does. However, having said all that, we'll be the first to admit that the flashlight still reigns supreme as the most common second source of light.

Probably one of the most popular flashlights today is the Eveready Skipper model. It is waterproof, shockproof, and floats in water. It comes in both the D and C sizes. Again, alkaline batteries are best. The C cells have less life than the Ds, but the smaller size and weight are convenient in caving since they are not going to be the main source of light anyway. If you are using D cells in your main light (as in a Justrite), you may prefer to carry a D size flashlight as a spare. An advantage of the Skipper light is its recessed pushbutton-type switch. Not only has this proven reliable for us, but it is nearly impossible to switch on accidentally. If you use a flashlight with a conventional surface-mounted switch, we suggest you reverse one of the batteries when it's not in actual use. By doing this, the batteries won't drain unexpectedly in case the switch is accidentally turned on while bouncing around in your pack.

As the third light source, the Cyalume-brand chemical light stick is a good choice. To use it, you just remove the wrapper, bend it till the inner cylinder breaks, and shake vigorously. It gives a surprising amount of light and it keeps glowing for at least sixteen to eighteen hours. We tested one in a cave when we were about an hour from the entrance. With no other lights, it enabled three of us to get out without mishap through a relatively easy walking and scrambling passage. Incidentally, the thing was still giving off some light after twenty-six hours.

One problem with light sticks is that you can't test them before you use them to be sure they'll work. Since they lose some light output as they age, it's best if you put a fresh one in your pack every year or so just to be safe. We always carry two in each of our packs.

Candles used to be the odds-on favorite for a third source of light and are still widely used. Carry both a candle and a light stick. Common types are 4- or 5-inch long (100- to 125-millimeter) plumber's candles, one-by-two-inch (25-by-50-millimeter) food-warming candles, and votive or religious candles (1½ inches high by 2 inches in diameter—35 by 50 millimeters). These are available in hardware stores and some supermarkets. With the longer candles, it's best to cut them to an inch or an inch-and-a-half long. Dig the wick out carefully so it can be easily lit. Candles should be carried in 35mm film cans or plastic bags to keep everything else in your pack from getting all waxed up. Matches stored in a waterproof container accompany the candles in the caver's pack. These can also be handy for starting a carbide lamp in case the flint or striker assembly fails due to mud or disagreeableness.

Personal Gear

Packs

Besides muddy clothes and a hard hat, another item in the typical caver's kit is a cave pack. Check the surplus stores for sturdy canvas types like the navy gas mask bags or marine fanny packs. A good cave pack should have three general characteristics. It needs a wide (2 inches or so) shoulder strap, long enough so that it can be put over the head and across the chest. In this configuration, the strap won't slip off your shoulder, and it leaves both hands free for crawling or scrambling. Besides a strap, the pack should have a handle or another short strap so it can be carried by hand or tossed forward in a tight spot. Some cavers like an extra strap long enough to use around the waist so the pack doesn't swing so freely from the shoulder. It should open and close easily yet securely. Cave mud can cause problems with certain types of fasteners, but the heavy duty snaps or buckles found on many surplus packs hold up pretty well.

The standard rucksack or weekend pack is also popular for carrying caving supplies to the entrance. However, unless you're blessed with a lot of large walking passages in your caves, you may find the rucksack too bulky and that a single over-the-shoulder strap is much handier. Rucksacks are also good for storing caving gear at home—including helmet, coveralls, and cave pack—so that everything is ready to throw in the car when the call comes.

Besides a pack for caving supplies, you often see people carrying a second pack. Most often, this contains specialized gear for technical vertical work, photography, or a special project. Separate small packs are better for extra gear than one

Fig. 7–7. The well equipped cave pack. *Bottom row:* spare batteries, flashlight, matches in waterproof case, candles, spare parts for carbide lamp, extra carbide in lamp bottoms. *Middle row:* emergency blanket (space blanket), first aid kit, spare carbide in baby bottle, water in plastic bottle. *Top row:* 12 feet of 1-inch tubular nylon with locking carabiner (caver's sling), three Prusik slings of ¼-inch polypropylene or Tenstron, and army surplus gas mask bag with sturdy strap and heavy-duty snap fasteners.

large one because small packs fit through tight spots easier. In really wet conditions, waterproof containers like surplus ammunition cans or sealable plastic bags for boating and rafting are called into play.

Camera Packs and Cases. Minimal protection in easy horizontal caves can be provided by a canvas cave pack with the camera installed in its own leather case inside a plastic bag. However, for serious cave photography, a surplus army ammunition can padded with foam rubber is the most common item seen. Some cavers even make up fitted wooden or aluminum cases for their cameras.

We have had good luck with plastic refrigerator boxes (like Tupperware). These come in a multitude of sizes and have lids that are nearly water- and dust-proof. We select a size that will accommodate camera or flash and wrap each of the heavier pieces in thin (¼-inch—6-millimeter) foam rubber. Film is kept in a sealable plastic bag and goes in the main box or a smaller one like the size for sandwiches. To keep the top of the box in tow, a hinge of 2-inch (50-millimeter) wide plastic tape ("boiler or gaffer tape") is helpful. Finally, a canvas cave pack of appropriate size with wide shoulder strap and stout snaps encloses the plastic boxes.

Caver's Sling

A very useful addition to your personal equipment is a caver's sling made of 12 feet (4 meters) of one-inch (25-millimeter) tubular webbing plus a locking carabiner. It could also be a doubled 24-foot length. The caver's sling has many uses: it can be a waist loop, chest sling, rigging sling (runner), diaper sling, tie-in line, or hauling line. To make it into a loop it is first tied with a water or grapevine knot (see chapter 8). For a chest sling, the same loop can be worn over the shoulders in a crossed loop configuration (fig. 9–8).

Knee Pads

Another important item of personal gear is knee pads. These are absolutely indispensable in caves where any amount of crawling is to be done. After twenty years of living with "caver's knees," we have found the best pads to be wrestler's knee pads. Look for them in sporting goods stores. Of tubular construction, they contain an Ensolite pad (dense foam plastic) which gives excellent comfort and insulation from cold, wet cave floors. The pad is covered with a strong knit fabric which seems to be remarkably immune to cave damage. Probably their best design feature is the wide elastic band in the back. Look for the type with a large cutout in the middle. This keeps the band from bunching up or pinching the inside of your knee when you walk or move about. Recently, some excellent roller skating knee pads with high-impact plastic inserts in front have come on the market. These may be a little more expensive, but they are easy to walk upright in.

We wear knee pads under our coveralls to keep them from snagging or sliding around. However, they go over our inner layer of pants, to help reduce chafing on the back of the knees. For hiking to the cave or in big walking sections, we pull them down into a kind of parade rest position over the shins. Then for crawling and chimneying (they are *such* a comfort in narrow chimneys!), we pull them back up into the operating mode.

Industrial knee pads of thick rubber with straps in the back are also used by many cavers. If you get this type, try crossing the straps in back to help keep them in place. Most people wear these on the outside since they are quite bulky. Unfortunately, you can't easily slide them down when walking is required, so either they irritate the inside of your knees or you take them off and carry them when not crawling.

Other Items

A minimum first-aid kit should be carried by at least one member on each caving trip. Also, every caver should carry water in a canteen or plastic water bottle for drinking water, and many carry a pocketknife, can opener, paper and pencil, and a watch to keep track of time. Cavers who wear glasses outside had better plan to wear them inside caves, too. To guard against loss or breakage, sporting goods stores sell elastic glasses holders that attach to the ear pieces and drape loosely around the neck.

Cave Food. All cavers should carry high-energy food with them to snack on during cave trips. Energy-giving food keeps you going and helps keep body temperature up. It supplements a good meal eaten before the trip. On a long trip, bring enough food for one or more full meals. Cold caves and wet caves put more demands on our system both for energy and heat restoration. Thus you should bring more food on trips to these caves.

Generally, everybody has a favorite variety of cave food, but it all has two common characteristics: it provides high energy, and it is not easily damaged by the rigors of the wet, muddy cave environment. Sugary foods give quick energy. Proteins and fats stick to the ribs more and give longer-lasting energy. Some of each type are best for balance. Here are some of the more common foods seen on a typical cave trip: M & M candies, raisins, or nuts carried in a stout plastic container; canned meat such as tuna fish, Vienna sausage, deviled ham, or boned chicken; dried fruit like apricots or figs; breakfast foods such as granola mixed with nuts and coconut rolled in a plastic bag; small, canned snack-packs of pudding or fruit (beware of sharp edges inside the cans, though); and beef jerky or meat sticks, rolled in plastic.

If you want a sandwich for a snack, a freezer storage box of that size and shape is indispensable. If you have ever tried to enjoy a sandwich that has been smashed to one-eighth its size and is impregnated with cave grit, you will appreciate these handy little plastic boxes.

8

Caving Knots

Knots are vital for all cavers and should be mastered above ground by beginner and advanced caver alike.

Did you know that knots were one of humankind's first inventions and that primitive peoples could not have survived without them? Today, cavers regularly use knots that are direct descendants of the ones used to tie spearhead to spear, bowstring to bow, and hook to fishline.

At first glance, it might seem that knots are more in the province of the vertical caver for use where ascending and descending ropes are required. However, two of the most common situations you run into, even in so-called easy caves, are the short 10-foot drop that's too wide to chimney, or the muddy slope that's too slippery to negotiate because of the spring rains. At moments like this, a rope mysteriously appears from someone's pack and the first caver automatically ties in to be safetied or belayed down (see chapter 11).

So far, the scenario is more-or-less true to life. But suddenly, all action stops. Several cavers, even some of the supposedly experienced ones, don't know how to tie the right knot. Somehow, running a knot-tying class in the middle of a cave trip always seems a little after-the-fact.

Practicing at Home. Fortunately, you only need a few knots for caving and anyone can learn them at home with a little practice.

Start off by getting about 6 feet (2 meters) of 6- to 8-millimeter core-and-sheath Perlon sling rope (such as Edelrid or Mammut accessory cord) and about 12 feet (4 meters) of 1-inch (25-millimeter) tubular nylon webbing. They come in beautiful colors these days, so you can select your favorite hues. Use them to practice knots now. Then later, you can turn them into very useful slings and loops that will become your constant caving companions for years to come. The one-inch webbing will become your basic caver's sling (see chapter 9). It makes into a diaper sling which is one half of a rappelling sling—or a loop (runner) for rigging. The Perlon cord is good as a back-up waist loop, a necessary redundancy for the diaper sling, a rigging runner, or a safety loop (see chapter 9). You may also want to buy a short length (4 feet or 1 meter plus) of 4- or 5-millimeter Perlon. Take this along with you to school or work and practice your knots when you have a spare moment. You may get some blank stares, but it's a good way to start a conversation.

General Thoughts. For knot-tying purposes, the basic parts of the rope (fig. 8–1) are: the end (also called the free end); the standing or load-bearing part; the bight (a doubled section or turn in the rope that doesn't cross itself); and the loop (a turn that does cross itself). Incidentally, there are distinctions between a knot, a hitch, and a bend. At the risk of offending the purists, we're going to call them all knots.

With any knot, form it carefully as you tie it. Be especially cautious that it retains its shape as you tighten it up. This is important; otherwise it may distort its shape and not form correctly. Study the drawings for each knot closely, so you know exactly what it looks like when it's finished. If it doesn't look right, untie it and do it again. Also, keep the picture of it in your mind, so you don't forget to leave a big enough loop in

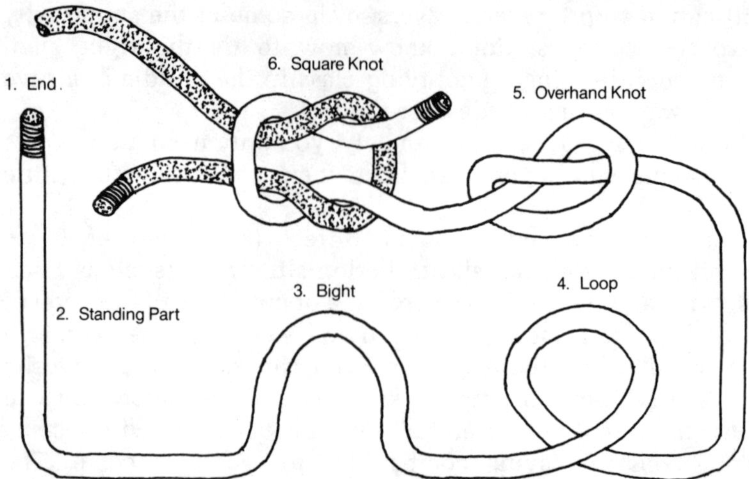

Fig. 8–1. Basic parts of a rope: *1)* end, *2)* standing or load-bearing part, *3)* bight, and *4)* loop. Also shown are *5)* an overhand knot, one of the simplest knots, used as a backup or keeper for several other knots and *6)* the square knot, not really a climbing knot, but useful when coiling rope (see chapter 9).

the middle or some extra at the end for back-up knots. Caving ropes are all made of artificial fibers these days. This means any knot that isn't self-locking must always have one or two back-up or keeper knots to prevent it from working loose.

After snugging a knot up, it should be set with a really hard pull. To set a knot forming a loop, put your foot in the loop and apply as much force as possible. With in-line knots, have someone else grab the rope on the other side of the knot and both of you pull hard. Later, check the knot regularly to be sure it's still tight. It can work loose in nylon. This is especially true with the rigging knot for a main rappelling or prusiking rope which has been loaded several times.

All knots weaken the rope because of their sharp bends and curves. As a rule of thumb, this weakening effect reduces the strength of a climbing rope by about 25 percent to 50 percent. However, modern ropes test at 4500 to 7000 pounds breaking strength. This is an adequate margin of safety. See chapter 9 for a discussion of ropes and their characteristics.

Tying any knot uses 6 to 18 inches of line, two knots proportionately more. Keep this in mind when taking up slack to tie a knot or buying webbing or cord for a sling.

One final caution: unless they're for permanent rigging, knots should not only be easy to tie, but also to untie. You will frequently load knots with your full body weight and more. So ease of untying is not to be taken lightly.

Tying into a Belay Line

Tying yourself into a safety line to be belayed on a tricky pitch (held safely if you fall) will probably be one of the very first applications of your knot-tying talents. Belays are given when you are free climbing a chimney, wall, or slope, traversing along a ledge, climbing a ladder, or any other time when you want the security of a safety line. The decision is up to you. Never be shy about asking to be belayed. It is better to belay than to risk a twisted ankle, broken leg, or worse.

Bowline. The proper knot for tying into a belay line is a form of the bowline, called the bowline-on-a-coil (fig. 8–2.2). The bowline is the closest thing we have to a universal caving knot. It can be used for four of the five basic situations that require knots in caves and is the recommended knot for three of those four. Basically, a bowline is a nonslipping loop that won't tighten like a hangman's noose when you tie it around your waist or chest. It can also be used for raising gear, tying in the belayer, tying two ropes together, and rigging the main rope. Finally, it is much easier to untie than most other knots, even after heavy loading. Simply turn it over, bend down on the back of the loop, and it unthreads quite easily.

The basic bowline is relatively easy to tie (see fig. 8–2.1). It can in fact be tied in more than one way. However, when it's finished, it has a very distinctive look that you should memorize. The important thing is that the free end of the rope must finish off inside the loop. If it does not, the knot is weakened by 50 percent (Wheelock 1967).

Right-handers will find the best way to tie a bowline is to hold the standing part upright in the left hand and lay a small

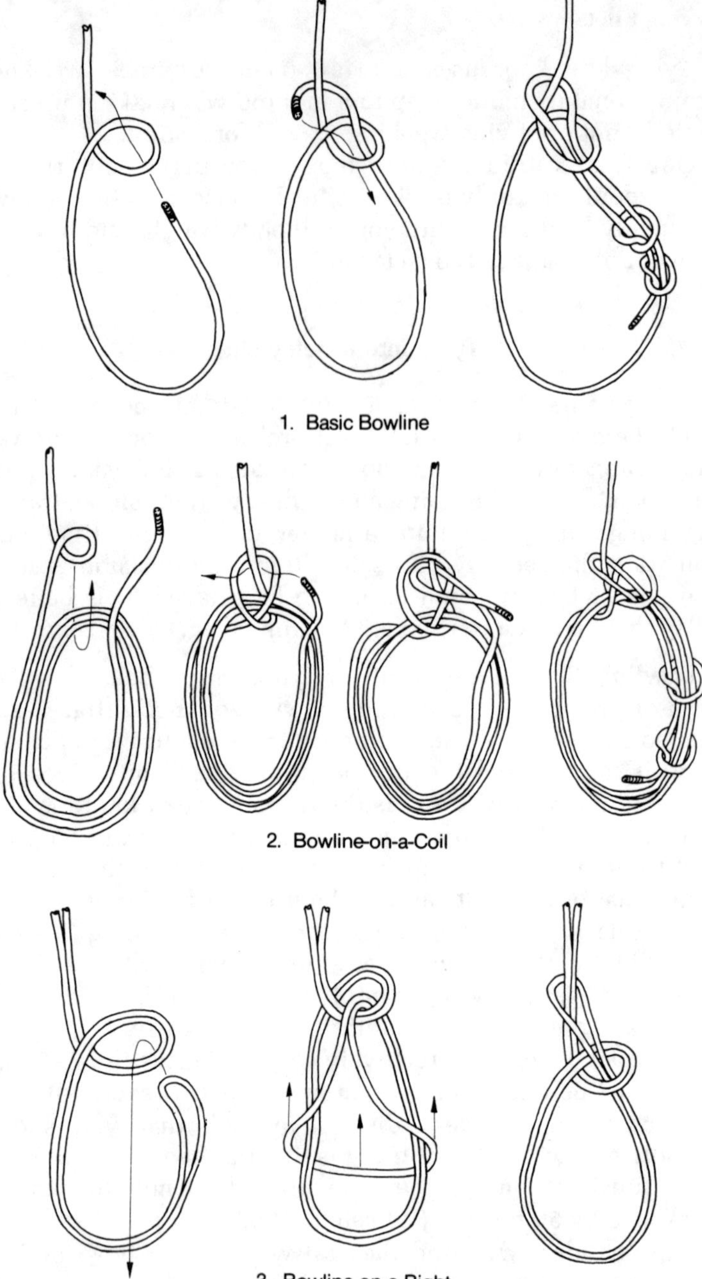

1. Basic Bowline

2. Bowline-on-a-Coil

3. Bowline-on-a-Bight

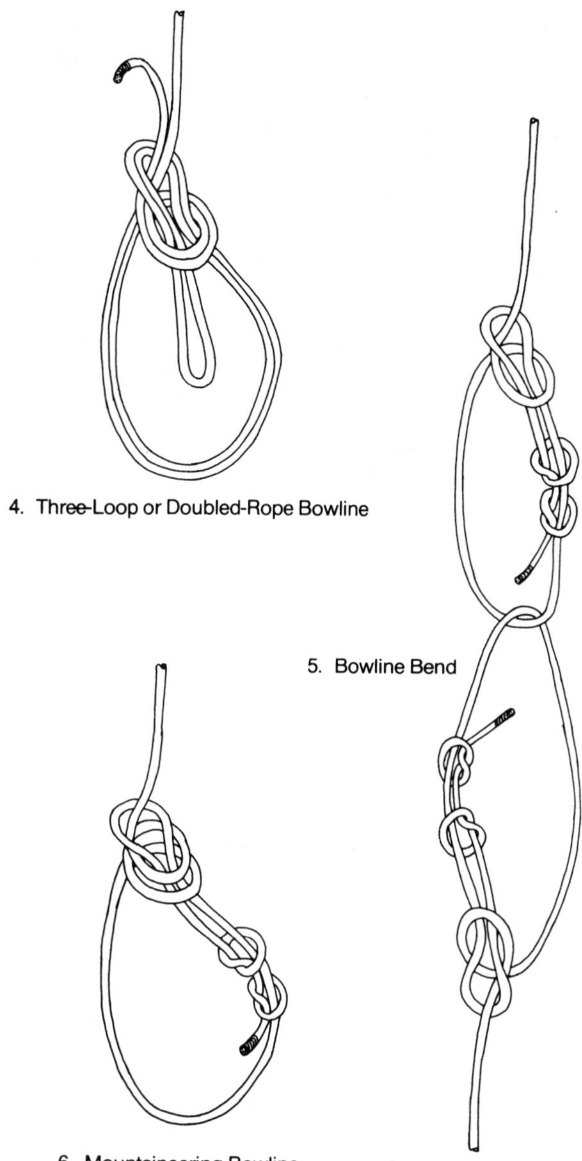

Fig. 8–2. The bowline in its several versions: *1)* basic bowline, *2)* bowline-on-a-coil, *3)* bowline-on-a-bight, *4)* three loop or doubled rope bowline, *5)* bowline bend, *6)* mountaineering bowline.

fist-sized loop over the standing part with the right hand. An alternate way to form this loop is to grasp the upright rope in the right hand with the thumb pointing down. Invert the hand so the thumb is up and you have formed the correct loop. Grasp the loop where the rope crosses itself with the thumb and forefinger of the left hand. Then thread the end of the line up through the loop with your right hand, around the back of the standing part of the line and back down through the loop again, ending up in the center of the main loop. Tighten it carefully and always secure it with two overhand knots. It can work loose in stiff line like new Goldline or PMI. Left-handers can follow the same steps by just reversing the hands.

Bowline-on-a-Coil. For tying into a belay line, the bowline-on-a-coil (fig. 8–2.2) is preferred. The extra coils reduce the shock to the body in case of a fall. It's tied the same way as the regular bowline, except that you first pay (feed) out about 10 or 12 feet of line. Then, while holding the standing part in the left hand, wind the end snuggly around the body four or five times in a counterclockwise motion (from right to left) with the right hand. Be sure the coils are tight around the body. Otherwise, the whole thing may pull right up over your arms and shoulders in a fall.

While still holding the standing part of the line in the left hand, form a loop over the standing part of the line and snake this loop up underneath the coils encircling the body. Be careful not to lose the twist when doing this. Center this loop tightly against the standing part. Then run the end of the line through this loop, behind the standing part, and out the other side of the loop. Finish off with two overhand knots around all the coils. Finally, study the finished knot to see if it has that distinctive bowline look. If not, try again. Your life may depend on it.

Tying Into a Seat Sling. There will be times when you are already wearing a seat harness (with leg loops sewn or tied to a waistband) and need to tie in for a belay. A good seat harness can support your weight even better than a bowline-on-a-coil, especially if you can't be lowered right away and have to hang on the line for any time. If you have on a seat harness you undoubtedly will have a locking carabiner attached to it. So all you need is a small loop to snap into the locking carabiner (a nonlocking carabiner is unsafe in this application). A standard bowline or a figure-of-eight loop would work equally well for this purpose. Some cavers and climbers recommend tying directly to the harness instead of interposing a carabiner, especially in rock climbing where the lead climber is some distance above the belayer. See the discussion in chapter 9 for the pros and cons. To tie directly to the seat harness, use the basic bowline or the rethreaded figure-of-eight loop (fig. 8–3.4).

Incidentally, this question of seat harnesses versus waistbands versus chest loops is complicated. See chapter 9 for a discussion. In general, only a seat harness is safe to hang in for longer than about ten to fifteen minutes. If the belay is set up in such a way that you can't be lowered or there are no ledges or footholds to support part of your weight, avoid tying directly or indirectly to a waistband or chest loop alone.

End Loops for Belayer or Gear

Probably the next most common thing you will need a cave knot for is to make a loop to haul up packs or to tie yourself in when you are a belayer. Ideally, everyone should carry his or her own pack. Nonetheless, it may be safer or more convenient to take off your pack so as not to be encumbered when climbing or chimneying. After three or four people are up, the packs are tied into a line or sling and pulled up. When you are a belayer, you need to tie yourself to an anchor so you don't get jerked off if the climber falls.

Usually, the loop is tied in the end of the rope. Sometimes, the end isn't available, and the loop is tied in the middle (see next section). For a loop at the end of the rope, you can use the figure-of-eight loop (fig. 8–3.2) or bowline-on-a-bight.

It may be tempting to use an overhand loop (fig. 8–3.5) rather than a figure-of-eight loop since it's easier to tie. However, if you've ever had to untie an overhand loop after it's been heavily loaded you won't be tempted to try it again. Ever.

1. Figure-of-Eight

2. Figure-of-Eight Loop

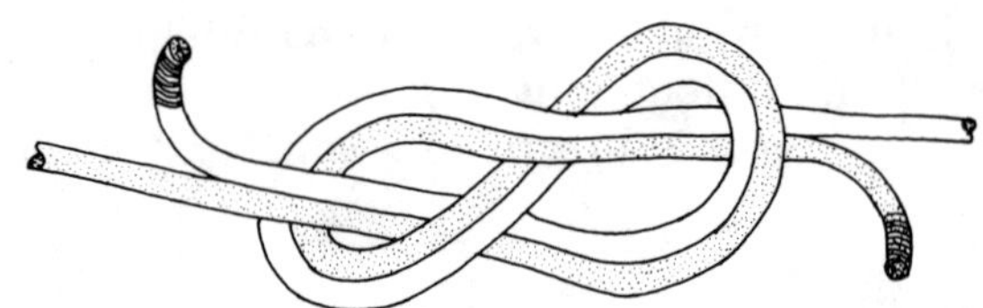

3. Figure-of-Eight or Flemish Bend

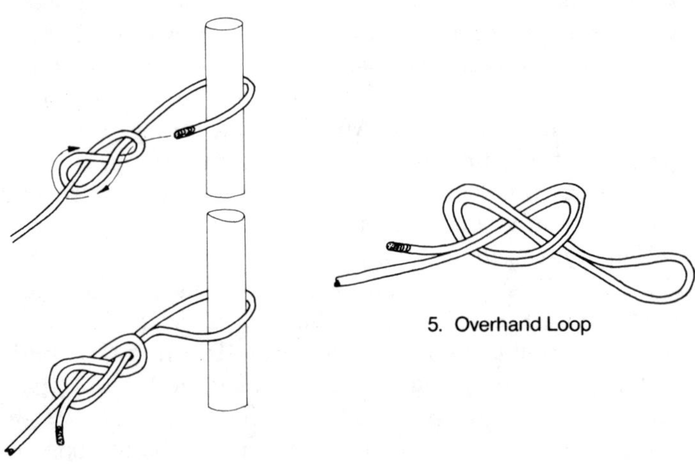

4. Rethreaded Figure-of-Eight Loop

5. Overhand Loop

Fig. 8–3. Figure-of-eight in its various forms: *1)* figure-of-eight, *2)* figure-of-eight loop, *3)* figure-of-eight or Flemish bend, and *4)* rethreaded figure-of-eight loop. Overhand loop (5), shown for comparison, is very hard to untie after loading.

Figure-of-Eight Loop. In recent years the figure-of-eight loop has gained in popularity because it seems easier to tie than a bowline and, like the bowline, it has several applications. You tie it the same way as a figure-of-eight knot, except you first double it into a bight instead of using the single line. It is also called the figure-of-eight-on-a-bight. Some prefer it because it doesn't seem to work loose and therefore doesn't require keeper knots, like a bowline does. When tied correctly, the load-bearing or standing part of the rope forms the outside of the loop of the knot. This subjects it to less bending or stressing than if it were more tightly coiled on the inside.

As with many knots, it's easier to tie than to explain. Refer to the drawing as you go through the steps. First, form a lazy horizontal bight to the right, long enough to contain a loop of the size you eventually need plus about 9 inches more in both top and bottom strands (18 inches total) for the knot itself.

Now—here's the trick to getting it right every time. Be sure that the end of the rope is the lower of the two strands of the bight, as shown in the drawing. Form an underhand loop, pass the bight around the back, under the loop, and finally through the loop. Pull the bight to the right and be careful that the load-bearing strand stays on the outside of the loop.

You can also tie it correctly by starting with an overhand loop (instead of an underhand), in which case the end starts out as the top strand of the bight.

Middle Loops. Oddly enough, the middle of the rope doesn't mean the exact middle by a long shot. It means anywhere in the rope *except* at the two ends. Most often when you tie yourself into the line preparatory to giving someone a belay, you use a middle loop around your waist or clipped into your seat harness with a locking carabiner. Even if you happen to be near the end, the chances are you will use the end to set up the belay anchor, and then tie yourself in a few feet away with a middle loop.

The two knots recommended for tying a loop in the middle are the figure-of-eight loop and the bowline-on-a-bight. To tie the bowline-on-a-bight, see figure 8–2.3. Note that it begins the same as a regular bowline, bringing the end up through the loop, but here it differs a little and is easiest to learn by practicing with the diagram. With the bowline-on-a-bight, you get two loops. If you need three loops, tie the three-loop or doubled-rope bowline (fig. 8–2.4) bringing the end down inside the first two loops so it forms a third long loop. This knot is also called the double bowline.

As when tying in to be belayed, instead of tying the line directly to your body, if you have a seat harness, attach yourself to the anchor point with a safety loop (see chapter 9) or rigging sling (runner).

Joining Two Ropes Together

The ropes you will most often be tying together are the ends of your slings—the general purpose caving sling, safety loop, and prusik (ascender) slings. To tie two main ropes together, use the water knot, grapevine knot, or bowline bend.

Water Knot. To tie the caving sling in 1-inch tubular webbing, the water knot is nearly perfect (only stitching would be better). It almost seems as if it was specifically invented for the flat surfaces of webbing. The water knot is also called the overhand bend, ring bend, sling knot, or tape knot. It is not especially easy to untie after loading, but then neither is the grapevine, another knot often used for webbing.

Tying it is simplicity itself. Tie an overhand knot in one end, leaving it fairly loose and open. Then take the other end, and starting at the point where the first end emerges from the first knot, thread the second end back through the first knot in the opposite direction. The ends will finish up on opposite sides of the knot. To tighten properly, attach the loop to a solid anchor, put your foot inside the loop, and bounce your full weight on it. Secure the water knot with an overhand keeper knot on each side. Otherwise it may work itself loose. If you don't tie a keeper knot, be sure to leave at least 2 inches of free end on each side. Check it regularly to be sure it is still tight. You can use this knot for other sizes of tubular webbing or flat braided webbing as well.

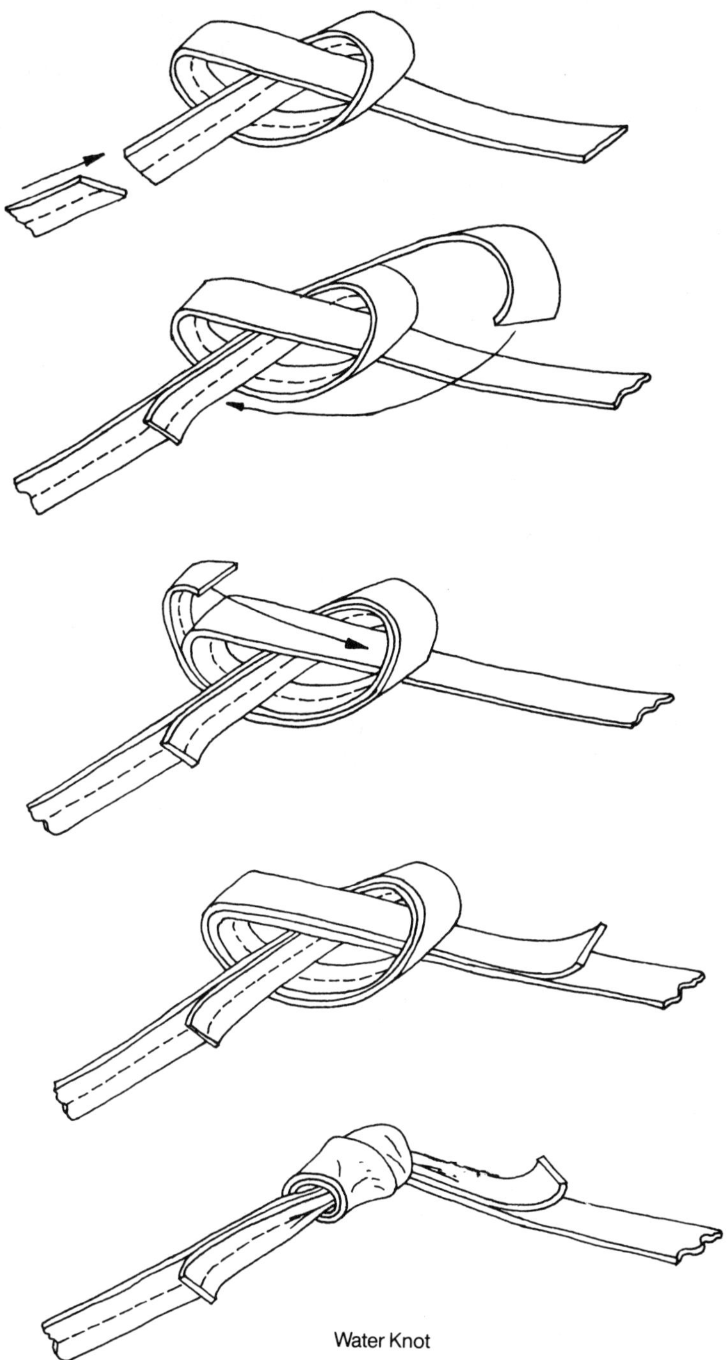

Fig. 8–4. Water knot. Especially good for webbing. Also known as the tape knot, sling knot, or webbing knot.

Grapevine Knot. Just as the water knot seems so perfect for webbing sling, so is the grapevine (fig. 8–5.1) perfect for medium-diameter safety loops and ascending or prusik slings. It is also called the double fisherman's knot and the double overhand knot. Although it resembles the fisherman's knot (fig. 8–5.2) in appearance and construction, the grapevine excels because it is self-locking and doesn't require keeper knots.

To fashion your 6- to 8-millimeter cord into a safety loop, tie the grapevine as shown in the drawing. Tie the first half on the right side, then flip the whole thing 180 degrees to tie the second half on that side too.

The grapevine is a little trickier to tie than the fisherman's knot but it is very pleasing aesthetically when tied right, with the two sides snugged up.

For ascending slings we recommend a $5/16$- or $3/8$-inch stranded or laid rope. We've had excellent luck with Tenstron, but Goldline is also used. Some prefer to use a core-and-sheath rope, like 7- to 9-millimeter Perlon or $5/16$-inch Bluewater (see chapter 9). Here again the ideal knot is the grapevine. A fisherman's knot is also good, but must be secured by an overhand keeper knot on each side.

Joining Two Main Ropes

Bowline Bend. You may have occasion to tie two main ropes together when more length is needed. Two regular bowlines, secured as always with overhand knots, are very good for this. Tie one bowline in the end of the first rope. Then simply pass the loop of the second through the first loop while the second is being tied. This is called a bowline bend (fig. 8–2.5). It is very strong and does not lose strength even if used with ropes of widely varying diameters or of different types, such as braided and laid. One text on knots (Irving 1968) cites this as the strongest knot for joining laid or hawser ropes. It is very easy to untie.

To make a somewhat more compact knot or to use up less rope, tie a grapevine knot. It's a little faster to tie than a

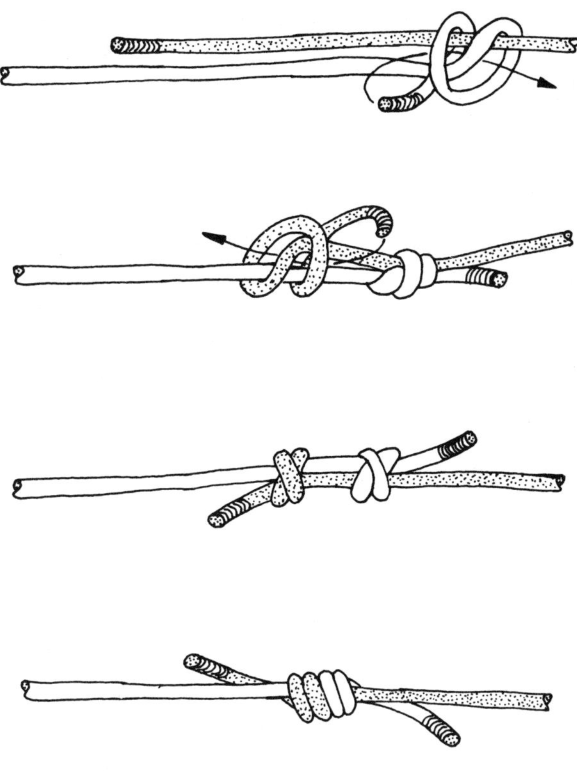

Grapevine or Double Fisherman's Knot

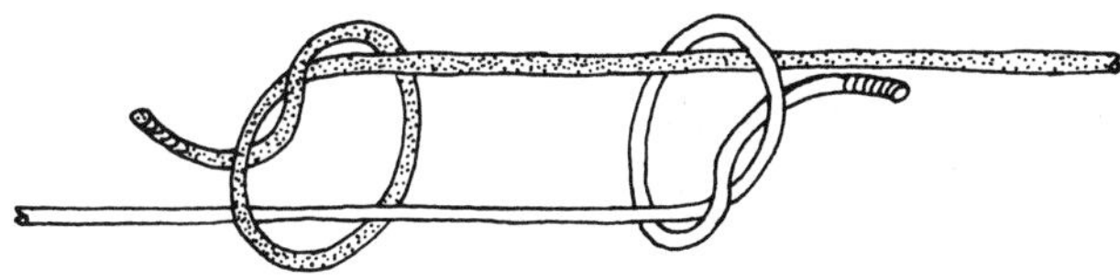

Fisherman's Knot

Fig. 8–5. *1)* **Grapevine Knot. Also called the double fisherman's knot.** *2)* **The fisherman's knot is shown for comparison.**

bowline bend and uses only about 28 inches of rope to tie in 11-millimeter rope, as against about 60 inches for the bowline bend. It can be hard to untie, however, after heavy loading.

A figure-of-eight bend (fig. 8–3.3), although harder to tie is another possibility, if both ropes are the same size. If not, stay with the bowline bend or grapevine. A figure-of-eight bend is tied like the water knot, except you begin with a figure-of-eight in one end instead of an overhand knot. Again, be sure the load-bearing strand is on the outside. A disadvantage of this knot is that it will be harder to untie than the grapevine or bowline.

Despite the fact that these three knots take different amounts of line to tie, they all extend about the same longitudinal distance or length when tied (about 8 to 12 inches from top to bottom of the knot). So longitudinal distance or length is not a factor as far as passing the knots when rappelling or ascending is concerned (see chapter 14).

Knots for Rigging

Rigging is covered in detail in chapter 12, but let us just remind you here that we recommend the use of two anchor points, one main and one back-up.

Our recommendation for an anchor tied around a fixed object like a large boulder or block, base of a stalagmite (if you're sure it's solid and there is no alternative), or tree, is the mountaineering bowline (fig. 8–2.6). This is also known as the double-knotted bowline. It should not be confused with the doubled-rope or three-loop bowline. The mountaineering bowline is often preferred by rock climbers because it is stronger than the regular bowline yet is no more difficult to tie. Simply make two loops over the main line and proceed as with the standard bowline. Like all bowlines, it is very easy to untie even after being severely loaded. The standard bowline is also widely used for anchoring.

For securing midrope anchors, as for example to a carabiner attached to a sling or bolt, either a bowline-on-a-bight, a figure-of-eight loop, or a three-loop bowline is good. The figure-of-eight loop probably deserves the edge in this application because it doesn't need the keeper knot of the three-loop bowline. However, its greater difficulty of untying should be taken into consideration.

Tying to a Fixed Line

To attach yourself to a static or fixed line—either to ascend with knots, or to tie in when you are a belayer or working near an edge—we favor the Prusik knot (fig. 8–6). It was first

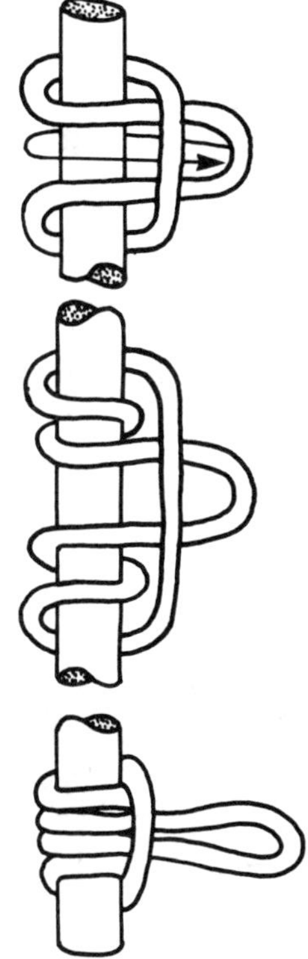

Fig. 8–6. Prusik knot. The original (and many believe the best) knot, named after Dr. Karl Prusik.

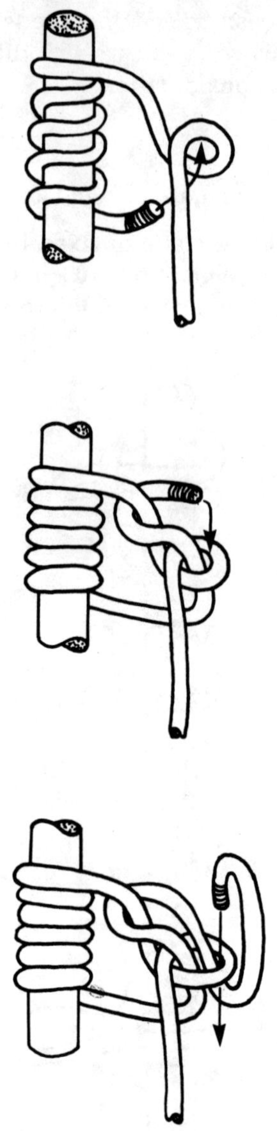

Helical Knot

Fig. 8–7. Helical knot. Also called the ascender knot, Pemberthy knot, P–H knot, and several other names.

described in 1931 by Dr. Karl Prusik for avalanche rescue. Although there have been numerous "improved" versions (some sixteen are listed by Thrun, *Prusiking*, 1971), we prefer to stay with the Prusik knot.

The basic idea of the Prusik knot is that it holds fast when your weight is on it. However, when you remove the pressure it can be slid upward, more or less painlessly. It's extremely easy to tie. Just remember how you used to wrap a rubber band around a pencil when you were daydreaming on a warm spring afternoon in the seventh grade. Remember? That's all there is to it.

Figure 8–6 shows it in a four-coil, right-handed version. On braided or core and sheath rope, it won't make any difference in holding power if it's right- or left-handed, but it may be better to use a right-hand version on laid rope. However, the right- or left-handed version may be easier for you to loosen. So, if you're going to ascend with it, see which is best for you. It can also be tucked through one more time to form a six-coil version, useful on slippery or icy ropes.

An alternative to the Prusik knot is the helical knot (fig. 8–7). It is called by a host of other names, including path, pemberthy, and ascender knot. Some claim it is stronger and easier to move up. If you ascend with knots often, this may be a better choice for you. But if you mainly want a knot to attach a safety loop to a static line, the added snugness of the Prusik may actually be an advantage over the floppy, loose-fitting helical knot.

Summary of Recommended Knots

Tying-in for a Belay	End:	Bowline-on-a-coil
	To Seat Sling:	Bowline, Figure-of-eight loop.
Loop for Belayer or Hauling	End:	Bowline
	Middle:	Figure-of-eight loop.
Tying Ends	Webbing:	Water knot
	Sling Cord:	Grapevine

	Main Rope:	Bowline bend, Grapevine, Figure-of-eight bend
Rigging	End:	Mountaineering bow-line
	Middle:	Figure-of-eight loop.
Tying to Static Line		Prusik

9

Caving Ropes

Ropes, slings, and harnesses for beginning and advanced caving.

Ropes are a caver's lifeline. Thus, there is great comfort in the fact that modern caving and climbing ropes do not break (Robbins 1979). They can be cut by abrasion, melted through by excessive friction, eaten away by chemicals like battery acid, or just plain worn out by misuse—but they don't break all by themselves.

For caving, ropes are used for four main purposes: descending, ascending, protection, and handlines. Rappelling and prusiking are descending and ascending techniques adapted from mountaineering, now highly developed by cavers. Protection for a climber is provided by belaying (stopping a fall with a rope tied to the waist). Hand lines are used to assist a climber on short slopes or tricky spots.

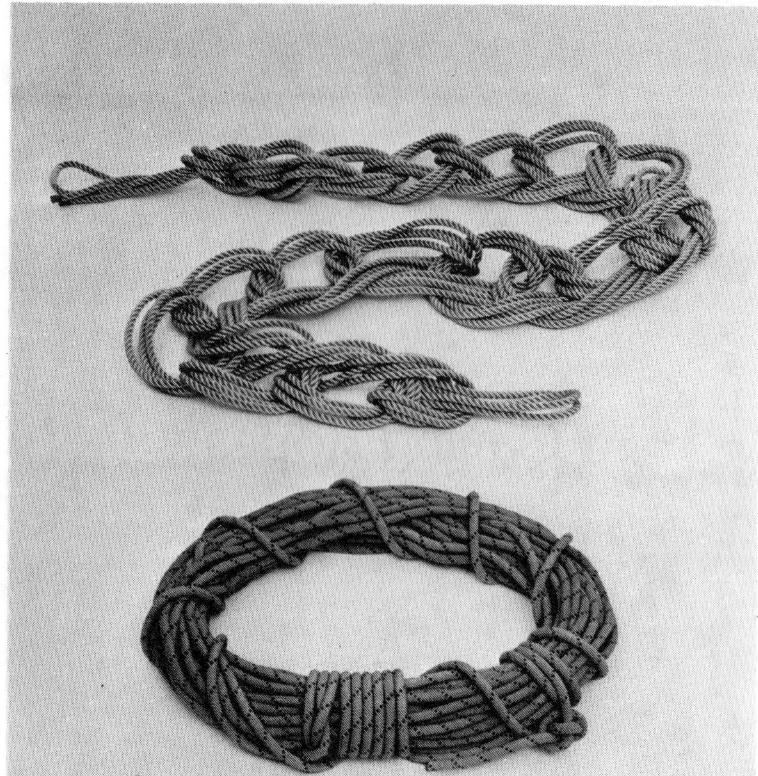

Fig. 9–1. Caving ropes. Breaking strengths are 6200 pounds or 2800 kilograms for Goldline *(above),* and 5700 pounds (at a knot) or 2588 kilograms for Blue Water II *(below).* Goldline is a mountain laid nylon climbing rope used in caving. Blue Water II, a low-stretch static rope made specifically for caving, is probably the most widely used caving rope. A new caving rope, Pigeon Mountain Industries (PMI), has recently been introduced. European alpine ropes, such as Edelrid and Mammut, use the same core and sheath construction as Blue Water and PMI.

Rope Characteristics

Static Caving Ropes. Caving and rock climbing ropes share many characteristics, but differ in one important way. Generally, climbing ropes need much greater stretch or shock-absorbing ability to protect a falling lead climber with a dynamic belay. A belay stops a falling climber by means of a rope tied to the waist. The idea of the dynamic belay is to stop the falling climber "softly," so the rope doesn't break, yet the climber's body (internal organs and skeletal structure) are not damaged either. Lead climbing, where the climber is some distance above the last anchor point of the rope, is not all that common in caving. In fact, a highly elastic or dynamic rope can be a distinct disadvantage in rappelling and prusiking, as explained later.

Ropes designed specifically for caving, like Bluewater and Pigeon Mountain, are static ropes rather than dynamic. They stretch less than 2 percent at low loads (200 pounds or 91 kilograms). At their breaking points, they stretch 15 to 20 percent. Dynamic climbing ropes have similar low-load stretch (typically 3 percent) but will elongate by as much as 80 percent before breaking. Goldline, an older rope than Bluewater or Pigeon Mountain, is also widely used by cavers, in its hard-lay mountaineering version. It is actually a dynamic rope with 7.2 percent elongation at low loads.

Rope Ratings: Breaking Strength. Ropes are rated in two ways: breaking strength and breaking elongation or the ability to sustain a certain number of leader falls. Static caving ropes are generally rated by average breaking strength. Their lower breaking/elongation characteristic causes them to fail the minimum rating of three leader falls.

Typically, caving ropes have an average breaking strength of about 6000 pounds (2721 kilograms). This strength is reduced in the cave environment because of the water, mud, and abrasion that ropes are subjected to. Also, remember there is a weakening effect caused by a knot or the sharp bend where a rope passes over a carabiner. These are estimated by the Plymouth Cordage Company (manufacturers of Goldline rope) and others to reduce the average breaking strength of a rope by about 25 to 50 percent. Conservatively, this turns a 6000 pound rope into a 3000 pound rope. This in turn must be diminished by a safety factor. British cavers recommend a safety factor of at least 12 for ropes handling human beings (plus any shock load on the rope when catching a fall). A safety factor of 5 is specified for hauling ropes (Cullingford

1969). So, with the factor of 12 multiplied by a nominal caver weight of 200 pounds, this comes to 2400 pounds, not too far from the derated 3000 pound working strength of a rope.

UIAA Fall Absorption Tests. The Union of International Alpine Associations (UIAA) is a European organization that has set up standards for ropes and other technical climbing equipment. Its energy absorption tests involve attaching a rope to an anchor, then dropping an 80-kilogram load for 11-millimeter ropes (176-pounds), or 40-kilogram load for 9-millimeter (88-pounds) ropes for a distance of 5 meters (16.4 feet). A recovery time of five minutes is specified between drops. The minimum requirement is to sustain three drops. Goldline meets the minimum requirement, by withstanding three falls, but fails the overall test due to greater low-load stretch (7.2 percent as against a UIAA maximum of 3 percent). Bluewater sustains two falls, less than the minimum requirement, but meets the low-load stretch requirement.

Recommended Size and Length. For caving use, $^7/_{16}$-inch (11-millimeter) is the size recommended. Goldline and Bluewater also come in $^3/_8$-inch (about 9-millimeters). While this weight is somewhat less than the $^7/_{16}$-inch (about 2 pounds per 100 feet), it is significantly weaker. Goldline in $^3/_8$-inch tests at only 3700 pounds rather than 6200.

As far as length goes, climbing ropes are usually sold in lengths of 120, 150, 165 (50 meters) or 300 feet. For general caving use, the choice of one of these lengths really depends on the depth of the vertical pitches in your caves. In fact, if you only have 20-to 30-foot pitches, a 60-foot length of rope is often more than adequate and a lot easier to carry. For the long drops it is not unusual to see lengths of 500 to 1200 feet or more, depending on the cave.

Handlines are either $^3/_8$- or $^7/_{16}$-inch (9- or 11-millimeters) of 30 to 50 feet in length. The larger diameter is easier to hold on to, but takes up more room in a pack.

Types of Ropes

Manila, Sisal, and Hemp

None of the natural fiber ropes made of manila, sisal, or

CAVING ROPES AND SLINGS

| Rope | Diameter or Size | | Con-struction | Pounds per 100 feet | Breaking Strength | | Stretch with 200 pound (90 Kilogram) load | Maximum Elongation at B/S† | UIAA Falls | Price per Foot | Remarks |
	Inches	Milli-meters			Pounds	Kilo-grams					
Goldline	7/16	11	Mtn. Laid	6	6200	2815	7%	50%	3	$.35	General caving and climbing use, incl. dynamic belaying.
	3/8	9	(Three strand twisted)	4	3200	1453	NA	NA	NA	.25	
Blue Water II/III	7/16	11	Core and	6	5700	2585	2%	21%	2	.35	Rappelling and prusiking in caving and climbing.
PMI	7/16	11	Sheath	6	5500	2494	2%	15%	NA	.35	
Kernmantel (Mammut, Edelrid)	—	11	Core and Sheath	5	5000	2270	3%	55%	4–11	.53	General caving and climbing, incl. dynamic belaying.
	—	9		3½	3500	1590	3%	55%	10–30		
One inch Nylon Webbing	1	25	Tubular	—	4000	1816	—	—	—	.18	Rappel, waist, chest, seat, and tie-off slings. All purpose sling material.
Two inch Nylon Webbing	2	50	Flat	—	6000	2725	—	—	8	.25	Rappel and various body slings.
Perlon	—	6 to 8	Core and	—	2000	908	—	—	—	.28	Safety loops
Perlon	—	9	Sheath	—	3500	1590	—	—	—	.30	Hand lines
Tenstron	5/16	—	Laid	—	1900	863	—	—	—	.12	Prusik Slings
Blue Water II	5/16	—	Core and Sheath	—	3500	1590	—	—	—	.29	Prusik slings.

*Estimated. European ropes are not rated in total breaking strength, but in resistance to breakage when holding a fall. NA: Not Available. — Not applicable.
†(% of original length)
Source: Manufacturer's catalogs.

Fig. 9–2. Caving ropes and slings (from manufacturer's specifications).

hemp, are suitable for caving. Manila once was used for prusik slings, but even this usage has largely been discontinued. Artificial fibers are superior in every way for the wet, muddy conditions of caving, and have made natural-fiber ropes obsolete.

Nylon

Nylon ropes, as used in caving and mountaineering, were originally developed for the U.S. Army Mountaineering Corps during World War II. Nylon ropes have tremendous strength because each strand is made up of a series of continuous filaments running the entire length of the rope. Nylon yarns used for ropes are nylon Type 6, Type 66, and Variety 707, and Super 707. They differ somewhat in strength and resistance to heat and ultraviolet radiation, but have all been successfully used in climbing ropes.

The term Perlon (a European trade term for nylon Type 6) is sometimes loosely applied to all core and sheath rope. In today's usage, it often is used to describe the smaller diameter accessory cord (5- to 9-millimeter) used for slings.

Although nylon is unaffected by many chemicals, there are a few that can cause fatal damage. Therefore, we believe the best policy is not to mess around and just consider them all dangerous. Among these, the one you're most likely to run into is battery acid (electrolyte), NaOH, from electric helmet lamps or cars. Others to be especially careful about are phenols (carbolic acid—C_6H_5OH), cresols (C_2H_8O), household bleaches, and paints. Temperatures above 150 degrees C (302 degrees F) in air, which can easily be reached if nylon rubs against nylon, are also dangerous.

A word of caution: Don't let any synthetic fiber like nylon run against another synthetic fiber: it can melt and fuse together. Such a situation can occur in an out-of-control rappel where the main climbing rope is brought into a braking position against a nylon seat harness. The moving rope is not damaged, because the heat built up is distributed over the entire length. But the other half of the frictional heat is concentrated on one spot on the harness, and the temperature will quickly rise to 500 degrees F (260 degrees C), the melting point of nylon. Even under control, fast rappels (more than 40 feet or 12 meters per minute) generate excessive heat and can damage a rope. You can learn about weld abrasion quite easily. Tie a 1-inch (25-millimeter) sling to a tree or rock just out of reach. Take an old or retired rope and put your feet into loops in the end. Then saw back and forth with as much weight and force as possible. A few dozen strokes and the rope will cut right through the webbing.

Ultraviolet radiation from sunlight causes a gradual weakening of nylon. In caving, however, ropes will usually be retired for other reasons, such as abrasion, before deterioration from sunlight occurs. British mountaineering standards call for a limit of 100 days of outdoor rope use, and fewer days for slings.

Nylon stiffens with use. This can be offset by treatment with commercial fabric softeners during washing (see below under rope care). When wet, nylon is weakened by about 15 percent. This loss is not particularly significant in most cases, but keep it in mind in wet caves.

Handling characteristics of nylon ropes are also of importance. A rope that's too stiff or too limp doesn't handle as well as one of medium stiffness. If a rope is too stiff it's hard to tie knots in it and have them stay tied. If it's too soft, it's hard to keep in a neat coil, toss down a slope, or snake around projections. Handling is somewhat a matter of personal preference, so when buying a rope, check its feel and knot-holding abilities.

Laid or Hawser Ropes. The most outstanding example of the laid rope is Goldline Mountain Lay from the Plymouth Cordage Company. It is a harder, more tightly woven laid rope specifically designed for climbing use. Its breaking strength is 6200 pounds (2800 kilograms). In 1978, Goldline introduced a new rope called a Goldline II with improved resistance to ultraviolet radiation. Other characteristics are essentially the same. Goldline also used to be cheaper than kernmantel ropes, but the price is just about the same now. Despite the introduction of newer ropes, Goldline retains its popularity with some cavers because it is versatile and resists abrasion well. It can be used for dynamic belaying, prusiking, rappelling, and hauling.

Although Goldline is rather stiff and somewhat more difficult to coil or braid than core and sheath ropes, the surface becomes soft and quite pleasant to the touch after some use. This fuzzy surface is actually caused by abrasion, and it helps protect the surface against any further abrasion. Be careful when tying knots in Goldline or any other laid rope. The stiffness can make it hard to form the knot properly and keep its shape as it is tightened.

Goldline has two disadvantages: it has greater stretch than caving ropes, and it twists when it hangs free. Stretch makes beginning a roped ascent more difficult, because the slack has to be taken up by your body weight before you actually get going. More seriously, its stretching increases the sawing action of the rope against sharp or jagged surfaces, making good rope padding even more vital. Twisting is a real problem on free drops, but where most roped descents and ascents are against the wall, Goldline still finds application.

Kernmantel Ropes. Kernmantel or core and sheath ropes originated in Europe. The basic materials used by all manufacturers are similar, but construction details are different. The core accounts for about two-thirds of the total strength, the sheath the remaining third. In the United States, Bluewater II and Super III, and Pigeon Mountain Industries (PMI) are ropes designed specifically for caving that use this same type of construction. Common European climbing ropes seen in the United States are Edelrid, Mammut, and Edelweiss. Goldline also markets a gold-colored, core-and-sheath rope called Goldmantel which is manufactured in Europe.

Core-and-sheath construction uses an inside core of continuous filament nylon. The filaments are grouped into strands. Blue Water and Pigeon Mountain have about eighteen to twenty strands, untwisted. Other brands use from two to fourteen strands, twisted together. Mammut Dynamic uses a single tightly-braided strand. The difference in core construction accounts for the slight differences in resistance to twisting and energy-absorbing characteristics.

Over the entire central core is a protective sheath made of more or less tightly braided nylon. This holds the core together and protects it against abrasion and ultraviolet radiation. One of the main benefits of the core-and-sheath construction is that the core strands are laid in such a way that there is virtually no twisting or kinking of the line. This no-twist quality is extremely important in caving rope where long free rappels and prusiks are common. It is also somewhat easier to coil or braid these ropes for carrying and storage because they avoid the tendency to kink.

Blue Water and PMI. Blue Water was the first static rope developed specifically for caving by cavers and is undoubtedly the most widely used caving rope in North America. It is now available in two versions: Blue Water II and Super III. Both have nearly identical specifications for strength, elongation, and abrasion resistance. Super III is somewhat more flexible and softer to the touch. It is, however, faster on rappels when new.

More recently, a new static caving rope has appeared from Pigeon Mountain Industries (PMI). It shares characteristics with Blue Water.

Blue Water and PMI have several major benefits for caving. First, they are static ropes with less than 2 percent stretch at low loads (200 pounds or 91 kilograms). If you have clipped into a line to prusik and found yourself climbing 10 to 15 feet before you get off the ground, you will appreciate the low-stretch characteristics of static caving ropes. Blue Water and PMI are constructed with the core-and-sheath design to resist abrasion. This is very important when using mechanical ascenders which have teeth or grooves that bite into the rope to secure their grip. Blue Water and PMI ropes do not twist when hanging free as do laid ropes.

Static ropes like Blue Water and PMI are specifically not recommended for dynamic belaying in leader climbing. They are used, however, for static belaying on short pitches in caving using the sitting hip belay (see chapter 11).

Blue Water II and Super III in 7/16-inch diameter specify a breaking strength of 5700 pounds (2585 kilograms) at a steel bar with a midshipman's knot (a variety of bowline). PMI specifies 5500 pounds (2494 kilograms) under similar conditions with a bowline.

Dacron, Polypropylene, and Terylene

Dacron ropes, which are widely used in sailing, are not really suitable for caving. Even though they have very little stretch, they are usually too soft and limp for prusiking. Recently, polypropylene ropes such as Tenstron (a three-strand laid rope) have come into use in caving for Prusik knots. In general, these are excellent ropes for this purpose in either the 5/16- or 3/8-inch (8-to 9-millimeter) diameter. Polypropylene ropes test at approximately 1200 to 2000 pounds (550 to 900 kilograms) in these smaller diameters. Terylene (polyester) is another material used in some European yachting ropes. Its main potential attraction to cavers is its resistance to battery acid. So far there has not been enough experience to fully evaluate Terylene ropes for caving.

Care of Ropes

Don't Walk on the Rope. What's the first rule of rope care? Go to any climbing practice and you'll hear it echoed several times: Careful, don't walk on the rope! A related, but sometimes forgotten, precept is don't drag the rope across the ground. Pick it up and carry it instead. The reason for both these basic rules is that small chips of rock and dirt or grit can become lodged in the rope and actually cut the fibers.

Rope Pads. To protect a rope which runs over a sharp edge, some kind of padding must be used (see chapter 12). This can be something as prosaic as a jacket in an emergency, but we use specifically designed pads of canvas or leather, each with a tie-off cord to keep it in position.

Storing and Preparing Ropes

When not in use, a rope should be kept properly coiled or braided and stored out of the sunlight. Ultraviolet light damages synthetic ropes. Untie any knots immediately after use and remove any kinks. Otherwise the rope may take the shape of the knot or kink.

New ropes will usually have the ends properly treated to prevent unraveling. If not, or if you cut a rope into pieces, you can fuse the ends by using a flame from either a carbide lamp, a propane torch, or heat from a soldering iron.

Use a spatula or wet fingers to form the end and keep it from expanding larger than the original diameter of the rope. Be careful not to drip any hot nylon on the hands because it really burns. It has a tendency to stick to the skin and is very difficult to brush off. If you expect to run the rope through a pulley, try to form the ends to a blunt point. To do this, work slowly and keep the fingers wet to avoid getting burnt. With tubular nylon webbing, you may want to cut the end at an angle before fusing, which makes it easier to insert into a buckle. When fusing webbing, press the two sides of the ends together to form a neat seal.

Another method is using a heat cutter designed by John deBoer (1979). Like the ones used in rope supply stores, it fuses the loose ends of rope and webbing as they are being cut. Use 10-gauge solid copper wire about 5 or 6 inches long. Bend it into a smooth, broad tip as shown in figure 9–3, and install it in a soldering gun. Place the rope or webbing on a piece of glass or asbestos tile. Turn the gun on and apply pressure to the rope. While not as fast as the commercial heat cutters, this will do a good job if you don't rush things.

Avoid using any chemical or paint markers on rope which might weaken the nylon. Battery electrolyte is very damaging to nylon rope. Don't store ropes with head lamp batteries or transport them together in a car trunk. Also a trunk frequently gets extremely hot in the summertime, hot enough to be damaging to nylon ropes.

Braiding. When carrying a rope in a cave, the standard rope coil used by climbers can sometimes cause a problem with the rope snagging on projections. There are two good alternatives. The first is to carry the rope in a bag or gunny sack tied at the ends with parachute cord or thin Perlon sling, perhaps with a carabiner inserted for hauling purposes.

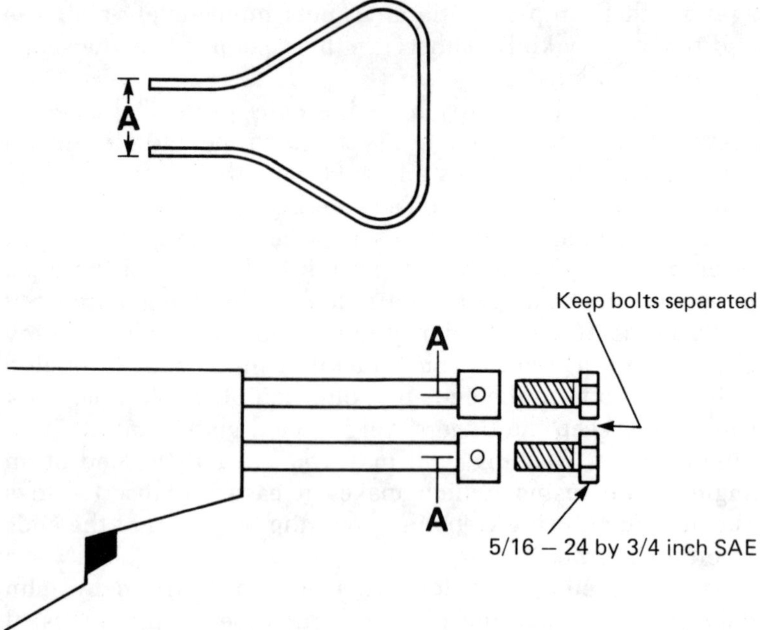

Fig. 9–3. Heat cutter made from #10 wire and a soldering gun, simultaneously cuts and fuses rope ends. *(Courtesy John de Boer)*

The second method is called braiding, which every beginning caver is urged to learn (figure 9–4). First remove any knots and kinks. Then double the rope several times, reducing its overall length to about 20 to 30 feet of doubled or quadrupled strands. After forming an overhand loop in the end, bring successive loops through each preceding loop as shown. By this technique, it is possible to reduce a 120-foot length of rope to about 8 to 9 feet. This resulting braid is relatively flat and fits easily across the shoulders for carrying. A braided rope is also easier to wash than a coiled rope.

Coiling. For open cave passages where the rope is not apt to snag, another technique to use is coiling. Several methods are in use today, but one of the simplest is where the rope is wound between the knee and foot as shown in figure 9–5.

First take out any knots and kinks. Then run two or three loops around knee and heel, and tie a square knot around the loop leaving the short end of the rope about 12 to 15 inches long. The remaining rope is carefully wound between knee and foot, using the heel to prevent the rope from sliding off, until about 10 feet are left. At this point, thread the remaining length around and around the coil until the square knot is reached. Here, wrap several tight loops around the rope and tie a square knot using this end and the remaining length of the short end. Wrapping the long end around the loose coils helps keep the rope from snagging when transporting it underground.

Fig. 9–4. Braiding a rope. A braided rope is less likely to snag or tangle in cave usage. It is especially useful for longer ropes, 200 feet and up.

Rope Washing

Mud and grit are problems for caving ropes for two reasons. First, a rope often gets completely coated with mud. It can get so bad that ascenders don't even move. We have had this happen often in muddy Sierra caves.

The second reason why grit on ropes is more damaging in cave usage is that ascenders are used much more by cavers than by climbers. The teeth of the ascenders grip the rope

Fig. 9–5. Coiling is the other common method of storing and transporting rope.

tightly and force dirt and rock particles into the rope under pressure. The moral: wash your ropes.

As far as cave ropes are concerned, cleanliness is next to godliness. A dirty caving rope is an unsafe caving rope. So, wash your rope after every muddy caving trip. There are two good ways to do it: in a washing machine or with a PMI rope washer. To wash in a machine, braid the rope first and select a large front-loading washer. Use a regular detergent with a cold or warm water setting (Isenhart 1974). Avoid chlorine bleaches. Plymouth Cordage recommends using cold water only with no soap or detergent for Goldline.

To soften a rope, use a commercial fabric softener such as Downey. This will also help reduce wear by forming a barrier between the rope fibers and dirt particles. After washing, unbraid the rope and stretch it out in the air to dry. Don't leave it exposed to the sunlight any longer than needed to dry, since you want to cut down on ultraviolet radiation. Also, avoid washing machines with plastic windows in the front door.

A second method of washing is provided by the ingenious rope washer made from a short length of ¾-inch water pipe by Pigeon Mountain Industries. A garden hose is attached to a fitting on the washer and the rope is drawn through the pipe where jets of water clean the rope. This seems to do an effective job and it's quite portable, being only about 5 inches long (fig. 9–6).

To use, tightly grasp the end of the washer where the water streams out with the index finger and thumb of your left hand (assuming you are right handed). Feed the rope into this end, passing it first through the other cupped fingers on your left hand. With your right hand, pull it through the washer for a distance of about 24 inches (60 centimeters). As you do this, apply pressure to the rope with the cupped fingers of your left hand to help loosen the dirt and grit. Pass each 24-inch section back and forth through your left hand and the washer at least twice, or more if the rope is especially dirty. You can judge the cleaning action by the brown color of the water streaming through your left hand.

Not only is it important to wash a caving rope every time it

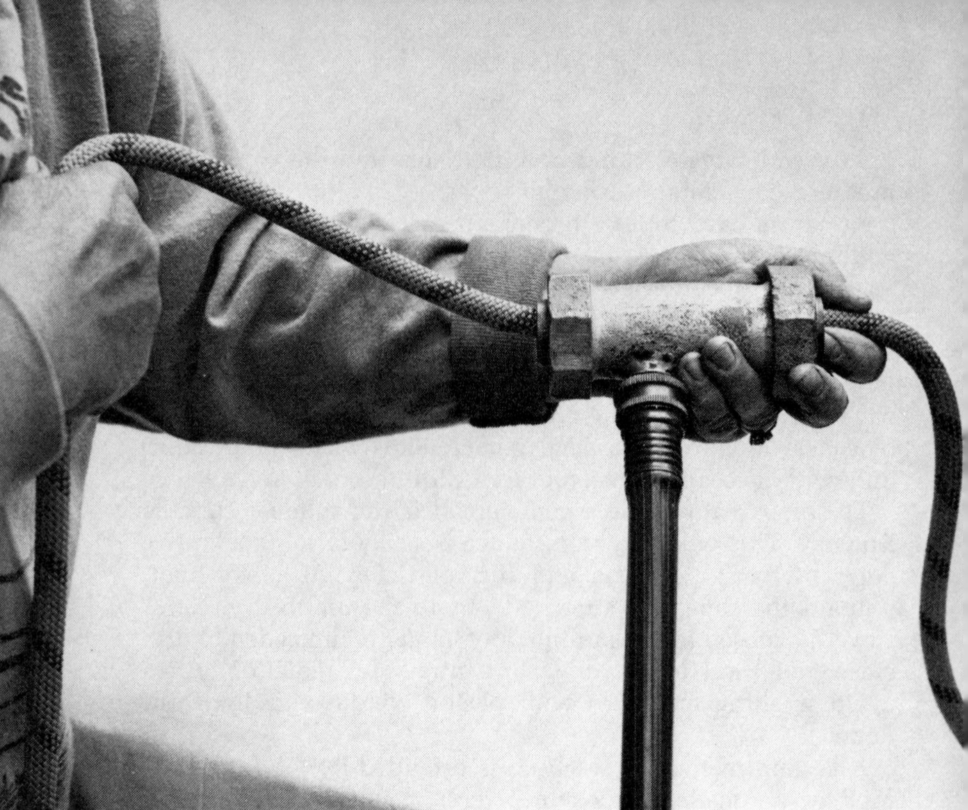

Fig. 9–6. Pigeon Mountain Industry rope washer forces water against the rope as it is drawn through.

gets dirty, some cavers like to wash new Bluewater and PMI ropes before using them. (Goldline doesn't recommend washing until the rope is dirty.) Washing removes oil and lubricants left over from manufacturing, and tightens the fibers and sheath to keep out dirt (Isenhart 1974).

Incidentally, a rope should be thoroughly dry before you use it. As mentioned earlier a wet rope is about 15 percent weaker. Rigging to avoid water in a cave thus becomes important to rope safety as well as to the comfort of the caver.

Inspection for Damage

To be completely safe, you should inspect every inch of caving ropes and slings before a trip or at least once a week during the heavy caving season. Figure on using a rope for only three or four heavy caving seasons, then retire it from critical use. The British Mountaineering Council tests in 1971 showed that at least 100 days of outdoor use could be expected before a rope became unsafe (Blackshaw 1975).

With laid ropes, the amount of wear can be judged by checking the outside yarns of each strand. When groups of strands are broken or if the strands stand out in lumps, the rope has been damaged (Aleith 1971).

With core-and-sheath ropes like Blue Water and PMI, abrasion damage is usually easier to see, because it will be to the outer sheath. Look for worn spots in the sheath where the white fibers of the core are visible. Even if the sheath is completely cut through, about two-thirds of the original strength remains. Nonetheless, if you detect a weak spot in the sheath where the core is showing through, it's best to retire the rope or convert it into two shorter ropes if the rest is undamaged. There could be internal damage to the core at or near the worn sheath location that is undetectable.

Ropes that have been subjected to severe elongation, as in stopping a long fall during dynamic belaying, should also be retired from active service. You can check laid ropes for wear caused by a severe shock by looking inside the strands. If a powdery fiber residue is visible the rope has probably been considerably stressed. Damage to webbing usually occurs at the edges. Any piece of webbing with the slightest cut at its edge should be discarded. It can easily tear and break if the cut enlarges.

Chemical attack on ropes and slings may show as a staining or softening of the fiber. Effects from heat are much more difficult to see. Excessive heat will cause fusing and glazing. Lesser heat, such as from a carbide lamp or an extremely fast rappel, can seriously weaken a rope without leaving any telltale signs.

Slings, Sling Materials, and Harnesses

Slings are multipurpose rigging tools made of short lengths of nylon webbing or Perlon accessory cord (fig. 9–7). Typical untied lengths are 5 to 12 feet (1¾ to 4 meters). Usually, they are formed into loops, and since they are multipurpose, are most often tied with a knot rather than sewn. Their function is to attach ropes or ladders to an anchor (to save rope or to position them better), or to attach ropes, ascenders, or descenders to a caver.

Harnesses are single-purpose devices, sewn into a specific configuration using 1- or 2-inch webbing. Thus, if a sling is sewn to a specific length, it might be more properly called a harness, especially if it is sewn at several points to form smaller loops as harnesses usually are. Seat and chest harnesses, made from the more comfortable 2-inch webbing are the types seen in caving for ascending, rappelling, and being belayed.

One of the most versatile slings used for caving is the basic sling (fig. 9–7). It is made from about 12 feet (4 meters) of 1-inch (25-millimeter) tubular webbing. Every caver should carry this sling plus a locking carabiner. A second common sling is the rigging runner, made from 6 to 12 feet (2 to 4 meters) of 1-inch webbing. Another popular sling is the safety

Fig. 9–7. Slings and loops. *From left to right: 1)* Safety sling of 5 feet of 7- or 8-millimeter Perlon accessory cord tied with two figure-of-eight loops; *2)* Safety loop tied as a continuous loop with a grapevine knot; *3)* Safety loop shortened by tying a figure-of-eight knot in the middle; *4)* Basic caver's sling of 12 feet of 1-inch tubular nylon, should be carried by every caver along with a locking carabiner.

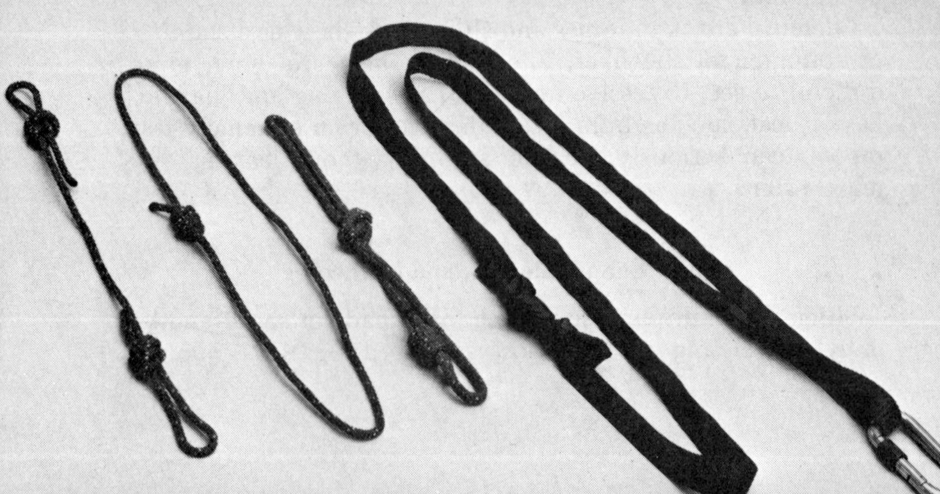

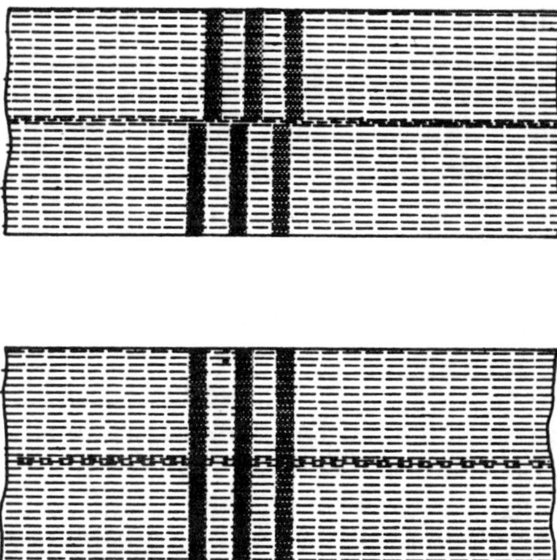

Fig. 9–8. Webbing edges. Top shows chained webbing construction which, in loosely-woven webbing, is less desirable. Bottom shows spiral construction which has greater abrasion resistance.

loop made from about 5 feet (1⅔ meters) of 6- to 8-millimeter Perlon (called a Claude loop by Montgomery, 1977). For technical vertical work, two or three safety loops plus five or six runners are extremely useful. A fourth type of sling is for prusiking with knots. If you plan to use knots as your primary prusiking method (instead of mechanical ascenders), ⅜-inch Tenstron is a good material for the slings.

Nylon Webbing

The webbing used for slings is made of nylon woven into a tubular construction. Flat webbing is also available but is stiffer and harder to tie knots in. You can get webbing in a veritable rainbow of colors instead of just white or olive drab. Webbing is woven in two different ways—spiral and chain (Davison 1978). If the weave is tight, either type is all right. However, if the weave is loose, the chain type will have a much more ragged edge structure and be much more easily damaged by abrasion (see fig. 9–8).

To tell spiral from chained, pinch the edges together and flatten down a small portion to expose the edge. If the weave is offset at the edge, the stitches won't line up with each other. This indicates the less-desirable chain structure. Also, it will usually have a definite ridge when the edge is pressed down and flattened out.

Webbing is more affected by ultraviolet deterioration than ropes because it has a larger surface area exposed to the sun. By the time 100 days of outdoor use rolls around, 25 to 30 percent of its strength will have been lost. Therefore, webbing should be retired sooner than the 100-day outdoor use limit for climbing ropes (Blackshaw 1975). Obviously, these outdoor exposure standards are not directly applicable because webbing and ropes are not subject to ultraviolet radiation underground. But the cave environment inflicts some special hazards of its own in the form of abrasion, dirt and mud particles embedded in the fiber, and repeated soaking in water. Thus, you must be especially conscious of the need for regular inspection and early retirement when wear is observed. As indicated, inspect webbing for cuts in the edges. Even the smallest cut is reason to throw the sling out.

Nine-sixteenths-inch (13-millimeter) tubular or flat webbing is also useful for mini-three-step aid slings (étriers), a kind of webbing ladder used in rock climbing (figure 9–9). You can make these from 20 feet (7 meters) of $9/16$-inch webbing. First double it, then tie a figure-of-eight loop in the top for carabiner attachment. Make three slightly offset steps about 12 to 14 inches (300 to 350 millimeters) apart in one leg and 10 inches (250 millimeters) apart in the other leg. Use figure-of-eight or overhand knots to form the loops. (See Robbins 1971a or Smutek 1978 for more details.)

Sewing on Webbing. Sewing the ends of webbing together, if done correctly, makes a much stronger joint and uses less material than a knot (Magnussen 1972).

You can sew webbing on a home sewing machine or have it done at an awning-maker, cobbler, or parachute harness shop. Magnussen recommends Number 24 Star Ultra Dee polyester thread. Paragear Equipment Company, 3839 West Oakton

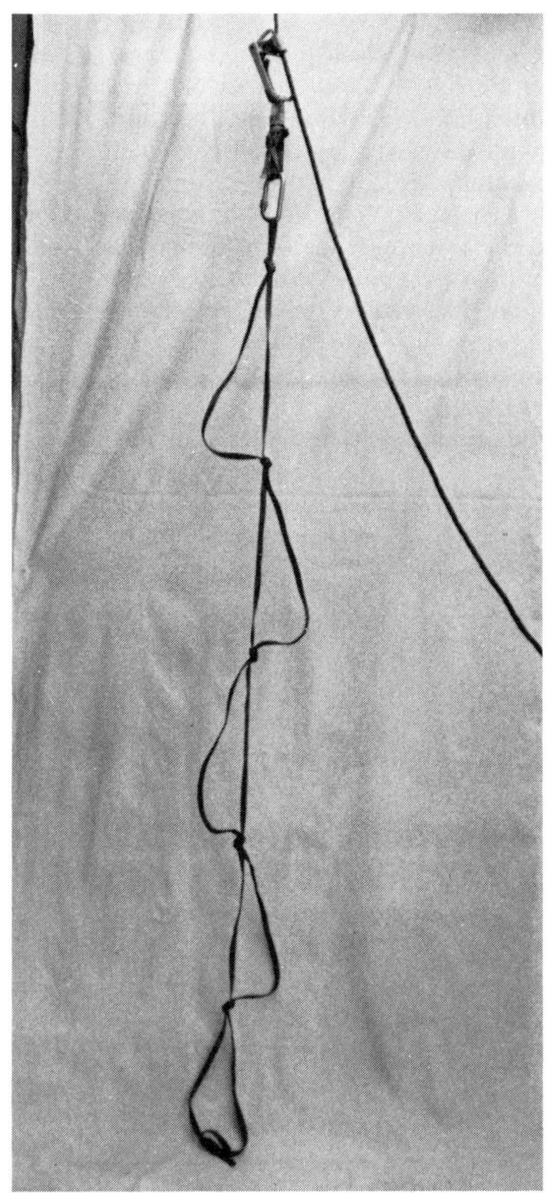

Fig. 9–9. Mini-etrier (webbing ladder) of three to five steps can be useful at the top of drops and for direct aid—a specialized technique used in rock climbing.

Street, Skokie, IL 60076 is a good source of nylon thread of many strengths and sizes (Nylon Highway #7, July 1977). Another option is 100 percent nylon thread (CONSO #16 nylon) which is available at some leather and craft shops. When sewing webbing with this thread, a slightly larger than normal needle with a larger threading eye is less likely to break. Set the machine for eight stitches per inch. A 3-inch overlap of the webbing ends is recommended (see fig. 9–10). Sew a two-inch-long splice with ten or more rows of longitudinal stitches. Two inch webbing isn't mentioned by Magnussen, but is presumably sewn with twenty or more rows. You'll find it isn't easy to crowd ten separate rows into a 1-inch-wide space, because the fabric is bumpy and the needle bounces, so some will overlap. If the first pass is made down the center, it's easy to keep the splice aligned. About half of the stitches are run out the full 3 inches to serve as indicator marks. These indicators will fail at a lower load than the breaking-strength of the splice.

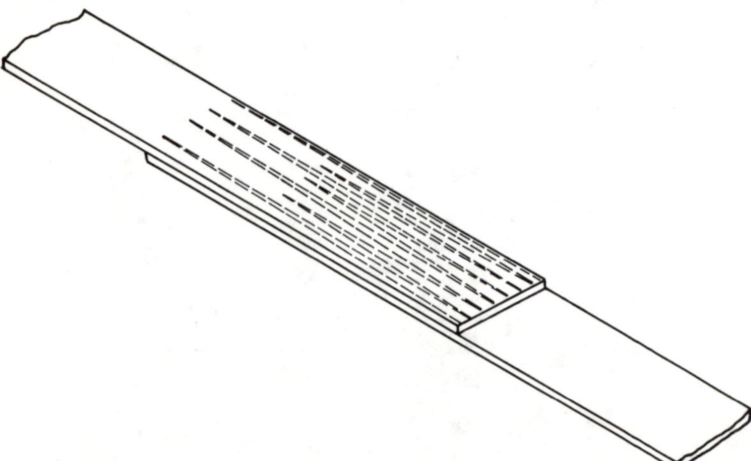

Fig. 9–10. Sewing webbing makes for a stronger joint than a knot, and uses less material. A 3-inch overlap with ten rows of longitudinal stitches, 2-inches long are recommended, with some rows extended the full 3 inches to serve as indicator stitches.

Fig. 9–11. Basic caver's sling tied around the waist as a diaper sling. This is one of the most common slings for rappelling but is potentially unsafe unless backed up by a separate waist loop of accessory cord (as shown) or another piece of webbing.

The Basic Caver's Sling

The versatile basic caver's sling is easily made from a 12-foot length (4-meters) of 1-inch tubular nylon. Webbing is preferred over rope because it is softer and spreads the load better, making it more comfortable when supporting your weight. For most uses, it will be tied into a loop with a water knot, secured with overhand knots on both sides of the water knot. One of its first jobs will be as a diaper sling (fig. 9–11). Specific tying directions are given below.

A word of caution—a diaper sling is only one-half of the required rappel sling. Always add a redundant waist loop as shown in figure 9–11. If the diaper breaks it will unravel, and you will come off the line if it is not backed up with a redundant loop. A way to avoid this eventuality is to use two basic slings or 25 feet of webbing to tie a swami seat instead (see below and fig. 9–13).

A second use of the basic sling is for a chest loop for belay tie-in or prusiking (fig. 9–12). Again, make a loop with a secured water knot to fit your chest size. Cross the loop in the middle and insert one arm in each half. Grasp the crossed strands in front of your chest and lift up over the head. This puts two vertical strands in front of each shoulder, which are drawn together and linked with a locking carabiner. Now you're ready to tie into a belay line or attach your chest prusik sling to the carabiner.

A slight variation of this (fig. 9–13) works well for attaching a Gibbs or Jumar mechanical ascender (see chapter 13). With the Gibbs, thread a bight through the hole in the cam. Then put the left half over the left arm and the head. Follow by putting the right half over the right arm and the head. Neither of these are as comfortable as a sewn 2-inch harness, but they are otherwise just as functional.

A third use for the basic caver's sling is to attach it to a hand line or other fixed line with a Prusik knot. Tie the other end around the waist or clip it into a seat harness. This is always a good safety practice when working near the lip of a pit or anywhere else where there is some vertical exposure. The safety loop, though shorter, is good for this too.

Another use is as a hauling line to raise and lower equipment over short pitches. If each caver in the party has this basic sling, several lengths can be knotted together with water knots to provide a suitable length.

A basic sling is also good as a runner around a rock or the base of a massive formation to position a ladder or rope at the proper place in a pit. If a lot of rigging is to be done, having five or six runner slings, either a full 12 feet or half-length 6 feet, is very useful.

Safety Loop

The safety loop is made from a five-foot piece of 7- or 8-millimeter Perlon (fig. 9–1). This can be fashioned into a

Fig. 9–12. Chest loop and swami seat. This configuration of the basic sling forms a chest loop linked by a carabiner in front. Swami seat around waist and thighs is tied from 25 feet of 1-inch tubular nylon. Swami seat is much safer than the diaper sling, because if one portion were to break, it would still remain attached to the body. Gibbs ascender shown on line can be used as a safety when climbing with a hand line. Note that chest sling and swami seat are tied together with a safety loop.

Fig. 9–13. Chest loop made from basic caver's sling shown in alternate configuration for Gibbs ascender.

loop to use as a prusik sling for knot climbing or protection with a spelean shunt (a protective device for rappelling—see chapter 13), and similar applications. Or, it can have small loops in each end as a longer sling to tie yourself into an anchor or static line.

To make it into a loop, tie the ends of the 5-foot length with a grapevine. The resulting loop will have a diameter of about 20 inches which is a good size for general use. You can shorten the loop by tying a figure-of-eight knot in it. (A figure-of-eight is better than an overhand because it's far easier to untie after loading.)

Seat Harnesses and Slings

A sewn seat harness that supports your entire body weight without danger of damaging internal organs is indispensable for technical vertical work. It is useful for ascending, descending, belaying, or tying into the line. Before deciding which harness is best for you, you will need to experiment with several types for comfort and balance. Put your weight fully into a harness to see where the strands cross your backside and hips. To check balance, hang on the line with an ascender or Prusik knot and see how far back the rig tilts your body. Generally, the more upright you are the better, both for comfort and efficiency of movement.

A harness must also be fail-safe. That is, if the webbing were to break at one point, the harness must still be attached to one or more other points and not unravel completely (as with a simple diaper sling). This would leave your body and your life unattached to the line.

Tying into a Harness. Is it safe to tie into a carabiner on a harness? Or is it better to tie directly to the harness? While it is undoubtedly safer to tie in directly, clipping in with a carabiner is probably well within the margin of safety, except for holding a leader fall. Using a carabiner is certainly faster and easier, especially if several are to tie in at the same point for a static belay.

The danger in using a carabiner clip-in for a dynamic leader belay lies in the possibility of the climbing motions twisting the carabiner around so that the load is applied to the gate. Although many carabiners now test at 4000 pounds (1814 kilograms) or more on the load-bearing axis, gates have failed at as low as 300 pounds (136 kilograms) (Blackshaw 1975). (See the discussion of carabiners in chapter 13).

For this reason, some climbers recommend against using a carabiner where the shock loading may be very high. They prefer to tie a rethreaded figure-of-eight loop or a bowline directly to the waistband or sewn loops of the harness. However, dynamic belays are seldom used in caving. Instead, we use static belays where the rope comes from above the climber and is normally kept quite snug with little or no slack. Thus there is little possibility of the load shifting to give lateral pressure on the gate.

Furthermore, there are several reasons why snapping into a

locking carabiner on a harness makes sense. In the first place, if you're really worried, you can use two locking carabiners and improve your chances greatly. The carabiner used, in any event, should be of the highest test types, such as an SMC locking D (5930 pounds or 2690 kilograms). Also, there may be some danger involved in trying to tie in with the rope if the space is limited on a ledge, if you are on a slick slope, or if you could get soaked in a waterfall. In these cases, the speed and convenience of clipping in versus the time and care required to tie in, weigh in favor of clipping in. Disengaging yourself is also faster, a useful benefit in an emergency.

Diaper Sling

A diaper sling (fig. 9–11) is quick and easy, but it is not safe by itself without a waist-loop backup. To make the diaper, form a loop from about 7½ to 8 feet (about 2½ meters) of 1-inch webbing (such as your caver's sling) using a water knot with back-up overhand knots. Wrap the doubled loop around your waist and put both ends in a locking carabiner. Pull one strand of the loop tight around your waist with the other strand hanging down loosely in the back. Reach between your legs with one hand and grasp the slack strand, bring it up in front, and attach it in the locking carabiner with the other two ends. To back up the diaper, wrap a piece of Perlon cord or another piece of webbing around the waist and pass it under or tie it to one or more of the strands of the diaper and also through the locking carabiner.

Fig. 9–14. Tying the swami seat. Figure 9–13 shows how to begin. Figure 9–14 shows the completed sling. See text for complete instructions.

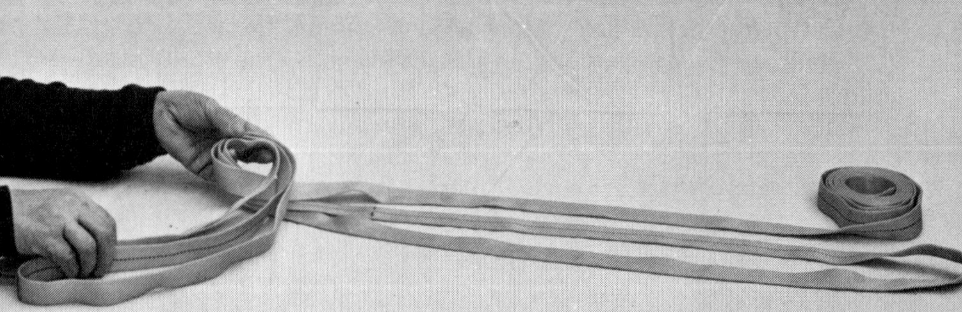

Fig. 9–15. Completed swami seat.

Swami Seat

A safer and more comfortable seat is the swami seat (figs. 9–12 and 9–14). This is also made from 1-inch webbing. You can try using 2-inch webbing but the knots are so bulky they're uncomfortable for many people. The swami is only a little harder to tie than a diaper, yet it won't come off you if a strand breaks. You need about 25 feet (64 centimeters) of 1-inch (25-millimeter) webbing for a swami. You can also tie it with two of the 12-foot basic slings.

There are several ways to tie a swami. The recommended way gives you three strands at the center point where the carabiner clips in. Find and mark the center of a 25-foot length of webbing with a pencil. Lay a length about 7 feet long (3½ feet on either side of the center mark), then double back a length above and below this center length. The next step is to tie the figure-of-eight leg loops. This is made a lot easier if the remaining ends are coiled as shown in figure 9–13. Tie the figure-of-eight loop using all three strands, placing the initial loop about 8 inches from the center mark as shown. Bring all three strands, including the coiled end, in back of and through the small loop. For the moment, don't tighten it down until the other one is tied. Then, if both loops are the right size for your legs and thighs, tighten them. When tying it on your body, run the ends around your waist several times and once or twice down through the leg loop and triple-thickness tie-off point. Finish it off with a secured square knot at your side (fig. 9–10). A locking carabiner attaches both the leg portion and waist portion together. A completed swami seat is shown in use with a Texas system in figure 15–7.

Texas Seat

Cavers who do a lot of technical vertical work often end up with two-inch slings. An inexpensive one is the Texas seat which comes with two rings for carabiner attachment and a buckle to tighten with. This sling has the advantage of being easy to adjust, so for practice sessions, several people can use it. However, it has the same failing as the diaper sling, in that it is not sewn at any point and could unravel. If you find the Texas seat to your liking, you can stitch the leg loops onto the waistband and turn it into a very respectable and inexpensive custom harness—tailored to your own measurements. It is available from Bob & Bob and the Speleoshoppe. The Swiss seat, also available from these suppliers, is similar but does not include the carabiner rings.

If you prefer to start from scratch, study the seats used by other cavers or the commercial models for ideas. In our case, we have found the REI Seat Harness (from Recreational Equipment Co, Seattle) to be extremely satisfactory. It comes in three sizes depending on waist and hip measurements. The cost is under twenty dollars. They designed it for belaying, aid climbing, and rappelling; if they knew about cavers, they'd know it's great for prusiking, too. This harness brings the center of gravity up higher in front of you (about waist or belly button level), somewhat higher than the diaper or Texas seat. You may or may not prefer this, so check it out.

Another excellent commercial harness is the Whillans Sit Harness, available from REI, Eastern Mountain Sports, Speleoshoppe, among several others. It's more expensive (about thirty dollars). Both a climber's version (in nylon) and a caver's version (in Terylene) are available. The Terylene may be of interest to electric cavers who use lead-acid cells. It is not damaged by lead-acid electrolyte. Forrest has a Swami Belt with separate leg loops which can be made into a complete seat sling. We have seen these used by several people very successfully.

Chest Harnesses

A good chest harness is a valuable addition for ascending with the preferred three-ascender systems. It's also good for rappelling, if you use the spelean shunt (a safety device for descending—see chapter 13), or need a higher, second point of attachment (in addition to the seat harness) for balance. A simple, crossed-loop chest sling can be made from the basic caver's sling.

A better chest harness can be made from 2-inch webbing and a buckle of the type sold by Bob & Bob and others. To keep the chest sling from riding down on your stomach, sew one or two shoulder loops of 1-inch or $^9/_{16}$-inch (25- or 13-millimeter) webbing to the 2-inch webbing. Incorporating a sewn loop or ring near the middle to attach a carabiner, ascender, or ascending box (see chapter 13), is a nice refinement. Or you can attach a Gibbs ascender cam directly to the chest sling with a $^9/_{16}$-inch webbing loop at the left shoulder to help you keep upright on the line. For added safety, separate or attached loops or belts can be run down to the seat sling to give redundancy to both slings. Commercial chest harnesses are not as common as seat harnesses but are sometimes available at mountaineering suppliers.

10

Basic Caving Techniques: Horizontal Caves

Here are the fundamentals you need for horizontal caves and the horizontal passages in larger systems.

To explore horizontal or so-called easy caves, you need these basic techniques: walking, crawling, squeezing through tight spots, and scrambling.

Learning in a Cave. Before getting into specifics, it should be reemphasized that the purpose of describing techniques in a book like this is to give you a familiarity with the structure and execution of the technique. Nothing can substitute for actual field training. Any skill needs to be practiced in a cave with an experienced instructor until it becomes second nature.

Walking

Horizontal Passages. What's an easy cave? Most cavers would automatically say a horizontal cave with passages big enough to walk in is easy. But even horizontal caves are not

144

that simple. They often descend gradually in a series of broad steps. Or, they may be comprised of several levels connected by shallow pits and slopes. Despite such vertical features, these caves are still considered basically horizontal, even though some scrambling is necessary to negotiate them.

Horizontal passages can be classified according to their height. However, cave passages don't continue at the same height for long. And, as the height changes, so do the techniques needed to traverse them.

Four to Six Feet: Cave Walking. Passages from 4- to 6-feet high can usually be walked with some stooping. Walking in a cave is a lot like cross-country hiking away from established trails. You scamper over boulders and outcroppings, climb small hills and rock faces, ford streams, and even walk right down the stream bed itself for fairly long distances—this sometimes being the only available trail.

Just like when you're on rough terrain above ground, always look before you step. By lighting the way in front, you can plan two or three steps ahead and let your feet follow. If you have to do a lot of stooping (like in the Backbreaker Passage in Sullivan Cave, Indiana), it may help to place your hands on your knees to rest and maintain balance. On really rough floors, you may have to move from rock to rock, testing each before applying weight, just like crossing a stream. In fact, you can expect to do quite a lot of actual stream crossing in the typical cave. Often, you will want to brace youself with a hand on the wall (unless in a fragile area) to keep good balance. If you want to study something, stop and look. You can't sightsee and walk at the same time over rough and slippery floors.

Crawling

Two to Four Feet: Crawling on All Fours. In passages 2- to 4-feet high, several methods can be used. Try to alternate them to avoid tiring. The most obvious method is to progress on all fours. But this puts your weight on your knees which should be avoided if possible.

Contrary to what you might think, it's not a good idea to crawl on the knees. The kneecaps are very delicate. A damaged kneecap can be so painful as to cause complete blackout. If a lot of crawling is expected, don't forget your knee pads.

A good way to relieve the knees, is to switch over to elbows and toes occasionally, or forearms and ankles. Sometimes lying on the side is preferable, shuffling the feet and pulling forward with the arms. Two other possibilities are to duck walk (squat down on the haunches) or to tuck one leg beneath and move forward on the other, in a kind of inching movement, using the hands for balance.

Under Two Feet: Belly Crawl. Crawling isn't the only thing that cavers do. It just seems that way sometimes! In passages from 10 inches to 2 feet high, the best method is probably the flat-out belly crawl. Just lie down on your stomach and go to it (see fig. 10–1). Nearly all caves require some crawling. At one extreme, you have short crawls, only a few feet long. At the other extreme are those crawling horrors which make you seem like an earthworm for hundreds of feet.

Returning to Babyhood. Fortunately, crawling is very easy to learn since most people seem to do it quite naturally. Merely allow atavism to take over and return to the belly-crawling age of six months. And this is very proper, too, since the stomach, arms, and feet are the best things to use for crawling.

For a belly crawl, the elbows go flat out to the side of the body, and the pack gets pushed in front. In many cases the helmet has to be removed and pushed ahead, too. However, movement in this manner is surprisingly easy if the floor is relatively smooth and the length doesn't exceed about 30 feet. It's only when the ceiling gets down below 12 inches or so that things get difficult for most people.

A word of caution in crawlways that go down. Never go headfirst down into a steep unknown crawlway. It's far too difficult to back out if you go in headfirst. Also, it sometimes happens that the passage bells out suddenly, leaving you with no support. So, unless a downward crawl is very well known and ends in a flat platform area, don't go in headfirst!

In a really tight passage, it's best to start off on the stomach. Push with the toes and pull with the arms while wriggling

Fig. 10–1. Belly crawl is the technique demonstrated by this caver as he emerges from a snug crawlway. Note that he has taken off his helmet and is pushing it in front of him.

like a snake with the rest of the body. Even the tightest crawlway normally has ledges and knobs that can be used to push-off with the feet and to pull-forward with the hands. Whenever possible, try to have the legs do most of the work, since they are far stronger than the arms.

Getting Stuck. Probably the spookiest part of caving to most beginners is the fear of getting stuck in a tight spot. However, the truth is that you can get through just about any squeeze with practice.

Here are some tricks of the trade. Before negotiating a tight crawl or fissure, empty your pockets and take off your helmet and pack. Then, think about which parts of your body are the widest. Normally, this will be the hips, chest, shoulders, or pelvis. Next, study the shape of the tight spot and plan the best way to fit your body through.

What you must do is learn to pour yourself into tight squeezes. Be as relaxed as possible. Then, as you ease yourself in, you can adjust your body to fit the passage as needed. Sometimes you have to narrow your shoulders by putting one arm ahead and dragging the other at your side (fig. 10–2). You will lose some of your pulling power when you do this, but quite often it's the only way.

If the squeeze is really tight, you will probably end up pushing your helmet ahead of you. Often a fellow caver in

Fig. 10–2. A trick for especially tight crawlways is to put one arm and shoulder through the hole and drag the other behind, as this caver is doing.

front will help by pulling your gear through for you. One way to move gear is to attach your pack to his or her foot (or to your own foot) and drag it along. Few crawlways are so tight that a dragging pack will get stuck, though it may slip off once or twice. If there are turns to be negotiated, lie on the side facing the direction of the turn. Once your hips are past the turn, you may have to turn over on the other side to get your knees to bend the right way. (Remember that they bend opposite to the waist.)

Learning Your Size Limit. We advise beginners to find out at an early date just how small a hole they can get through. You'll probably be pleasantly surprised at how small an opening that is.

The shoulders, rib cage, pelvis, and hips are usually the limiting dimensions. Typical vital statistics on cavers are about 7½ inches for small cavers, and 11½ to 12 inches for large cavers. Try measuring the thickness or width of these anatomical features on your own body. This way you can quickly find out which particular part is going to give you a problem.

On this point Moose Dawson (1979 NSS administrative vice president) has some light to shed. He distinguishes between a barrel chest and a square chest. Even though he takes a large suit size (46), he can make a 9¾-inch (24.8-centimeter) squeeze (with exhaling). Yet a friend with a smaller overall chest diameter is stopped at 11 inches (28 centimeters) even with exhaling. Mostly it's bone structure that holds you up. Nearly all your excess adipose tissue (also known as baby fat, beer belly, or hops hips) will compress. However, your bones don't give—without breaking.

With me, it's my chest. Once I get my shoulders and rib cage through a squeeze, I stop worrying and just squirm on through. Others can always seem to get the upper body through, but panic a bit when they have to force their lower abdomen past a constriction. Once you learn your limiting dimension, getting through is more a matter of getting the right push-off point for your feet. There may be pressure on your chest or pelvis, but if you can get the right purchase on a

foothold to shove on through you can usually make it un-
aided. If not, you may need someone to give you a foothold
with a hand or foot or use the webbing with foot loops
technique described below.

Exhaling Makes You Thinner. A trick that many of us
chest-limited types employ is the letting-out-the-breath ploy.
You can reduce your chest thickness by ½ to 1 inch (12 to 25
millimeters) by this means. When trying to inch through a
really tight spot, you let out all your breath, shove forward
with everything you've got, and take a small breath. Then let
it out, and shove again. Needless to say, this is not the
moment to panic.

I put this technique to good use each time we come to a
famous tight spot in California's Church Cave, known as the
Venturi Passage. The ceiling in this gently descending walking passage suddenly swoops down to a very nasty squeeze: 9
inches (23 centimeters) high, 14 inches (36 centimeters) wide,
and 20 inches (51 centimeters) long. The cave's natural wind
currents are funneled abruptly into this tiny orifice. The gale
that issues from it is often spirited enough to blow out your
carbide light.

The Venturi apparently floods during the snow run-off in
the spring. This flooding causes the bowl-shaped depression
to fill up with silt and rough rubble. So, the first thing you do
is sweep the larger pebbles and rocks out of the way. Of
course, if two or three people have already gone through, this
may have been done automatically.

On the other side of the constriction, the ceiling raises back
up just as sharply as on the entrance side. For that reason, I
like to approach it flat on my back. I put both hands over my
head, raise my knees, and push with my feet flat on the floor.
This works fine until the ceiling lowers and my knees touch
it. With some thrashing around, I can locate a much needed
foothold on the wall.

About this time, my chest hits the tightest part of the tube
so, to reduce the chest diameter, I exhale. Then using the
power of a straightleg push on that blessed foothold, I pop out
the other side. Dragging my legs and feet on through is easy,

since I can now sit up and use my arms on the floor for pushing.

I suppose if we had any sense, we'd bring along a small shovel and just dig the Venturi out before attempting it. But it's located about five hours into the cave and finding a volunteer to carry a shovel all that way isn't easy.

Boot-size Crawls. We used to say that if you could get your helmet through a tight spot you could get yourself through. However, that's a little optimistic, since most helmets are only about 7 or 8 inches high.

What is true, generally, is that if your upturned boot can make it, you can too. However, this assumes that only one of the two dimensions is as small as the length of your boot (about 10 to 13 inches—25 to 33 centimeters). The other dimension must still be wide enough for shoulders or hips. Even so, its a happy thought that if your muddy boot can do it, the rest of you can probably make it too, one way or another.

The Button Hole. For my wife, Janet, and myself, it was almost the other way once. It was in a cave called One–Two–Three in the high Sierra. The easy way was to forget the squeeze that puts you near entrance number three, and go back out entrance number two, as others have done in the past.

This squeeze has been dubbed the Button Hole (fig. 10–3). It's a vertical slot about 36 inches (91 centimeters) high and some 10 or 12 inches (25 or 30 centimeters) wide. Except at the very narrowest spot, that is. Horizontally, from the beginning to the wonderful end when you're finally out, it extends about one body length.

Ten inches is not all that snug to a caver, assuming you take off your helmet, battery pack, and coveralls first. But in the Button Hole, you have to pour yourself in sideways at the upper part of the slot, then snake downwards. It's at that spot where you have to pass a 20-inch long knife-edged flake that juts out from the wall and hits you right in the center of your chest. By actual measurement, the edge of this jolly little item is only 8½ inches across from the opposite wall and exactly 8 inches from the floor (22 and 20 centimeters).

Fig. 10–3. Getting through the Buttonhole in 1–2–3 Cave calls for another tight squeeze trick: shedding your coveralls. *Photo by Bruce Rogers.*

Knife-like flakes with deep pockets or scallops are often found protruding from the limestone bedrock in alpine caves, evidence of the mighty flow of water that rushes through them in the spring runoff. On the floor of this slot is additional evidence of fast-moving water—gravel and stones.

After one bout with coveralls on and one with coveralls off, Janet decided to try mind over matter. She was determined not to let a stupid squeeze get the better of her. After some cogitation, she could be seen on hands and knees furiously digging stream debris from the floor of the slot barehanded.

Several minutes later, she had scooped out another 2 inches of clearance from flake to floor. This accomplished, she popped through and coolly called back to me that it was a piece of cake. And so it was. Except that my rib cage is bigger: that flake scribed the neatest thin, red line down my breast bone from collar bone to belly button!

Freeing a Stuck Caver. What do you do if you really get stuck? First, be sure you really are hung up. Sometimes simply unhooking pack or clothes will free you.

If you are stuck, the most obvious remedy is for other cavers to grab you and pull. This works in five cases out of six. If it doesn't, another successful technique is to run a length of rope or webbing through the passageway with a figure-of-eight loop tied into the line so that you can get a good hold on the rope and the others can pull you out.

If this is to no avail, you or a caver on the other side can place the loop around one of your feet. This allows you to use the line as a foothold. Push hard with your foot until you move forward 2 or 3 feet. Then raise your knee again, have the others take up the slack, and repeat the process. Surprisingly enough, this will usually free the stuck caver in the worst situations. In fact, in any crawlway known to be tight, a line with or without loops can be carried through by the first caver for the others to use for hand or foot holds.

Scrambling

Scrambling is a technique used when a passage is too steep to walk up, yet not steep enough to require classic rock-climbing skills. It combines several types of movements, including walking, climbing, sliding, bridging (applying pressure to two points with extended limbs or back), and jamming (inserting hand, knee, or foot into a crack or slot). Generally speaking, any downward or upward cave passage of less than 45 or 50 degrees can be negotiated by scrambling. If it's steeper than that, chances are it will have to be climbed using rock climbing or other techniques. But a surprising number of slopes that seem very steep at first glance can be easily scrambled using a combination of balance, three-point suspension from rock climbing, and the seat of your pants.

Another word about conservation at this point. Any movement in a cave can cause damage, but this is especially true of

Fig. 10–4. Scrambling is the technique used for this short descending slope. The caver is maintaining several secure points of contact and is inching forward to gain another.

scrambling. Avoid scrambling techniques in formation areas where delicate speleothems could be destroyed by a careless movement. Use an alternate technique like roped climbing or seek another route.

When scrambling down, gravity and friction are on your side, so it's sometimes easier than going up. The trick is to stretch out one limb at a time leaving the rest of the body to hold fast in a secure position (fig. 10–4). This is the so-called three-point climbing technique used by rock climbers and it's quite easy to adapt to scrambling down a 45 degree angle. Use the entire body, arms, legs, feet, back, shoulders, seat, and even your helmeted head once in a while for balance. Then, stretch an arm or a leg down to the next handhold or flat area keeping the other three in close contact until the new hold is secured.

As with all new skills, its best to practice outdoors to get a feeling for the basic technique. Almost any area has some large boulders along the shore of a lake or in nearby hills. Gradually descending blocks are very similar to the type of pitch found in caves and make excellent practice for learning to scramble in a cave.

In scrambling, as in climbing, the arms are used primarily for balance. This means that the legs support the weight, not the arms and hands, although for the short time of a few seconds up to a minute maximum, you can use an arm or hand if necessary. As in any kind of climbing, never lunge or jump. Speed is not the object. Plan the route of movement ahead, checking each move while proceeding and the next level will be reached in no time.

Climbing back up a slope is more strenuous because gravity is against you, but in some ways it is easier because you can see the holds better. One caution—if you have to scramble up rather than down on the way into the cave, keep this rock-climbing rule in mind. You must be able to climb back down any pitch that you climb up, in case it dead-ends. Rock climbers consider going down harder because it's harder to locate holds. Admittedly, this is not true for scrambling as for vertical climbing, but it's still a precaution to keep in mind in those caves where the passage goes up, not down.

11

Intermediate and Advanced Skills

The next level of skills enables you to tackle difficult caves with considerable vertical extent using belays, chimneying, and free climbing.

Drawing the line between basic, intermediate, and advanced techniques is difficult to do precisely. The skills really overlap and develop from each other. Also, all of us learn at different rates. At any one time we may be ahead in one skill and behind in another.

With these thoughts in mind, the skills we have categorized as intermediate are belaying, knowledge of climbing signals, climbing with a handline, and the hasty rappel. Chimneying, traversing, and free climbing are classed as advanced.

Intermediate Skills

Belaying

Belaying is a way to protect a climber in case of a fall by means of a safety rope. It works like this—when you're climbing, tie a rope around your waist or to a seat sling. A belayer situated above controls the rope so that if you lose your footing, the belayer and the rope keep you from falling.

Two types of belay are given—static and dynamic. A static belay is the primary one used in cave climbing. The maximum amount a climber is likely to fall is only 1 or 2 feet (⅓ to ⅔ meter) before the belayer stops the fall. For a static belay the belayer is located above the climber and the rope is kept quite tight with very little slack. Static belays are also used in rock climbing when the second or third person on a climbing team is climbing up to where the lead or first climber is.

Dynamic belaying is used to protect the lead climber, who is climbing above the belayer. In this situation, the lead climber may be several feet (10 feet—3 meters—or more) above the belayer or the last anchor point, so the maximum fall will be *twice* that distance. The rope is also left purposely loose or slack between the anchor and the climber, so he or she can climb freely and not be pulled off the face by the drag of the rope. This kind of fall puts a severe load on the line. For example, a 200-pound (91-kilogram) caver falling from ten feet above the anchor could potentially generate 4000 foot-pounds of energy—200 × 10 × 2 (twice the distance). It is the belayer's responsibility not only to stop the fall, but to stop it softly in such a way that the forces on the climber, the protection chain (anchor, rope, and belayer's harness), and on himself are kept within acceptable limits. This technique is called dynamic belaying and involves a limited slippage of rope under control of the belayer.

Lead climbing is quite rare in caves. The exceptions are where a new cave passage is being sought high up on a wall, or where an entrance to a new cave is being looked for on a cliff or up a steep slope. (It is fair to say that even in these latter cases, most cavers will find some way to rappel down to an entrance, then prusik back up, rather than climb up a sheer face.)

Since static belaying does not generate severe loads on the rope, low-stretch static caving ropes like Blue Water and Pigeon Mountain Industries are sometimes used for static belays on very short (no more than 20 to 25 feet or 7 to 9 meters) drops. Never use them for dynamic belays. If there is any doubt about which rope to use for a belay, choose Goldline or one of the kernmantle dynamic ropes.

How is it that the belayer is almost always above the climber in caving? In rock climbing, belay points leapfrog up the slope, alternating below and above the climber. But in caving the first direction is usually down. So, if it's a climbable pitch, belaying is from above. After the others have made the climb down, the last person (who is often the best at climbing down) descends with a self-belay, such as a Gibbs ascender on the line, attached to a seat harness. Similarly, going back out, the best climber will climb the pitch with or without a self-belay depending on the difficulty, then belay the others up. In both cases the belayer is above.

There are times (see fig. 15–3) when the belay line is run through an upper pulley down to a free climber or a ladder climber, and the belayer is below. Even so, the belay point is at the pulley above the climber, and the belay given is a tight static belay.

Sitting Hip Belay. For a static belay, the best and safest position—both for belayer and climber—is the sitting hip belay (fig. 11–1). The first requirement is to tie yourself to a secure, slack-free anchor. Why is this so important? Without a good anchor, the pit could as easily claim two victims instead of none if the climber falls. To attach yourself to the anchor, you can tie-in directly to your waist using a bowline on a coil. If you have a waist loop or seat sling, you can tie or clip into it. Since this is a static not a leader or dynamic belay, a carabiner snapped to a sling or harness has enough margin of safety (see chapter 9).

The rope from the anchor to you can be a separate sling or the rope itself. If the rope is used, tie a figure-of-eight loop in the line at the belaying position. Alternatively, a tail in the end of the rope can be brought back out from the anchor and a figure-of-eight loop tied into that for you to clip into. If you prefer to tie directly to waist loop or seat harness, a rethreaded figure-of-eight can be used.

Regardless of the tie-in used, locate the knot so there is as

Fig. 11-1. Sitting hip static belay. Belayer is tied with a slack-free sling to the anchor point coming from behind at his right side. The direction of his pointing (right) hand and his right leg are in the same direct line to the climber and the expected line of pull in case of a fall. Thus he will not be rotated out of position by a fall. There is no slack in the belay line, so the climber cannot fall for any distance and thereby overload the static belay. Both feet are firmly anchored: the left against an adjacent surface, the right in a foot stirrup especially rigged from the anchor for that purpose because no natural surface was available in the direct line of climb. Note that the position of the anchor and especially the direction of the fall dictate which hand will be used as the pointing hand and which will be the braking hand. Practice alternating hands so that you are proficient with both for either job. The rope is coiled loosely in a "messy" coil so that it can be drawn from the coil without snagging.

little slack as possible in the line. After clipping or tying in, inch forward a bit to take any remaining slack out of the tie-in line. When tying in, an important consideration to remember is the possibility of being rotated out of position in a fall. If the anchor is directly behind you and your tie-in sling is clipped or tied into your harness in the center of your back and the pull from a falling climber comes directly from the front, the danger of rotating away from your belaying position would be minimal. Unfortunately, this isn't usually the case. Therefore, the side the anchor is on and the hand closest to the climber (the pointing or feeling hand) need to be—*as nearly as possible*—in a straight line. Thus, if the anchor is on the right, choose the right hand for the pointing hand and vice versa. Finally, be sure to aim your pointing hand and body in the expected direction of the fall.

Choose a position (fig. 11–2) where you can sit back from the edge of the drop with legs spread apart somewhat, knees flexed but not locked, and feet braced against a solid object like a wall, rock, or in a crack. Be *sure* to wear gloves. Arrange the rope on your braking hand side in a loose, sloppy coil, free enough so it doesn't snag during a descent. Similarly, when taking it up with an ascending climber, try to keep it from getting too snarled up. The line down to the climber is held by the pointing hand. The rope then passes around your back into the other or braking hand. *Never* let go of the rope with your braking hand under any circumstance.

When belaying an ascending climber, pull up the slack in the rope so there is never more than a foot or two of slack in the line. Taking the rope up while never letting go of it with the braking hand requires attention and practice. See figure 11–2 for a description of the proper hand movements.

When you are belaying someone climbing down, feed the rope out slowly. Keep the rope snug but not too tight unless the climber requests more tension. Develop a feel for the rate of climb so that the climber isn't held back, yet there is no slack. Don't make the climber pull the rope around your body.

To stop a fall, the braking hand is brought quickly across the chest and further if necessary, all the way down to the ground on the opposite side. At the same time, both hands

Fig. 11–2.1.

Fig. 11–2.3.

Fig. 11–2.2.

Fig. 11–2. Taking up the slack from an ascending climber during a static belay calls for a repetitive sequence of hand movements. The vital point is never to let go of the rope with the braking hand (the left hand in this case). In 11–2.1, the right or pointing hand is reaching forward as far as it can to begin drawing up the line. In 11–2.2, the left or braking hand has pulled the rope around the body until the hands meet. Here, the right hand grasps both ropes together for a moment to allow the left hand to slide smoothly back to the waist position, still holding onto the line yet ever alert for a fall. In 11–2.3, the left hand has been drawn across the chest to lock the rope and arrest a fall. The legs tense and apply pressure to the foot brace. The Mountain School (Renton, Washington) recommends that the braking hand be quickly brought across the chest and shoulder while turning the body at the waist in the same direction. This allows the hand to be pinned down to the ground and provides greater braking action.

squeeze the rope. Surprisingly, even a small caver weighing only 125 pounds can safely stop the fall of a climber weighing 200 pounds or more. After you have stopped a falling caver, hold him or her tight to allow the caver to regain a secure footing or slowly lower the caver back to the bottom.

Dynamic Belaying. The principle of the dynamic belay is that if you are a lead climber and you fall, you are gently arrested by the belay rope and belayer rather than coming to a sudden stop, as would happen if you were tied into a fixed rope. Factors that make a slower stop possible are the stretch of the rope, the friction around the belayer's body, and the natural reaction time needed to bring the rope to a stop. Thus, the belayer's body acts as a combination shock absorber and friction brake.

The actual mechanism is complex, and at least one respected climber contends that dynamic belaying has never followed its own theory (Robbins 1979). The fact is, according to Robbins, it is the rope that gives an automatic dynamic belay and not the efforts of the belayer, successful or otherwise, to let the rope run through the hands for a few feet. Whatever the merits of these arguments, since dynamic belaying is so seldom required in caving, we're not going to say much more about it. Those interested in pursuing this subject are advised to consult Robbins (1971, 1973, 1979), Aleith (1975), Blackshaw (1977), and others.

Mechanical Dynamic Belay Devices. Several devices and techniques have been devised for dynamic belaying of lead climbers. These include the Sticht and Edelrid/Bankl belay plates as well as several others. A method of wrapping the rope around a carabiner with a half-ring bend or friction hitch (Baumgartner 1974) has received UIAA (International Alpine Association) approval and is widely used on the European continent. While these devices can also be used for static belaying, the sitting hip belay is recommended and should be learned by all serious cavers first, before experimenting with the newer mechanical aids.

Tying in to be Belayed. When you are the climber and you are getting ready to tie in for a belay, stand clear of the edge in a secure position. To tie in, the preferred knot is a bowline on a coil. Or, if you have a seat harness, you can snap into a bowline or figure-of-eight loop with a locking carabiner. If you will be doing a leader climb, tying directly to the harness with a rethreaded figure-of-eight is recommended (see above and chapter 9).

If it's much of a drop, we recommend a seat harness rather than the bowline, waist loop, or chest sling. If you will have to hang in the rope for any length of time, a seat harness won't damage your internal organs or chest like the others will (see chapter 9).

If you have a long enough rope, there is some advantage to tying it in the middle to be belayed rather than the end. That way, the rope doesn't have to be thrown back down (and be subject to snagging), but often can be pulled back down by the next climber using the free end at the bottom.

Climbing Signals

Climbing signals are a kind of verbal shorthand that simplifies communication and avoids confusion. Signals differ a bit in different parts of the world. The ones we have found successful are as follows.

When you are tied in, your first signal is *ready* or *ready on belay*. The belayer answers when ready, and not before, *belay on*. It's possible that several seconds or minutes may pass before the belayer is ready to give the *belay on* signal. However, under no circumstances should you assume that you are being belayed until you hear the return call. Then, when you are ready to climb, you move over to the beginning of the pitch and call *ready to climb*. The belayer answers, *climb*.

These initial calls can be shortened to *ready to climb* on your part (meaning you are ready on belay and ready to climb) and and *climb* on the part of the belayer when he or she is ready. Other important signals are *falling* when you lose your footing, *tension* when you want tension on the rope, or *slack* when you want slack. Don't say *take up slack* when you want tension, because the belayer may only hear *slack*. Also don't use *up rope* to indicate tension. *Up rope* means to take up the excess slack before beginning to climb and to raise the rope after the climb has been completed or when hauling equipment.

When you reach the end of the climb, call *off belay* to tell the belayer to relax. However, never give the signal *off belay* until you are perfectly secure, preferably sitting down. Finally the belayer calls *belay is off* to indicate you are no longer protected. After untying, the next call is *off rope* meaning the rope is free for the next person.

Two other calls are useful, not for belaying as above, but for rigging. Before lowering a rope or ladder down a drop, ask *all clear?* The answer is *clear* (or silence if no one is in the immediate drop zone). Then, just before you lower the rope—or ladder—call *rope!* Finally, don't forget to yell *rock* anytime you dislodge *any* object into the drop.

Climbing with a Hand line

A hand line is a length of rope used to give an extra assist on a slippery slope or on an otherwise climbable pitch at a spot where there aren't any good holds. A hand line can be either a regular climbing rope or a piece of webbing. Typically, the length is 30 to 50 feet, which will handle the common 10- to 20-foot pitches nicely and leave enough extra to tie to a secure anchor.

We should distinguish between climbing with a hand line and climbing a rope hand-over-hand. The latter is nearly impossible and very dangerous. A hand line is used when you are climbing a wall or slope and your feet are touching the wall, so your legs help support your weight. Climbing a line hand-over-hand is when the rope is hanging free and you have little or no help from your legs at all. Instead, you have to rely entirely on your arms. This is why only decathlon athletes can climb a free hanging rope for more than a few feet.

While the overuse of hand lines in caving is not to be encouraged—since at best the holds they offer are a little shaky and a natural hold is always better—there is an essential difference in philosophy between caving and rock climbing. In caves, the act of climbing is not an end in itself, as it is in rock climbing. Rather, the end of the cave is the end that a caver seeks. For this reason hand lines, ladders, and other types of mechanical aids are perhaps more common in caving than in classic rock climbing.

To use a hand line, first tie it off to a suitable anchor (see chapter 12). Then wrap the line around your forearm and wrist two or three times to increase friction. On especially tricky or muddy slopes, tie a series of figure eight loops in the line spaced about 3 feet (1 meter) apart or less to provide extra handholds and footholds. Remember to move your hand or hands along the line as you proceed. The line can only give you a hold at one point. Also, before putting your weight on the line, be sure you have two other good footholds or handholds. Often the rope will shift on you unexpectedly and throw you off balance.

You can increase the safety of a hand line immeasurably by clipping yourself to the line using an ascender, your safety loop, and a seat harness (see fig. 11–3) or a chest sling and seat sling (see fig. 9–11). A Jumar or Gibbs ascender (see chapter 13) or a Prusik knot (chapter 8) can be used. The Jumar and Prusik knot must be moved by hand, but the Gibbs will trail along without an assist. However, the Jumar also serves as a very convenient handhold all by itself because of its handle construction.

Two notes of caution: First, the Jumar ascender is safe in this situation only if the safety loop is short and keeps you within 1½ to 2 feet (½ meter) of the line. If it were possible for you to fall much more than this, you could put a shock load on the Jumar above its 600-pound (300-kilogram) rating. A Gibbs, the newer Jumar 79, and the CMI ascenders (see chapter 13), all test at 1000 pounds (454 kilograms) or higher and are safer. Second, this technique assumes that you are up against the wall and won't be hanging free from the rope. If you were hanging free, unloosening the Prusik knot or ascender would be next to impossible with your full weight on it.

Generally, hand line ascending or descending is best done on moderate (up to 50-degree) slopes or slides. You can hand line climb a steeper slope (60 degree) or use the hand line for a hasty rappel (see next section) to go down such a slope, but

Fig. 11–3. A hand line can be used as an assist when climbing short, moderate slopes which are too steep or slippery for scrambling. Safety can be increased by the use of an ascender (as shown) or Prusik knot attached from the line to the seat harness.

it's dangerous for more than 10 or 15 feet without an ascender attached to your seat harness. To go up a steep slope, hold the rope tightly in both hands and try to lean back away from the slope. This puts your weight more at right angles to the surface. With practice, you can just walk on up, though it is strenuous and more than 15 feet or so is not a good idea.

Hasty Rappel

To descend 10- to 20-foot slopes of not more than 50-degree or 60-degree steepness, the hasty rappel or French rappel is useful (fig. 11–4). For longer pitches, the regular rappel is safer (chapter 14).

Fig. 11–4. Hasty or French arm rappel for moderate slopes. After crossing the rope behind the upper back, it is wrapped around the wrists and forearms. Gloves are always worn to prevent rope burn.

To do a hasty rappel, simply run the rope across your shoulders and extend your arms as far as possible. Gloves must be worn. Grasp the rope in each hand, taking one or more turns around the forearm and wrist. Take care that the rope runs on your sleeves and that the sleeves don't ride up exposing your skin to painful rope burns.

You can face either left or right depending on which way the slope runs. Then, just walk down sideways tilting the head away from the body to see where you're going. To stop, bring the lower hand up to the chest.

Advanced Skills

In our experience, some caver training programs seem to concentrate a bit too heavily on the technical vertical skills of roped descents and ascents, at the expense of the physical skills of chimneying and climbing. Many caves with considerable vertical extent can be explored completely—and in less time—by scrambling, climbing, and chimneying. In some places, a hand line may be rigged to speed up the process or to belay someone who is less experienced on a muddy or slippery slope, but roped ascents or descents are not needed. This kind of cave may even be more difficult than one requiring rope work.

That's why we encourage you to practice and perfect your physical climbing skills, even though technical vertical work may seem more glamorous. Both types of skills must be in the arsenal of any well-rounded caver who expects to explore all parts of the cave.

In discussing cave climbing we distinguish between it and rock climbing. In the first place, caves go down, mountains go up. Put another way, cavers usually climb down to get into a cave and climb up to get back out. With rock climbers, it's the other way around. They go up, then come back down. This may sound a little simpleminded, but it helps to explain somethings if you keep it in mind. Secondly, cavers climb in the dark. At first glance this may seem harder, since the holds are more difficult to see, but it has a major benefit. You can't see how far up you are. In rock climbing terms, this is called exposure—the expanse of free air below you. Because you can't see as well, the exposure *seems* less dangerous. And, in point of fact, the heights are usually on a much less grand scale than in mountaineering. For every 150- to 500-foot drop in caves there are hundreds of 20- to 60-foot pitches.

Finally, rock climbing is generally more two-dimensional than cave climbing. Classic rock climbing often includes the process of climbing up a sheer wall or open face which is at a 90 degree angle or nearly so. Cave climbing, on the other hand, is most often done not on walls so much as in fissures, cracks, chimneys, and piles of breakdown. This is not to say that there aren't a lot of pitches on mountains where two walls come close together and chimneying techniques are used. Similarly, there are times in caves where sheer walls must be climbed, to push a high passage, for example. Nonetheless, we like to characterize cave climbing as mainly three-dimensional, where you are climbing close to the opposite wall—close enough to stretch out arm or leg to reach a ledge, knob of rock, or, shelf. Then with back, arm, elbow, or even head on the other wall, you inch forward to get to the next spot. This spider-like movement is best exemplified in negotiating chimneys.

Chimneying

Chimneys are quite common in caves. They include narrow vertical passages, sometimes tubular, sometimes slots or fissures, sometimes where two walls or large breakdown blocks come together. Chimneying is used to move down or up between such walls. The horizontal movement in a traverse can be quite similar. In Britain, chimneying is sometimes referred to as "back and footing." Actually, the British term is quite descriptive because it is the back and the feet that do the work, with the arms being used mostly for balance (fig. 11–5). Chimneys range in size from about 18 inches to 36 inches in width (½ to 1 meter).

The exact technique used in each chimney depends a lot on the distance between the walls. Descending a really narrow chimney (about 14 to 24 inches or ⅓ to ⅔ meter) is fairly easy

Fig. 11−5. Chimneying calls for a coordinated series of moves as shown. Note that only in Figure 11−5.1 is there a flat foothold. The other holds are all jam or pressure holds. Jam holds, each successively higher, are shown by the left foot in each of the pictures. Pressure holds are shown by the hands in each picture, and by the right foot in Figures 11−5.2 and 11−5.3.

because gravity helps do the work and friction keeps you from falling. However, they are quite a bit harder to climb up, because the legs can't do their job as well in such a narrow space.

When chimneying in a really narrow spot, an aided ascent can be used with loops tied into a line for footholds. The technique is to raise the foot and have cavers above take up the slack in the line. Then you stand in the loop and raise yourself 2 or 3 feet to a fully standing position. Raise your foot again while bracing yourself in the chimney (which isn't hard if it's really snug) and repeat the cycle. In this way you can move quickly up a chimney too tight for regular chimneying techniques.

When a chimney widens to about 24 inches (⅔ meter), put one foot under your body on the back wall and the other foot on the facing wall. This tends to require more downward pressure with the hands but it's still easy to do. Remember to brace firmly with your back against the wall, move your feet one at a time, then squirm up, down, or sideways with your back. For better control, try to keep your knees bent a little, if possible, like a skier or dancer, rather than straight out. Also, keep the knees at about waist level but not any higher, otherwise, the seat may slip down. When a rest is needed, simply put your feet about level with your seat or waist. You can stay in this position safely and comfortably for several minutes without strain.

In wider chimneys, put both feet on one wall and the back on the other wall. You'll find it more comfortable to put your back against the smooth wall. This is easier on the spine in case there are knobs or rough spots. Besides, knobs or ledges are good for footholds and handholds. Even though you can chimney up on completely smooth walls, a few good ledges and crannies sure make it easier. In fact, if you have a lot of holds, you can go up with one foot on each side in a straddling motion which is faster and less strenuous than chimneying.

One problem with chimneys is that they have a disconcerting habit of widening or belling out into passages near the bottom. With practice, you'll find that you can often chimney sideways to a corner or a narrower spot and continue on down. After you're down, study the pitch and try to remember how you did it. It will help you get started right when you come back later. Often when you chimney up, getting started is the hardest part. Sometimes a leg up from a fellow caver is the only way to do it, so don't be shy about asking.

One final point—because you usually have good support from the walls in a chimney, you can often lean forward or wiggle around to get a better angle on a hold. For example, some small ledges are too steep to hold your boot if you're standing vertically. But you can often twist yourself at a crazy angle or lean way forward and use that hold after all.

A modified chimneying technique can also be used to slide down a smooth-floored slope if the roof is close to the floor and irregular enough to offer some holds. By lying down with your back on the floor and feet on the ceiling, you can negotiate a difficult slope that is impossible to climb any other way. A word of caution again—don't descend headfirst in a slope because it may be impossible to get back out.

Traversing

Traversing is a sideways movement somewhat similar to chimneying if the walls are close together, or similar to free climbing if they are not. In either case, the movement is horizontal rather than vertical. In caving, traversing is often done while straddling a narrow passage, but it can also involve stepping sideways along a narrow ledge, using handholds on the wall as in rock climbing (fig. 11–6). Often traverses are used to avoid climbing down to floor level and then back up again when it's clear that the passage simply dips down for a short distance. It's also quite common to use a traversing technique along the walls of a passage to avoid water down below, assuming that this can be done relatively safely and that eventually the route leaves the stream.

When moving on a ledge, the best technique is to move the feet in a shuffling motion (fig. 11–6). Don't try to cross one leg over the other if the ledge is especially narrow and if you are

Fig. 11–6. Traversing a narrow ledge above a 30-foot (10-meter) pit. The climber is safetied with separate belays from either side to prevent penduluming. Note how he shuffles his feet along the ledge instead of trying to cross one leg over the other which can cause tripping. Handholds are plentiful between the massive flowstone ribs. In some places jam holds are used.

facing the wall. Shuffling the feet tends to keep the balance, while crossing the legs invites tripping.

Traverses along very narrow ledges or a series of small footholds can be safetied in two ways. Separate belay lines (fig. 11–6) can be set up on either side (after the best climber has made the traverse belayed from one side). The two-sided belay keeps a climber from swinging like a pendulum in case of a fall some distance along the ledge. Alternatively, it can be rigged with a hand line tied off at both sides (sometimes called a fixed line in rock climbing). Each caver should clip into it from a chest loop or seat harness with a locking carabiner. On a particularly dangerous traverse, the first person to cross will be rigging the fixed hand line so he or she should be belayed with a safety line. In a cave under intensive study, where traffic along a certain route may be heavy, it's not uncommon to rig a more or less permanent fixed line using bolts and bolt hangers to speed traffic and minimize the danger. Such a line should be removed, however, if the situation changes.

Free Climbing

Free climbing—also called three-point-climbing or classic rock climbing—is a skill that novices should learn in practice climbs above ground before trying their prowess underground. Free climbing can't be learned from a book. A book—or a good instructor—can outline the principles. But the only way to learn the technique is by doing it yourself under the guidance of an experienced instructor.

Free climbing does not mean climbing without a belay. When rock climbers use the term free climbing, they mean without artificial aids such as *étriers* (webbing ladders), rope stirrups, or hardware. Except in special cases, nuts, chocks, pitons, and bolts (which are inserted or driven into the rock face) are not used as direct climbing aids, but only as anchors for ropes and belaying. Cave climbs are usually made up of short pitches of 10 to 30 feet (3 to 10 meters) rather than the longer ascents found in mountain climbing. Depending on the skill of the group, short climbs in caves may or may not be belayed. However, if there is any doubt, rig a belay line and be safe.

Free climbing pitches are found in pits or fissures too wide for chimneying, walls, breakdown areas with large fallen slabs and blocks, and steep slopes. Holds are usually large and muddy rather than small and dry as in rock climbing. Wide pits and walls are negotiated with a combination of chimneying and free climbing using ledges and holds. Breakdown blocks have sharp edges that are good for pulling yourself up and cracks between the blocks that a boot, knee, or shoulder can be jammed into. Flowstone slopes (which shouldn't be climbed at all if likely to be damaged or dirtied) are made up of ascending ledges that look like easy steps, but are sometimes too narrow or sloping to serve as good footholds. Between the ledges, small ribs or knobby columns offer handholds or fingerholds for balance. Other useful flowstone holds are larger columns and stalagmites which can be hugged with both arms when swinging up onto a ledge.

Free climbing is based on the principle of always having three points of contact (fig. 11–7). The feet and legs do the lifting. The hands take care of the balance. For example, starting with secure footholds and handholds, one of your hands probes upward to a knob or crack. When a good one is found, hold tight with both hands and look for the next foothold. It helps a lot to lean out from the rock so you can see the holds better. You can almost always tell an inexperienced climber by the way he or she clings too closely to the rock. Once a good foothold is located, the weight is shifted upward and one of the hands starts probing again. Movement is smooth, sure, and graceful. Lunging, jumping, or rushing are dangerous and counterproductive.

Before starting up a climb, plan the route ahead, but allow for an alternate route if possible. Select footholds and handholds carefully, but test them before putting full weight on them. Surprisingly enough, footholds so small as to be barely noticeable are used every day by experienced climbers.

For footholds, the side of the foot is better than the toe because the toeholds put greater strain on the leg muscles. When first placing the foot onto a foothold, flex the ankle a few times to be sure to get as much boot as possible on the hold. This helps you sense the hold with the sole of the boot. But don't shuffle around once the foot is positioned or traction may be lost. For balance, keep the knees bent slightly.

When no ledge or knob presents itself, a hold can sometimes be created by jamming the hand or foot into a crack (fig. 11–5). This is an important technique and is the only way some climbs can be made. For foot jams, insert the boot at an angle, then twist it into the crack. This makes it easier to get out after you put your full weight on it. Hand and fist jams are also very useful. Gloves are essential for jam holds, although bare hands are better for most climbing.

Generally, climbing up is easier than climbing down because you can see the holds better. When descending, try to face outward when it's relatively easy going, move sideways when it's a little harder, and face in (as when climbing

Fig. 11–7. Free climbing a muddy wall. Caver has three points of contact with two feet and the left hand and is reaching for a new hold with his right hand.

upward) when it's very difficult. Whenever possible, face outward, or get a firm grip and lean outward, so you can look down and see the holds better.

How about belaying with a safety line? On all but the shortest ascents (less than 10 feet), a belay is standard and even on the short ones it is a good idea. Never be afraid to ask for a belay if you feel uncertain about the safety of the ascent. When climbing down, always use a belay if there is real danger. On a tricky descent, you can ask for tension from the belayer so that you can lean out and look over your shoulder to find the next hold. Or, the belayer can hold you securely so you can probe around with your foot until you find the next hold. Be sure the belayer understands what is happening before doing this.

As with tight crawls and chimneys, the experienced cavers should talk a new caver down a slope, explaining where the holds are and where to make the next move. Others in the party can also help out by shining their lights on the holds so that they can be seen more easily in the darkness.

In caving, when a climb down is much more than 25 to 30 feet, a line is usually rigged, and the descent is made by rappelling. Similarly, if a particularly long upward climb is necessary, it will often be rigged for a ladder or prusik ascent.

A final note of caution. Never climb up a slope or pitch that you won't be able to climb back down easily. Sometimes it will run into a dead end and it will be necessary to climb back down. If it's not too long a pitch, it can sometimes be rigged for a hasty rappel, using a handline or the caver slings carried by two or three cavers. Always carry a hand line in caves where climbing and scrambling are required.

12

Anchors and Rigging

Familiarity with proper rigging techniques is important not only for the person doing the rigging but for all cavers who put their lives on the line.

Rigging is the technique of securely attaching climbing ropes, ladders, and sometimes cavers to safe anchoring points. If you're a beginning caver, you might well ask, "Why should I bother to learn about anchors and rigging?" Rigging a cave properly is often a complex task. It requires experience, judgment, and assistance.

You need to know about rigging for three reasons. First, you must be able to do it yourself as the main rigger or in an emergency. Second, all rigging needs to be routinely checked by at least one other knowledgeable caver. In other words, you should be prepared to serve as a back-up person to the main rigger. Anyone can make a mistake; the time to find out is when you're alive and well at the top of the drop, not when you're half dead at the bottom. Third, it will contribute to your peace of mind. There's no substitute for confidence in your

Fig. 12–1. Primary and back-up anchors using bolts, bolt hangers, carabiners, and figure-of-eight loops. Note that there should be little or no extra slack between the primary (lower) anchor knot and the secondary (higher) anchor, but that the knots face downward in line with the main load.

equipment coupled with your own experience gained through good training.

Anchors

An anchor is a secure point to which rigging is attached. For safety, especially with man-made anchors, one or more backup anchors are advisable (fig. 12–1). Backups can sometimes turn a questionable anchor into a reasonably safe one if the load is evenly distributed (fig. 12–4). Anchors are used to rig a climbing rope to rappel (descend) or prusik (ascend), to attach a ladder, or to tie yourself into when you are belaying.

Natural anchors are preferred to artificial ones for conservation and aesthetic reasons—artificial anchors damage the cave or the surface area near the entrance. Outside a cave, suitable natural anchors for rigging an entrance drop can often be found on the large rocks or trees nearby. Avoid precariously balanced rocks or shallow-rooted trees. Inside a cave, break-down boulders, limestone knobs and flakes, and certain massive formations can also be used. However, be wary of formations. They often have a concealed structure that is quite irregular and makes them susceptible to breaking. With any anchor, tie around the bottom or maximum cross section. Run your hand over the entire surface to check for sharp edges or prickly knobs. Pad if necessary to protect the rope or webbing.

When no suitable natural anchor can be found and there is no other safe alternative, an artificial anchor, such as a bolt, is usually installed. However, indiscriminate bolt installation is not recommended unless careful consideration is first given to safety and conservation.

For safety's sake, each primary anchor should have at least one back-up anchor to catch the fall if the primary anchor fails (fig. 12–1). With artificial anchors, this is an absolute necessity. If possible, place primary and secondary bolts in different bedding planes (sections of rock) to lessen the chance of simultaneous failures (Isenhart 1976).

To attach the main rope or a ladder to the anchor, short lengths of sling called runners are often used. The purpose is either to save some length on the main climbing rope or to place the rope where it is easier to get over a lip, out of a waterfall, away from a sharp edge, or closer to a ledge that the climber can sit on to get on or off the rope (fig. 12–2). Three or four single runners made from 6 feet (2 meters) each of 1-inch webbing tied with a secured water knot and a like number of double runners made from 10 to 12 feet (3 to 4 meters) of webbing are very handy for cave rigging.

Montgomery (1977) cautions that you should always ask the question, "What would happen if . . . ?" when picking anchors and placing slings for rigging. For example, you should always use separate runners from each anchor point to the line or ladder (fig. 12–3). With only a single runner connected to each anchor point, if one anchor fails, the others may be

Fig. 12–2. Rigging runners around boulder conserve climbing rope and position the rope better to get on or off, or to avoid a sharp edge.

subjected to a substantial shock load. To equalize the load between two or more points, figure 12–4 offers two alternatives (Hansen 1977). These would be very effective where the choice of anchors is less than perfect or a heavy load is expected as during a rescue.

When running the rope through the connecting carabiner on a runner, be sure the direction of the load won't force against the gate. Also, resist the temptation to make a chain of three or more nonlocking carabiners to add length to a sling. If twisted, the gates can quite easily open up. Finally, always attach the main rope to the runner with a carabiner, not directly. This is especially true if you use a doubled rope and intend to pull it down. Running a nylon rope against a fixed nylon runner or cord may cause fusion and breakage.

When rigging, always clear away all loose rocks and debris from the edge of a drop. Falling rocks are the cause of many accidents. Always yell *rock* when you dislodge anything into the drop. If you're on the bottom during rigging, stay out of the drop zone. Before lowering a rope (or ladder), call down and see if the drop is *clear*. Is so, yell *rope* before actually lowering it.

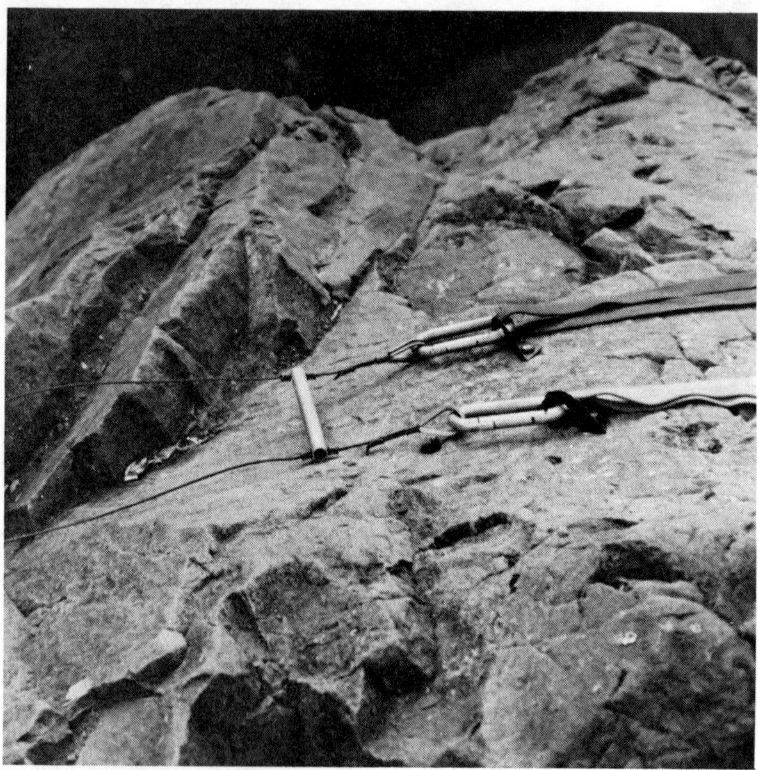

Fig. 12–3. Ladder rigged to separate bolt anchors with carabiners. Note runner slings going to additional back up points (at some distance to right, out of picture). See also figure 15–4 for ladder rigging details.

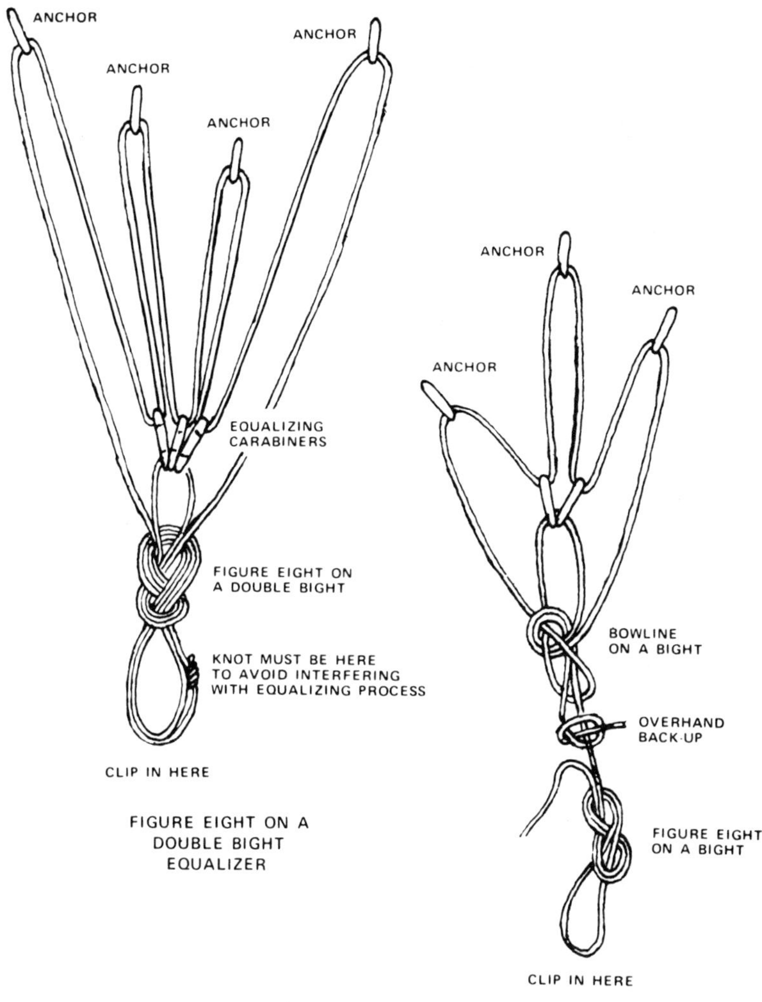

Fig. 12–4. Load equalizing systems for multiple (more than two) anchors. Should one anchor go, the system will automatically spread the load between the remaining anchors. Perlon cord, or webbing, can be used. With webbing, the figure-of-eight on a double bight works better than the bowline-on-a-bight version. *Courtesy "Off Belay."*

Bolts

First choice among most North American cavers for artificial anchors are expansion bolts. These are driven or tapped into predrilled holes and expand against the walls or rear of the hole to lock in place. Bolts are preferred to the pitons (flat, knife-bladelike metal wedges) formerly much used by mountain climbers. It is seldom that a suitable crack for piton driving can be found in the limestone of caves. The newer "clean climbing" chocks (irregularly shaped metal devices for larger cracks and holes) have never found much application in caves. This is probably because cavers do so little pure rock climbing on sheer faces where temporary, removable (hence "clean") anchors like chocks can prove their value. One advantage of bolts is that they can often be placed so that the line is positioned properly for the drop, that is, out of the water or free of sharp edges, something you often can't do with a natural anchor.

Two types of expansion bolts seem to be the most popular: the self-drilling or Red Head brand concrete anchor and the Rawl Drive-In contraction stud. We prefer the self-drilling anchors (fig. 12–5) in the ⅜-inch (9-millimeter) size. Recommended safe working load is 1544 pounds (700 kilograms) in 3500 pounds per square inch (normal) concrete according to ITT Phillips, manufacturer of the Red Head brand. This is 25 percent of their test results. Other producers of similarly constructed bolts are: Rawl Products Sabre-Tooth, Star Concrete Anchors, and VSI Fasterners Corporation Concrete Anchors. This type of bolt gains its strength from the rear of the hole by means of a conical wedge that expands as the shield is driven home into the hole. Because the strength comes from deep inside the hole, this type is advantageous where the outer layer of rock may be weathered or softer.

Second in popularity is the Rawl Products ¼-inch (6-millimeter) Rawl-Drive contraction stud. This has an offset split shaft that jams and locks into the predrilled hole. They come in 1½- or 2-inch (37- or 50-millimeter) long versions with the end threaded to accept a nut for use with removable hangers. Another version comes in a 1¼-inch (30-millimeter)

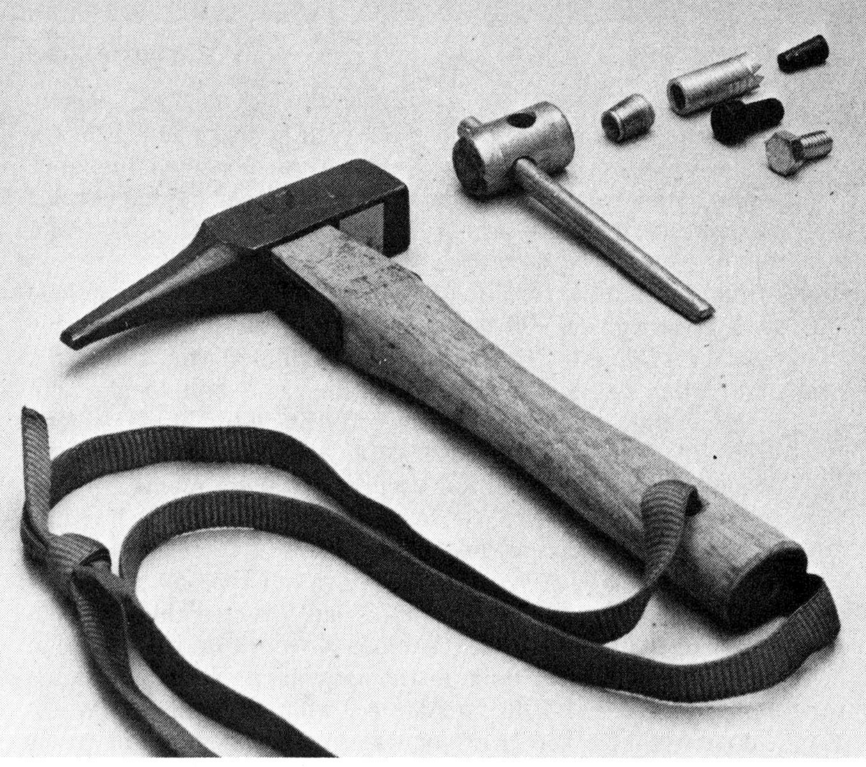

Fig. 12–5. Expansion bolt anchor. *From left to right:* piton hammer with 5 feet of ½-inch nylon webbing, driver with rotating handle, tapered collar (shown broken off), drill shield with teeth at one end, and conical-shaped "red head" plug which expands the shield to lock it in place. Below the shield is a case hardened bolt with an allen key head; beneath that is a standard bolt with a hex head.

length. It has a head and is already installed in an SMC hanger. There is some evidence that the split shank of the Rawl Drive-In fatigues (weakens) with age. For this reason, these are not considered as permanent as the self-drilling anchors.

Types of bolts to be avoided are the lead-lag shield, plastic insert, fiber-screw anchors, or the Star Dryvin, which is nail-driven into a soft metal shield.

In setting any bolt, try to confine the damage to the cave wall to as small an area as possible. Before beginning to drill, study the bedrock carefully for cracks and evidence of loose surface flakes or crumbly rock (or on the surface, badly weathered rock). Pound the surface with your hammer and listen for solid sounding areas. While not 100 percent reliable, rock sounds can be helpful to an experienced ear. As mentioned earlier, try to place primary and back-up bolts in different bedding planes or sections of rock.

Bolts should be installed in the wall or floor where the load will be at right angles to their axis. Most bolts are noticeably weaker if subjected to a straight-out pull along the axis of the bolt. Thus ceilings are not suggested as a bolt location. In walls, a slight (5 degree) downward drift to the hole is a good idea. Then if the bolt loosens, it won't fall out under load (Montgomery 1977). Proper hammer weight seems to be a subject of some debate. We use a piton hammer, with a 13-ounce (¼-kilogram) head. This is about average (although the Chouinard boasts an 18-ounce head). Other cavers recommend at least a 16-ounce (½-kilogram), the weight of a standard carpenter's hammer. Hammer blows should be hard but not hard enough to fracture the rock at the surface near the hole. Rotate the drill 120 degrees after each blow. Do not lubricate the drill with oil or water. Instead, blow out debris every few minutes with a small hose. Wear safety glasses or goggles to protect the eyes.

The self-drilling anchors are driven with a hammer and a holder or driver that fits over the tapered collar. The other end contains the drilling teeth. Drill by striking and rotating until you reach the depth of the break groove on the tapered top (fig. 12–6). Remove the shield and install the conical plug in the toothed end. Replace the shield in the hole and drive it in with several sharp blows until the break groove is again flush. Then with a sideways blow, snap off the tapered top, and the anchor is ready for use. The snapped-off top can be removed from the holder by putting the chisel end of the turning handle in the lower hole of the holder and tapping the end of the handle sharply.

It usually takes 15 to 20 minutes to set a bolt, but it can take longer in especially hard limestone. Hole depth is critical and must allow the final position of the anchor to be such that the hanger is flush with the surface. Some recommend a gap of

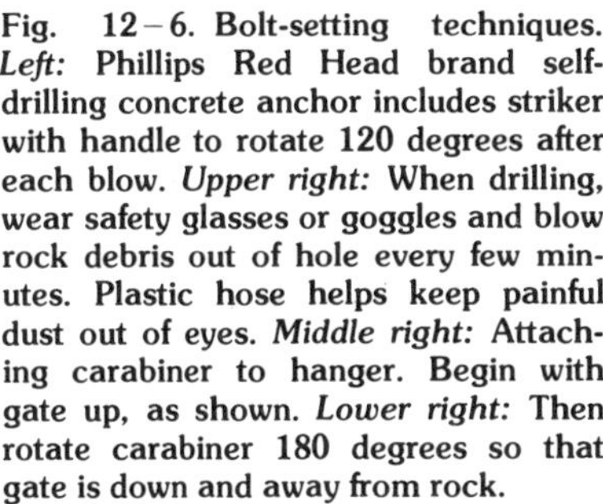

Fig. 12–6. Bolt-setting techniques. *Left:* Phillips Red Head brand self-drilling concrete anchor includes striker with handle to rotate 120 degrees after each blow. *Upper right:* When drilling, wear safety glasses or goggles and blow rock debris out of hole every few minutes. Plastic hose helps keep painful dust out of eyes. *Middle right:* Attaching carabiner to hanger. Begin with gate up, as shown. *Lower right:* Then rotate carabiner 180 degrees so that gate is down and away from rock.

about ⅛ inch between the hanger and surface rather than tightening the hanger tight up against the rock. This is so the hanger can remain tight yet is free to adjust itself to the movements of the load and not force the bolt loose when the load shifts. This is probably still true with older, angled hangers. But the newer, flat-mounting SMC type can be flush-mounted and will not stress the anchor. High-tensile strength (Grade 9) bolts should be used. Whether the standard hex-head or allen-head type is used, be sure to bring the proper wrench to tighten it up. Montgomery (1977) recommends coating the bolt and end of the casing with grease. This is probably a good idea although we haven't come across any vertical cavers who do this in our part of the world.

When attaching the carabiner to the hanger, be sure that its final position is down and out—that is, with the gate down and away from the rock. This keeps it from opening if the rope or sling twists under load (fig. 12–6).

After drilling the hole and installing the hanger, should you leave the hanger there or remove it? You can get an instant difference of opinion among vertical cavers on this point. If you do decide to leave the hanger in place, you can apply Locktite to the threads to prevent theft. Whether you leave it or not, it's a good idea to install a small metal tag stamped with the date of installation and your club's initials or other identification.

What if you find a bolt already installed? Is it safe to use? You should certainly be suspicious if you don't know its history. To find out whether it's safe, attach a rigging runner with a carabiner and load it fully by jumping up and down on the sling. If it moves, better forget it. If it doesn't move it's probably okay. Nevertheless, it bears repeating that you should not rely on any *single* artificial anchor. Always have at least one backup.

Rope Abrasion and Pads

To prevent rope abrasion, rope pads must be installed wherever the rope is subjected to pressure against a sharp

Fig. 12–7. Leather rope pads protect rope at lip and other points of abrasion. Both are attached to the anchor with thin cord. Other rope pad materials are rug remnants, blue jean legs, and slit garden hose.

surface. The primary place will usually be up near the anchor. Note that the longer the drop the greater the abrasion potential. Montgomery cites drops of over 75 to 100 feet as cases where the abrasion risk must be carefully studied. He also points out that where the rope makes a sharp angle over an edge is more dangerous than where it only touches the wall.

Prusiking, with its constant up and down sawing motion, is potentially more damaging to ropes than rappelling, assuming a steady rappel rate. All cavers should learn to rappel smoothly and avoid the kind of jumping and bouncing that pulls anchors out and abrades ropes severely.

We routinely pad all drops with leather, canvas, or rug pads. (fig. 12–7). Old blue-jeans legs, cut open at the seam, make good pads. Size should be about 12 inches (⅓ meter) wide and about 3 feet (1 meter) long. Old cut up rug remnants—except those made of nylon—are also good but are heavier and bulkier to carry. Leather wears really well; its only disadvantage is its higher cost. Whatever you use, attach a 10-to 15-foot (3- to 5-meter) length of parachute cord so the pad can be tied off and positioned properly. In cloth pads, metal eyelets are helpful to prevent tearing.

Montgomery (1977) describes a "Jerry" protector made from a piece of heavy material about 5 inches (125 mm) wide by 2 feet (600 mm) long, and held together with Velcro strips. It is tied to the line or anchor with a short cord, and folds around the rope. To pass it, you simply unzip the Velcro.

When rappelling down or prusiking up, carefully reposition the rope on the pad after passing it. If there are several pads, for example at the top of the drop, it may be worth rigging a short tail of rope from the anchor so you can transfer to this and avoid the pads completely. Don't forget to tie a figure-of-eight loop in the bottom of the tail to keep from accidentally coming off the end, just as you do with the main rope.

Garden hose slit in a longitudinal or spiral cut is also sometimes used to pad ropes. While simple and relatively cheap, we've had a problem with it coming off the rope if a stiff plastic hose is used. When used on edges, it can bend and separate at the slit, exposing the rope (Montgomery 1977).

13

Vertical Gear

Equipment for technical vertical caving: ladder climbing, rappelling, and ascending.

The specialized gear for vertical caving is loosely called climbing hardware. It includes carabiners, pulleys, cable ladders, descenders, and ascenders. Some of this equipment has been borrowed from rock climbing, but there have also been some significant developments by cavers, particularly in the area of prusiking devices and low-elasticity ropes. This chapter covers hardware. Ropes, slings, and harnesses are found in chapter 9. Anchors, bolts, and rigging are covered in chapter 12.

Carabiners

Carabiners are oval rings of special alloy aluminum or steel with a spring-loaded, inward-opening gate on one side. Specific uses for carabiners in caving include rigging to hang-

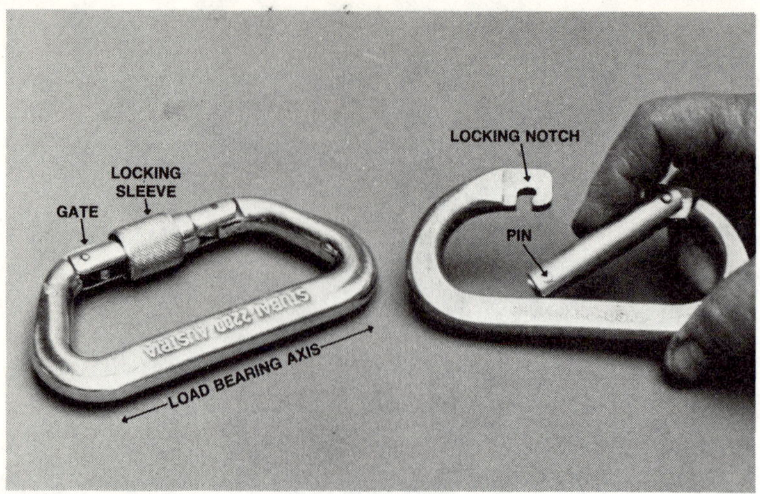

Fig. 13–1. Locking and standard carabiners. The standard carabiner gate has a pin which fits into a slot with a notch as shown. Check to be sure that locking carabiners have this same construction. Modern carabiners test at 3000 to 5500 pounds (1350 to 2500 kilograms). Locking carabiners without threads use a pin inside the sleeve. When the pin wears, the sleeve can jam and become hard to open without pliers.

ers or runners, rappelling, snapping into a line on a horizontal traverse, attaching to a belay line, lowering gear, and attaching gloves or equipment to cave packs. Present day carabiners test from 3000 to 5500 pounds (1350 to 2500 kilograms) and cost anywhere from four to eight dollars (fig. 13–1 and 13–2). A carabiner is only about half as strong when the gate is open as when it is closed. However, they are designed so that they can be opened under a nominal working load of up to about 200 pounds (90 kilograms). This is one of the characteristics important in rock climbing, where ropes are often snapped into the gate under load.

UIAA (Union of International Alpine Association) standards call for strength along the major axis (the long or load-bearing side) to be 4850 pounds (2200 kilograms) open, 2646 pounds (1200 kilograms) closed. Many current brands meet these standards, and those made in Europe may be marked to that effect. Because there is still some variability in carabiner

BRAND		AVERAGE RATED LOAD	
		Pounds	*Kilograms*
SMC/REI	Locking D, bright finish	5635	2558
SMC/REI	Standard D, bright finish	4790	2175
SMC/REI	Standard oval, bright finish	3795	1723
Chouinard	Oval	4435	2013
Chouinard	D	4000 (min)	1816 (min)
Bonaiti	Locking D	5500 (min)	2500 (min)
Bonaiti	Locking D (steel)	11,000	5000
Bonaiti	D	5500 (min)	2500 (min)
Stubai	Locking D (steel)	11,000	5000
Stubai	Locking D (steel)	5400	2450
Hiatt	Locking D	4850 (min)	2200 (min)
Liberty (Eiger)	Locking D	5500	2500
Liberty	D	4500	2041
Liberty	Oval	3200	1452
Clog	Offset D	4850	2200
Clog	Standard D	4620 (min)	2100
SMC	Bolt Hanger	4800	2180
SMC	Aluminum Descending Ring	3320	1508

Fig. 13–2. Rated load of carabiners (from manufacturer and dealer catalogs). All are aluminum except as noted.

manufacturing, it is best to stay away from those without a brand name. In North America, the major brands available are SMC, REI (made by SMC), Chouinard, Bonaiti, Stubai, Hiatt, Clog, and Liberty (Eiger).

Although carabiners are designed to take some side loading, the fact is the gate is unquestionably the weakest spot. When rigging you must be very careful that the load can't shift and be applied directly against the gate (fig. 13–3).

Failure of a gate at a load as low as 300 pounds has been reported (Blackshaw 1975). Many carabiners have a locking sleeve to keep the gate closed. However, despite what you may think, the locking sleeve doesn't make the gate—and hence the locking carabiner—any stronger than the gate on a nonlocking carabiner. Where a gate fails, test results suggest it is the hinge pin that most often breaks (Blackshaw 1975). Thus, the sleeve serves to keep the gate from opening accidentally, but it could be a tragic mistake to think that a locking carabiner is automatically stronger.

Locking carabiners screw shut on exposed threads or on an internal pin in the sleeve housing. Check to be sure the threads are flat-topped, not crested, to avoid abrasion on webbing (fig. 13–4). Threaded types seem more reliable than the pin types, which tend to jam.

Carabiners come in several shapes: oval, kidney, pear, or D. Blackshaw cites the D as being the best shape because it assures that the load will most often be applied to the load-bearing (nongated) side. The oval shape is also very popular.

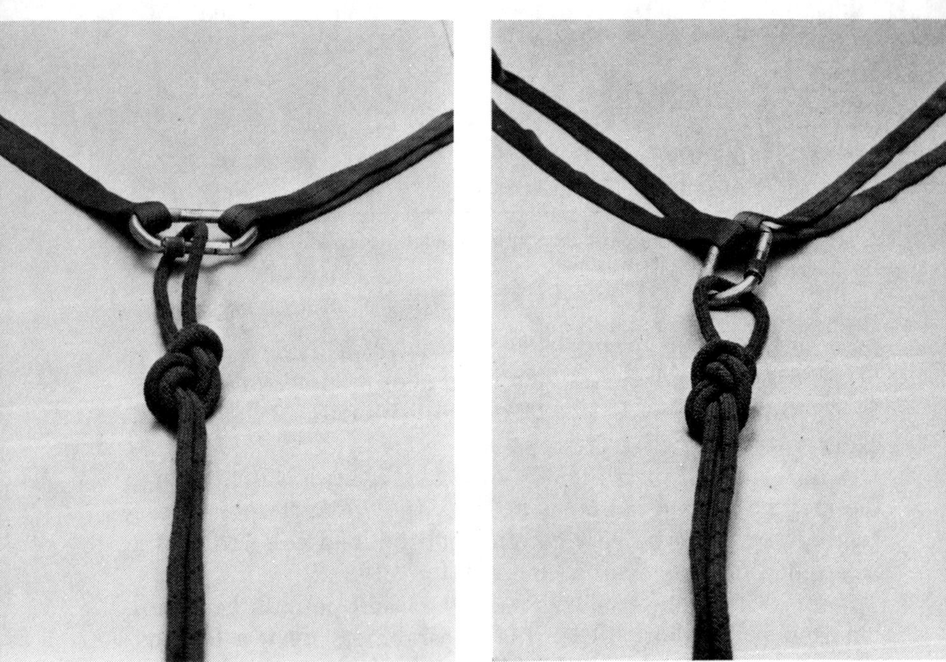

Fig. 13–3. *Left,* improper rigging, showing how the load is applied directly to the gate, the weakest point on a carabiner. *Right,* slings and rope are arranged correctly on the load-bearing axis.

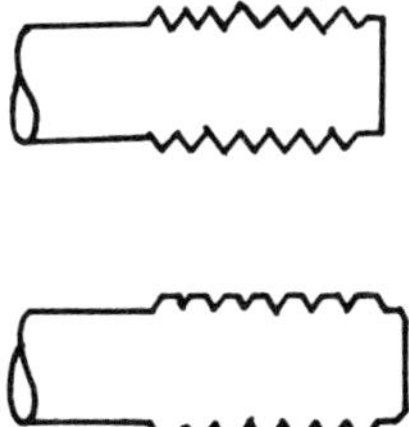

Fig. 13–4. Threads for the sleeves on threaded locking carabiners. The sharply crested threads at top can cut through webbing. Flat crested threads are much safer.

At a minimum, each caver should have three carabiners, two of the locking type and one of the standard D or oval type. These three carabiners are exclusive of any used for rappelling with break bars (see below). For main rigging to anchors or to your seat harness, we recommend a locking carabiner meeting the UIAA standard of 4850 pounds (2200 kilograms) or higher. For the most part, cavers tend to need fewer carabiners than rock climbers. It is not unusual for climbers to buy ten at a crack. Climbers also seem to use more nonlocking types because they often only have one hand free to snap in a carabiner and lockings often need two hands.

While clipping two carabiners together is okay, avoid making a chain of three or more (unless they are locking types). Twisting of the chain will easily open one or more gates. Remember, too, our earlier warning about always having the gate opening face downward and away from the rock. Like the boxer going for the long count, the final position is *down and out*.

Taking care of carabiners is relatively simple, but don't suffer from the delusion that they are indestructable. Carefully wash off all mud with water or a solvent such as paint thinner. Lubricate the gate lightly with a penetrating oil like WD-40. One particular caution: a carabiner that has fallen any distance or bounced hard on the rock should be retired. Invisible cracks may develop from even a short drop (Wollock 1978).

Rapid Links

A very strong (10,000-pounds or 4540-kilograms) rigging device for main ropes that shares several characteristics with the carabiner is the quick link or rapid link. It can be found in hardware, boating, and some auto supply stores. Most of these seem to be of French manufacture, the Maillon Rapide Link.

Unlike a carabiner, it derives a large part of its strength from its locking mechanism which in effect makes it into a continuous oval. Since it has no gate, it avoids the hinge pin, the weak point of a carabiner. Nevertheless, don't forget that the screw sleeve is integral to the design and function. The #9 size of the Maillon Rapide (about two-thirds the size of an SMC oval carabiner) tested to 10,000 pounds, whether finger-tight or wrench-tight. However, with the sleeve unscrewed, the link failed far lower—1100 pounds or 500 kilograms (Davison 1979). Mountain Safety Research (MSR) sells what it calls a Lock Link Carabiner for rigging and harnesses at $8.50. With the lock closed, MSR says it tests at 5000 pounds (2270 kilograms).

We have used rapid links for several years to attach main ropes and pulleys to anchors. The one shown in figure 13–5 was purchased at a towing hitch shop. The principle disadvantage we have found is that the opening is only about half as big as a carabiner ($\frac{3}{8}$ to $\frac{7}{16}$ inches—10 to 13 millimeters—compared to 1 to $1\frac{1}{4}$ inches). This makes it harder to fit ropes and harnesses inside. On the other hand, there's no gate to bump into ropes that are already inside.

In the balance, we definitely prefer carabiners because they are more fail-safe. If you forget to lock a locking carabiner, you haven't lost any strength. You have given up the advantage of the gate being harder to open, but you're no worse off than if it was a nonlocking carabiner. If you forget to lock a rapid link, the strength drops to one-ninth of what it is when locked. And if you load a rapid link when it's not screwed shut with even a light load, you may find that it will never screw together again.

Pulleys

Pulleys are useful in caves for hauling and rescue opera-

Fig. 13–5. Rescue pulleys are of special design with flanges that can be rotated to allow the pulley to be put on the rope at any point. Pulleys typically test at above 5000 pounds (2270 kilograms). Rapid link shown above pulley at left is a carabiner-like device that tests at 10,000 pounds (4540 kilograms) but must be screwed shut to achieve rated strength.

tions (fig. 13–5). The best types are usually called rescue pulleys. They consist of two flanges enclosing a nylon or metal pulley wheel to protect the rope from abrasion. The flanges are hinged so you can put the pulley on the line anywhere and not have to thread the end through. Strength of the pulley sold by REI and EMS is stated to be near 5000 pounds (2270 kilograms). A rapid link might be a good means of attaching a pulley in rescue situations where its additional strength could be an advantage. Some of the best pulleys are those made by Search & Rescue Associates and H. R. Anderson.

When buying a pulley be sure that the pulley wheel turns freely. If it binds, it can overheat and possibly fuse nylon. Some can be disassembled for cleaning. Use Locktite when reassembling to secure the nut and take care that the wheel runs freely.

Ladders

Do cavers still use cable ladders? You bet they do. Oddly enough, it appears to us that they are used more by experienced vertical cavers than by those newer to the game. This could be because seasoned cavers have learned through field use which particular piece of equipment is best for each situation and choose accordingly. Or it could be that these cavers are more likely to have grown up with ladders and therefore accept them as a standard piece of gear. Whatever the reason, cable ladders are still very much in use despite the recent developments in vertical gear which have tended to eclipse them.

Most often today, they are used in one-pit caves where it's easier for everyone to climb out on a ladder rather than to take the time to put on ascending gear. Even in this case, the way down the pit usually is via rappelling. Cavers rarely climb down ladders, since it's a lot easier and more fun to rappel down. Note that you have to have a line for belaying a ladder ascent anyway, so it gets pressed into double service as a rappel line for the descent. Ladders are also useful for waterfalls or muddy slopes; they're easier to hang on to.

Even with groups that still use ladders, one or at most two lengths (30 to 60 feet—10 to 20 meters) are all that anyone wants to climb anymore. Beyond climbs of 60 feet (20 meters), most North American cavers prefer mechanical ascenders.

Types of Ladders. Modern caving has now standardized on the cable ladder. Rope ladders (also known as rubber bands) with wooden, metal, or rubber rungs are seldom seen anymore. Since nylon stretches so much, you needed to climb the first 8 or 10 feet twice just to take up the slack in the rope.

Cable ladders are made of high-grade aircraft cable (standard or stainless) with rungs of aluminum alloy measuring about 5 inches wide. The ends are finished off in metal eyes for attachment to two carabiners and thence to two anchors. Length is usually 33 feet (10 meters), with a spacing of about 12 to 15 inches between rungs. In Britain, where cable ladders are still used more extensively than here, many clubs make their own ladders and prefer shorter rung spacings of 10 inches or so.

Cable ladders test at about 1000 pounds for each of the cables and 650 pounds for each rung and clamp that attaches the rungs to the cable. You should be especially wary of older cable ladders, particularly those made in the 1950s and early 1960s. Some of these ladders had a breaking problem from a chemical reaction taking place between the different types of metal used in the rungs, clips, and cable. But even a brand-new ladder still only tests at 650 pounds. Therefore, all ladder climbs, even as short as 10 or 15 feet, should be belayed without exception.

The ladders most commonly sold in this country are made by a French manufacturer, Pierre Allain. They are available through caving suppliers shown in the Appendix. Cost is about $1.25 a foot or $40.00 for a 10-meter length.

Care of Ladders. In a cave, protect a ladder from damage and abrasion by carrying it in a cloth sack, cave pack, or rubber inner tube. When installing a ladder down a pitch, lower it gently, don't throw it over the edge. It doesn't pay to bang it up on rocks and ledges. Besides, it can easily get caught on projections if you're not careful when you lower it.

(The same cautions are applicable to lowering, not throwing, ropes.) Try not to step on a ladder when it's stretched out on the passage floor. You might kink the cable or bend it over a sharp rock edge.

After use, wash all the mud off and inspect it when it's dry for loose cable strands and other signs of wear. To test it before use, rig it to a solid anchor, stand on the bottom rung and bounce on it with your full weight a few times. For storage and transport, coil a ladder by twisting each of the rungs in the opposite direction to form a crisscross pattern in the cable (fig. 13–6).

Rappelling Devices

Rappelling is a technique of safely sliding down a fixed rope (chapter 14). In this chapter, we will review the mechan-

Fig. 13–6. Steel cable ladder. For carrying and storage, twist ladder as shown, roll snugly but not tightly, and tie with a short length of sling or cord. Ladders test at about 650 pounds and occasionally break, so a belay is always used.

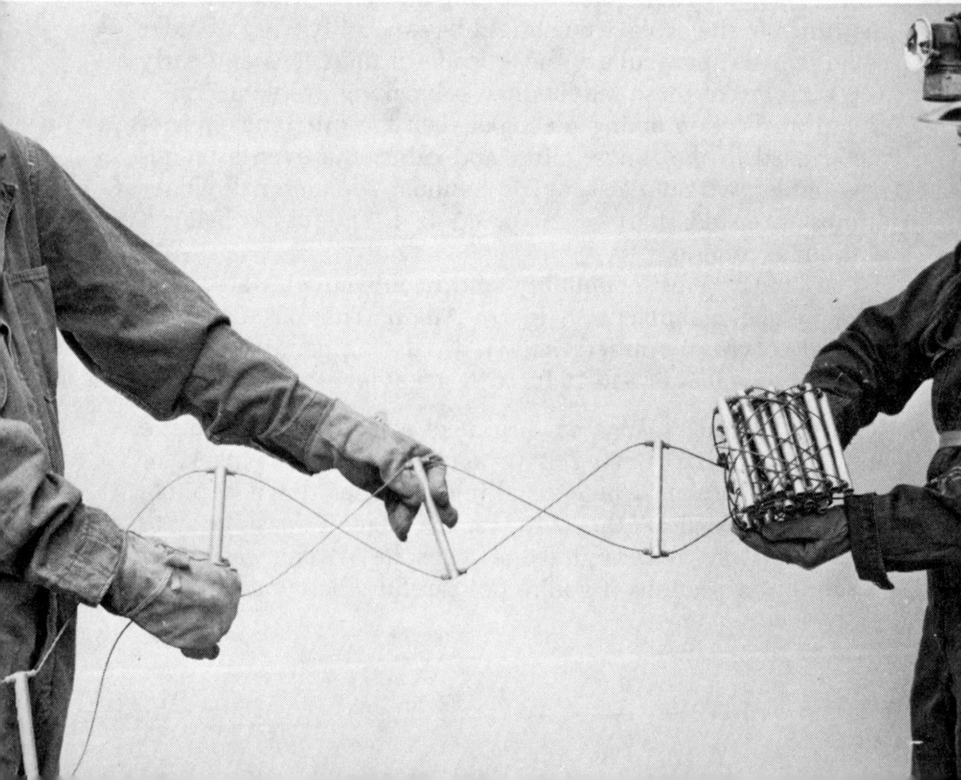

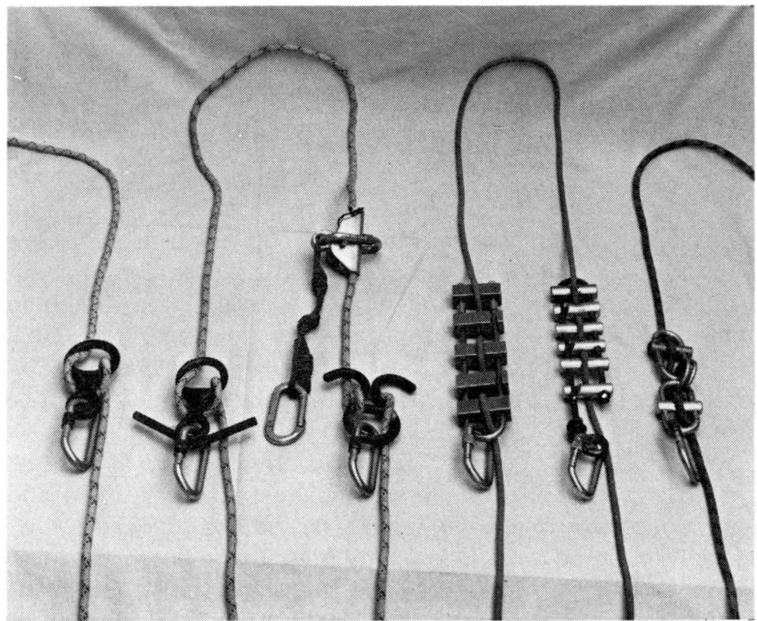

Fig. 13–7. Rappelling (descending) devices. *Shown from right to left,* each with its own high strength locking carabiner: double carabiner/brake bars, Blue Water rappel rack, super rack, MSR Longhorn with spelean shunt above it, MSR combined Longhorn and Figure–8, Clog Figure–8. Note that first two bars on rappel rack are the grooved type which help center the rope in the rack for better guiding. For long drops (over 150 feet or 50 meters), a rack is necessary. Neither the Longhorn nor the Figure–8 can dissipate enough heat or are rugged enough for long drops.

ical devices used for this technique. Figure 13–7 shows an assortment of the currently used equipment.

Double Brake Bars

One of the earliest and still very popular rappelling devices is the double carabiner/brake bar. These are standard oval carabiners supplied with tubular bars of the same brand that fit onto the gate side of the carabiner and lock across on the other (long) side. The rope is threaded through as shown in figure 13–7, so it applies pressure onto the bar and keeps it locked in place. If threaded upside down, in the so-called suicide rig, the bars will flip up and the rope will come out of the device. This is why you must always check for proper rigging before starting down the drop. Also note that the carabiner gates must be up (i.e., away from your harness). The reason for this is that the rope tends to pull the bar upward and this will help keep the gate closed if it is also on the up side. We also usually put the gates on opposite sides (as shown in fig. 13–7); but this is a habit from earlier, crossed-carabiner rappels and is not really necessary with carabiner/ brake bars. To connect the two carabiners together, a ring such as the SMC aluminum descending ring, a ⅜-inch (9-millimeter) diameter welded chain link, or a rapid link can be used.

When rigging, open both bars and bring a bight of rope up through the outside carabiner first. Snap the bar down and then thread the rope through the closer carabiner. Take out the slack in the rope so there is steady pressure on both bars.

While they are widely used, we can't recommend brake bars without some reservations. The possibility of threading them in a suicide rig is one thing, but you could do the same with just about any other descender as well. What bothers us is that they rely on cross-loading (between gate and long side), instead of along the main or load-bearing axis.

For this reason above all, we must caution you to never rappel with a single carabiner/brake bar rig. You're stacking the odds way against yourself if you do this.

Another less serious but still troublesome problem with brake bar rigs is the lack of a really easy-to-use lock-off position for resting or emergencies. With the rappel rack and MSR Longhorn this is simplicity itself. But with a brake bar rig, the best possibility seems to be to wrap the rappel line around one leg. This works and is essentially safe, but isn't all that easy to do. Later, we will describe the spelean shunt, a rappelling safety device that can add a convenient and safe resting position for brake bars afficionados.

Rappel Racks

In addition to brake bars that snap across carabiners, caving has developed some specialized rappelling devices called rappel racks. When making a long drop, the length of rope hanging below you increases the friction between a rope and rappelling device to the point where you may not be able to move at all. Sometimes you have to force the rope through the rappel device. Then, when you get near the bottom, the friction is much lower. Clearly a variable friction device would be useful, hence the development of rappel racks.

Rappel racks (fig. 13–6) are essentially long U-shaped devices usually having six brake bars that can be controlled by hand pressure or by adding or subtracting bars as needed (see chapter 14). The best method of control is by pressure on the bars. The instruction sheet with the Blue Water rack advises you to start off with five or six bars spread apart over the entire length of the rack. You control descent by shifting the bars up and down with one hand, the other hand holding onto the rope at some point below the rack. In this mode you can use all the bars and yet get surprisingly good control by changing the spacing of the bars: apart at the beginning, tighter later on.

Note that the rope must always be threaded so it passes over the top bar, not between the steel rack and the top bar. This is important, because the heat-dissipating ability of aluminum is much better than steel and where the rope first contacts the descender is where it's hottest. Also, when you lock the rack by wrapping the rope up over the oval end, the standing part of the rope pinches the overlapped end, making it nearly impossible to unlock the rack.

In normal use, the rope will soon wear a groove in the first two bars (assuming they are aluminum, not steel, as is most often the case). These can be switched with the last two bars to equalize wear (Montgomery 1977). In addition, Padgett and Padgett (1975) advise that the rope should always run down the center of the bars. Otherwise, offset grooves will develop which make it difficult to shift the bars under load. They recommend that you file shallow grooves in the middle of the first three bars to guide the rope properly. Bars with such grooves already provided are available from the Speleoshoppe. (See Appendix.)

Heating of the first two bars can be a problem on long drops (150 to 1000 feet—50 to 300 meters). One good solution is to add ¾-inch aluminum tubing spacers to the rack frame between bars one and two to keep the bars separated (Montgomery 1977).

Although originally devised for deep pits, rappel racks can be used just as well on short drops, so they are really a universal rappelling device. A major supplier of racks is Blue Water Ltd. The standard size is 14 inches, with six bars. PMI also produces a rack. Other racks, some homemade, are seen from time to time. We advise you to stay away from any that have an open eye for carabiner attachment rather than an eye with a double loop or several wraps around the frame (Davison 1976).

Super Rack

A modified rack with several unique features has recently been introduced by Isenhart (1973 and 1977) and marketed by the Speleoshoppe. Features include a heavier rack, four or five massive square bars with center positioning grooves, and aluminum spacers between first and second bars. The first and third bars are permanently attached, the others are open. Control is very smooth and is done entirely by shifting the bars. It has been reported (Davison 1977) that some people have experienced control problems with the Super Rack. Others have reported no difficulties at all. As with all technical vertical equipment, it is essential that you try each type yourself, under controlled conditions above ground, to find what suits you best.

Longhorn and Figure–8 Ring

For short and medium drops (less than 150 feet or 50 meters) new lightweight descenders of safer design than the popular double carabiner/brake bar rig are now coming into use. (For longer drops, a rack should be used.) The first is Figure–8 Ring from Colorado Mountain Industries, Clog

Climbing Gear, and SMC. Another is the Longhorn (and Longhorn/Figure–8 combined), which until recently was sold by MSR and will still be available at least until the present stock runs out.

We have used the MSR Longhorn extensively and prefer it to the Figure–8 Ring. It is very easy to rig, much easier than brake bars or a rack. For us, the control is better than with a Figure–8, but others find the control with the Figure–8 to be excellent. Montgomery (1977) reports that British cavers have experienced great success with Figure–8s on the short and medium drops common in Britain.

An important benefit of the Longhorn is the ease of adding friction. Simply take another loop around the horns and it slows you down. To stop and secure a rappel is equally simple (fig. 13–7). After wrapping one loop around the horns, you pull up some more slack to form an underhand loop and hook it over the top horn. For resting or changing over this is as secure as a rack and easier to do. Unlocking is almost as simple: squeeze the rope where it passes through the horn and undo the locking loop.

A potential problem of the Longhorn (and perhaps the reason MSR is discontinuing it) is the remote possibility of the rope popping off one of the horns if your weight is removed from the line. However, this hazard is also present with carabiner brake bars. For that reason, we always caution trainees about how the brake bars could loosen (as you maneuver into position at the top of the drop, for example). Nonetheless, we have never known it to happen; nor have we had any problems with the Longhorn.

With the Figure–8 Ring, this hazard doesn't exist at all. Thus, excellent security is the best selling point for this descender. Its main disadvantage is that it must be unclipped from your carabiner to thread, and the possibility of dropping it is ever present. There also doesn't seem to be any way to lock it off for resting or emergencies, except wrapping the rope below around your leg. It should be threaded as shown in figure 13–6. If this doesn't provide enough friction, it can be rotated one or two full 360 degree turns to the left or right before clipping into the carabiner.

Again, try both of these out and see if either is better for you than a rack or brake bars.

Spelean Shunt—Rappel Safety Device

The spelean shunt is an ingenious new rappel safety device invented by two Australian cavers using standard and readily available gear. (Toomer and Welch 1978). But first a little background on rappel safety. As should be obvious, when you rappel, your entire life rides on the descender, the sling attaching the descender to your body, and the rope itself. These are all part of one system, and no separate or back-up safety is provided.

In the early days of cave rappelling (late 1950s and early 1960s), it was not uncommon to use a separate belay line to safety the rappeller. Many of us were worried about the sling/bars hazard and a belay line seemed logical. However, it was soon found, after one or two mishaps, that using a second line could be more hazardous than going it alone. The belay line often got all tangled up with the rappel line and people got stranded in midair.

Then, several cavers (including ourselves) started using the so-called prusik safety. This was simplicity itself: tie a loose Prusik knot on the line using your safety loop, hold the knot gently in one hand, and connect the other end into your seat sling or a separate chest sling (or both). If the brake bar rig failed, you would be saved.

None of us gave much thought to how we'd get out of this secure spot on the line. What if we were in the middle of a free rappel (away from the wall) 60 feet from the floor and with no second rope to transfer to? The fact is, when that Prusik knot locks, you can't get down or up unless you've brought other gear with you for a changeover. Neither can someone easily lower you, because the line is loaded (by you) and tied off. Furthermore, if you are dangling from a chest sling or waist loop (instead of a seat harness), the pressure on your internal organs will literally kill you in *minutes* if the squeezing isn't relieved.

And that's not all. The worst part is that it doesn't work. It won't stop you. In an actual rappelling accident back in 1964, a falling caver could not let go of her Prusik safety knot. She rode it a full 100 feet down and only dropped it when she hit her head on a ledge 20 feet from the floor. This accident was fully documented and reported, but its lesson has not been learned even today. Simply stated, it is this: Taking your hand off the knot is a negative action, and under stress you can't do it (Tech Troglodite 1964). A nearly identical accident took place in Cass Cave, West Virginia (Smutek 1976).

However, there is even more. Calculations based on the analysis of a fatal accident in Britain concluded that if a Prusik safety knot slips along the rope for as little as one foot before it grabs, the heat generated by the friction will melt the sling and the knot will fail. In this case, it was a 4-millimeter Perlon sling attached to an 11-millimeter kernmantle rope. The climber fell and was killed. Either way, Prusik safeties are a bust. Incidentally the reason the caver's prusik sling didn't fuse to the rope in the 1964 accident is that it was made of natural fiber (manila) rope, not nylon.

In 1976, Don Davison, then the NSS Safety and Techniques Chairman, came up with one answer to this problem (1976a). This is called the safety rappel cam. It has an ingenious trigger mechanism activated by striking a cord with your hand. Thus, a positive action is taken which locks the mechanism. Also, if you are injured and lean back from the rope, the trigger cord, which is attached to your chest sling, will trip the cam.

We built one of these and tried it out on several occasions. It worked very well, except it's not as easy to reset as the spelean shunt. In addition, it seems a little complex for the average caver to build and use. So far we haven't seen a commercial version of it, but for a time the Speleoshoppe offered a kit.

In the meantime, along came the spelean shunt (fig. 13–8), a simpler device. It only needs a Gibbs ascender, a locking carabiner, and your safety loop sling or flat nylon sling. The carabiner acts as a very effective release mechanism after the shunt has locked. It takes a minute to get used to fitting the shunt on the line until you've done it a few times. First the safety or webbing loop is attached to seat and chest sling. Then it is threaded through the hole in the Gibbs cam, fol-

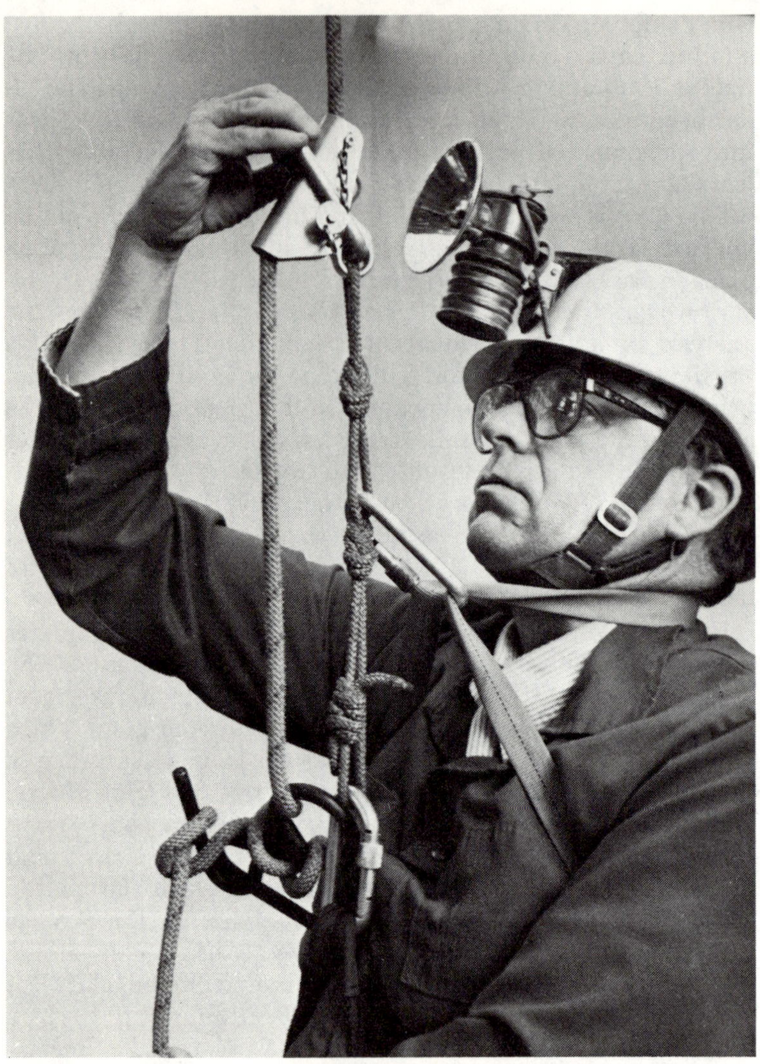

Fig. 13–8. Spelean shunt made up of a Gibbs ascender, locking carabiner, and safety loop connected to chest and seat harness. Carabiner serves as a handle to release the shunt after it has locked. A 12-inch (300-millimeter) long loop of 7-millimeter cord (not shown) attached to the carabiner further aids unlocking. Not only is it an excellent safety device, it can provide a good resting position for Figure–8 Ring or carabiner/brake bar descenders. Note MSR Longhorn locked off with an underhand knot over one of the horns for a safety after shunt is released.

Fig. 13–9. Assembling the shunt on the line is easy if you practice it a few times. (See text.)

lowed by the carabiner as shown in figure 13–7. Next, the rope is snapped through the carabiner and the shell of the Gibbs is slid upward into the rope, through the carabiner and into its regular position over the cam. Then the quick-release pin is inserted so that the nongated (long) side of the carabiner rests on the pin.

Length of the safety loop should be enough so the shunt rides comfortably on the top of your descender. The weight of the carabiner will keep the cam from locking, so you can almost forget the shunt is there.

If you want to lock it to rest, or in an emergency, just grab the Gibbs housing or the carabiner and it will lock. Be sure the sling is short enough so the shunt won't be out of your reach when it tightens on the line above you. The only time it may lock unexpectedly is near the top of the drop, if you jerk the line suddenly or if it hits the wall when you have to squeeze through a tight spot. Since it locks so easily, it can provide a good resting position for a brake-bar or Figure–8 rappeller. (As we have pointed out, you can't lock the carabiner/brake bar rig like you can a rack or Longhorn.)

To release, take your weight off the line for an instant and pull down on the carabiner. There are several ways to do this. If you're near the wall and have any kind of foothold, you can push up with your feet. To assist in pulling down on the carabiner, especially if you have much rope weight below you, you may want to attach a 12-inch (300-millimeter) diameter loop of 6- or 7-millimeter cord to the carabiner to grab onto and add leverage. Releasing the shunt doesn't take much effort at all. It can even be done in free rappel by just bouncing gently on the line. If you have any trouble releasing it, try adding the pull cord or try taking a wrap around your foot with the trailing line and step up for an instant.

You'll like the spelean shunt for medium and deep drops. There is some question as to whether carrying one more piece of technical gear is justified for short 20- to 60-foot pitches, however.

Mechanical Ascenders

For prusiking, two types of mechanical ascenders have

largely replaced the Prusik knot. These are the Jumar ascender (and the Jumar 79 and CMI 5000 just introduced) and the Gibbs ascender (fig. 13–9). Basically, they are devices that can be easily moved up the rope, but when the upward motion is stopped, they grip the rope securely and will not slip. This is the same action as the Prusik knot. Both have their pros and cons, which will be outlined here in some detail. Systems for their use will be found in chapter 15.

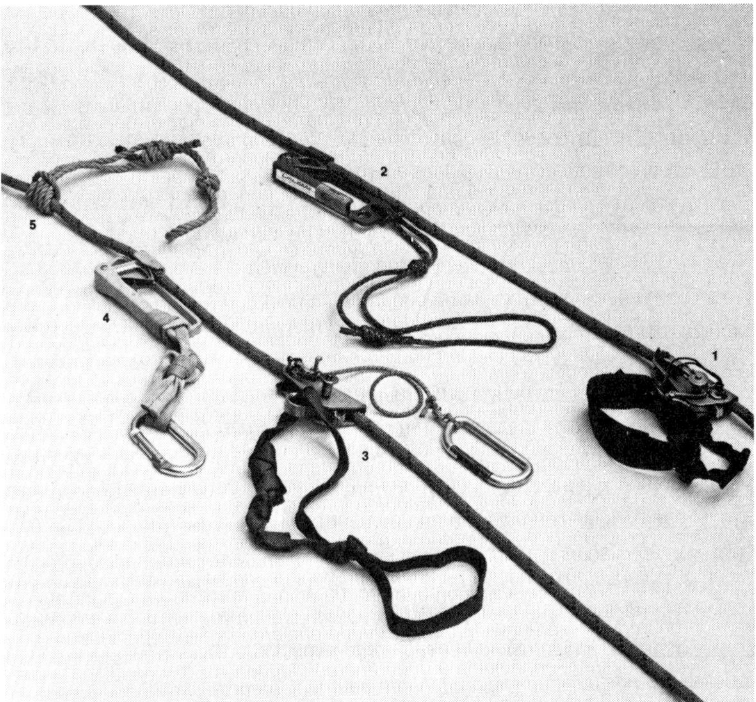

Fig. 13–10. Ascenders: *1)* Gibbs ascender, attached to 2-inch webbing for right foot with sewn-on retaining strap (chicken loop), *2)* CMI-5000 ascender with 7-millimeter Perlon cord, *3)* Gibbs ascender with sling for left foot and elastic shock cord with carabiner for "floating" the ascender, *4)* Jumar ascender with carabiner sling properly tied around back (strongest) part of assembly then down through bottom strut (carabiner is then attached to sling, not directly to Jumar), and *5)* Prusik knot in ⅜-inch Tenstron line.

Jumar Ascenders

Jumars were the first mechanical ascenders. They remain very popular with climbers and cavers. They consist of cast-aluminum frames and steel, spring-loaded cams. Their big advantage over Gibbs is they are much easier to put on and take off the line. With only a little practice, you can do it one-handed. This is a real plus when you need to come up over a lip, pass a knot, or cross an overhang. Because they're so easy to put on, many Gibbs-system cavers (like us) carry one in a handy pocket or clipped to our seat slings for just such exigencies. To help keep the ascender on the line, a plastic safety catch is provided. Always be sure this is in the locked position before applying your weight. Be especially careful when grasping the Jumar to slide it up that you don't accidentally unlock the safety catch. Jumars will work equally well on ropes from 7 to 11 millimeters.

Jumars are sold singly in right- and left-hand versions and in pairs, at a cost of about sixty dollars a pair. Jumar has just introduced a new, stronger version, with improved cam and three-position safety catch, that tests at 1100 pounds (500 kilograms). Both the standard and Jumar 79 will be available for some time to come. The older Jumar frame was factory-tested to 660 pounds (300 kilograms) which is considerably lower than other climbing gear. With either Jumar, the test figures assume that the main force is in a more or less downward direction as in normal use. When tested at an angle, as on a traverse rope or ascending a slope, two problems arise: the Jumar is considerably weaker since it twists under loading (Ullin 1973), and it has a tendency to pop off the line. This latter condition is, however, quite easy to overcome by use of a carabiner attached between line and Jumar sling.

Attaching the sling to the standard Jumar must always be done as shown by threading it up through the hole in the handle and around the back (fig. 13–10). Never clip a carabiner to the bottom brace. Loading the bottom brace directly with sling or carabiner is very dangerous because the brace is much weaker than the main frame. It is also the area most likely to be damaged from a drop or sudden shock loading. For the same reasons, the hole in the top is not strong enough to support your full weight. In some floating ascender rigs (see chapter 15), a shock cord is attached to the top hole. It is more than adequate for this purpose.

If properly cared for, Jumars will provide good service for years. Cams should last for several seasons and are replaceable if they begin to slip. The top Jumar cam will probably wear out first. In an emergency it can be exchanged with the lower.

Be especially careful not to drop a Jumar. The frame is quite brittle and can develop hairline cracks quite easily if dropped. If used on muddy ropes, the cam teeth will fill up and may slip. They can be successfully cleaned with a toothbrush, a regular preventive maintenance procedure highly recommended.

The Jumar 79 is at least twice as strong as the standard Jumar. It can be safely rigged through the single hole in the bottom brace or around the brace with a carabiner or sling. Similarly, the top hole is strong enough for a carabiner or sling.

CMI 5000

A new ascender from Colorado Mountain Industries (CMI) has just appeared on the market. It seems to have overcome several of the more serious problems of the Jumar. In essence, it is far stronger (5000 pound test) and has three strong tie-off points, two on the bottom and one on top. Priced at sixty dollars per pair, they compete directly with the Jumars.

When they first came out we bought a pair to try them. So far they seem superior to the Jumars, and we are eager to see if the interior parts will offer the same degree of reliability that the rugged frame appears to provide.

Gibbs Ascenders

Gibbs ascenders were first introduced in the late 1960s, and were quickly accepted by cavers in North America as an alternative to the Jumar because they are cheaper and offer several real advantages. Nevertheless, the Jumar continues to be at least as popular (certainly on a worldwide basis) because many feel it has greater versatility. Before getting into a detailed comparison, though, let's look at the Gibbs and its advantages.

Probably the stellar attraction of the Gibbs is that it doesn't have to be raised up the rope. It literally follows you as you climb. For this reason, Gibbs ascenders are undoubtedly the fastest way to climb up a rope. Gibbs systems consistently win the climbing contests at NSS conventions, often setting new speed records.

The Gibbs technique is aptly named rope walking. Your feet and chest are attached directly to the cams. As you raise your feet and chest, the cam comes up with them. Since your body weight, rather than a spring, operates the cams, the Gibbs will almost never slip, even on wet, muddy, or icy rope. Furthermore, wear on the rope and cam is less, because the cams don't drag on the rope as they are moving upward. Most people find Gibbs less strenuous and easier to use (once they are on the line) than Jumars. This is somewhat misleading, though, because it does take longer to rig them.

The main problem area with the Gibbs is the three-piece design which makes it more difficult to put on the line. Two hands must be used. The Gibbs consists of a U-shaped shell bent from aluminum plate, a cast aluminum cam, and a stainless-steel lock pin. We have always preferred the slightly-more-expensive quick-release model rather than the spring-wire version. (It is understood that the latter will be discontinued soon.) All three pieces are attached together, so you aren't in any danger of dropping them. The original model, which we are still using, did not come with cam attached to the shell (we have since modified it). Several years back we dropped the shell down a 110 foot pit. It was not damaged, however, which points up another basic advantage of the Gibbs over the Jumar. They don't break, and they always seem to work. About the only operational difficulty we have experienced is with mud fouling the quick-release pin. This is easily cured by giving the Gibbs a nice warm bath (followed by a *light* oiling of the pin).

Gibbs ascenders sell for about fifteen dollars and will work with rope sizes from 5 millimeters to 14 millimeters. They are individually tested to 1000 pounds (454 kilograms) compared to 660 pounds (300 kilograms) for the standard Jumar. Cams are easily replaced in the Gibbs. Davison (1975) recommends replacement when you first notice polishing (a shiny spot) on the seventh tooth (or on the seventh tooth mold line ridge, if there is one). (See fig. 13–11.) He reports that by this stage, the higher teeth (numbers 1 through 6) will show marked grooves. On the question of wear, Gibbs recently brought out an alternate model with a spring-loaded cam. We have installed one of these on our right (lower) foot. It definitely reduces the need to kick out with the right foot and is therefore more convenient to use. It remains to be seen, however, just how

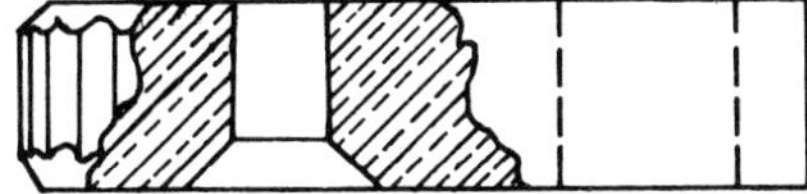

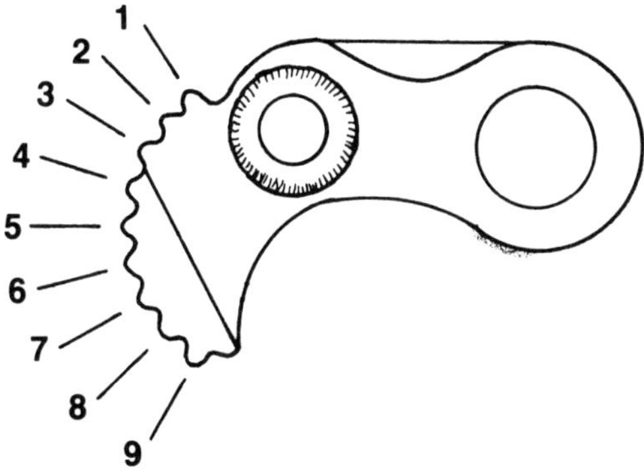

Fig. 13–11. Gibbs cam numbering. When wear on the seventh tooth is detected, cam should be replaced. Top shows the hole in the right-hand side drilled out with a countersink to facilitate inserting the quick-release pin (a modification suggested by Kirk McGregor at the 1976 NSS Convention, and others).

much this spring pressure might increase the wear, if any. Incidentally, we don't find any advantage in using spring-loaded Gibbs for our floating (attached with flexible cord) knee or shoulder Gibbs. Figure 13–11 shows how to bevel the hole so it's easier to install the quick-release pin.

The Jumar/Gibbs Debate. The main advantage of the Jumars is their ease of handling and versatility. They are much easier to put on and take off the line, and a Jumar system (ascenders and slings) is easier and faster to put on and take off yourself. Thus, Jumars are preferred where you have a series of ascents separated by tight passages or climbing that require taking off your ascending rig. However, Jumars can slip off the rope if not installed properly with the safety catch latched, particularly on nonvertical pitches.

Their versatility allows you to descend almost as easily as to ascend. That is, by removing the downward pressure from the sling, the Jumar catch can be released and moved downward as easily as upward. Now, this doesn't mean that cavers have taken to rappelling with Jumar ascenders. But you could go all the way back if you had to. Furthermore, there are situations at overhangs and outcroppings where it is sometimes better or more convenient to go back down a few feet and either readjust your rigging or choose another route. Getting up over the lip and passing rope knots is also easier, because the Jumar can easily be unclipped (assuming the other ascenders are still secure) and put back on the rope above the lip or knot.

Gibbs ascenders, on the other hand, are faster (at least for short drops) and work on muddy or icy rope. They are cheaper and stronger than standard Jumars. Gibbs test up to 2200 pounds (1000 kilograms) and are all individually tested to 1000 pounds (454 kilograms). They can also be used to descend, but not as easily as Jumars. The major disadvantage of Gibbs ascenders is that they are more awkward to put on the rope since they have to be partially disassembled. It is also quite hard to pass a knot with the foot and knee Gibbs since the rope must be pulled up. It is nearly impossible on really long drops or when more than one person is ascending the same line.

The consensus seems to be that the Gibbs are superior for deep pits and pitches where both hands are needed to push away from the wall. However, the Jumars are probably more versatile because they can be used in multipitch caves, with several different types of systems, and are more easily clipped on and off the line. Our personal preference for caves with only one or two drops is for a Gibbs system with spare Jumar and safety loops for overhangs and lips.

As for the old-fashioned Prusik knots, they are still in use today, particularly for shorter drops where the added complexity of rigging into the line with ascenders is too much trouble. Also when equipment weight and bulk looms large or where backpacking trips call for minimum equipment, prusik slings may be taken along in preference to the heavier Jumars or Gibbs.

Ascender Boxes. An ascender box is used with some mechanical ascending systems (chapter 15) to keep your body as close to the line and thus as nearly upright as possible. The box has two sections: the main rope goes through one, and with a Mitchell system, the ascender cord from the upper Jumar to the right foot goes through the other.

Two boxes are currently available commercially, the Bluewater (about ten dollars), and the Gossett (about twenty-five dollars). Despite its higher price, the Gossett is probably worth it because of these advantages: more rugged construction, separately latched rope compartments allowing the main rope or sling to be rigged or derigged independently, and a one piece assembly eliminating the possibility of dropping parts during rigging (the Bluewater box has four parts). About the only problem with the Gossett box is that after long ascents (several hundred feet) or under muddy conditions, the knurled tightening screws are sometimes hard to loosen. We have found that if during rigging you tighten them up then back them off about one-eighth turn, they are much easier to loosen after loading with your full climbing weight.

Rigging Knife. A useful accessory for vertical caving is the rigging knife. Available from yachting supply outlets and some hardware stores, these knives have a lockable marlin spike, one regular blade, and a lanyard ring. The marlin spike is very handy for untying knots after they've been loaded. The blade is good if you ever have to cut a sling or rope in an emergency. To keep it handy and prevent it from dropping, attach it to your seat harness or belt in an out-of-the-way place with a short (18-inch or ½-meter) piece of parachute or accessory cord.

Summary of Vertical Equipment Required

This is a run-down on the vertical gear we take along on cave trips. For caves where we know we'll be doing vertical work, we carry a separate pack for vertical gear in addition to our cave pack.

Horizontal Caves—No pits expected. Caver's sling (12 feet of 1-inch webbing or 4 meters of 25-millimeter webbing), and locking carabiner (we always carry this sling).

Intermediate Caves—Small drops (25 or 30 feet—8 to 10 meters) or a new cave with unknown but expected vertical extent.

    50-foot 9-millimeter hand line

    MSR Longhorn or other descender

    Caver's sling and locking carabiner

    Prusik slings (5/16-inch Tenstron)

    9/16-inch mini-étrier (fig. 9–8) (attach with Prusik knot or Jumar to line)

    Safety loop (20-inch diameter) 7-millimeter Perlon; two carabiners

    Rigging knife

Advanced Caves—Short and medium vertical pits (20 to 150 feet—6 to 50 meters).

    MSR Longhorn

    Spelean shunt

    Chest sling, home-made 2-inch with loop for Gibbs cam

    Seat sling, REI, attached to chest sling

    Three Gibbs ascenders, safety loop on line for fourth point

    Shock cord for knee Gibbs (left knee)

One-inch étrier with Jumar, plus 9/16-inch mini-étrier
Two extra safety loops, with four carabiners, rigging knife
Spare Gibbs (part of spelean shunt)

Really Big Ones—Deep vertical pits of 150 to over 1000 feet (50 to over 300 meters).

Rappel rack
Spelean shunt
Chest and seat slings as above
Gibbs as above except float both knee and foot Gibbs
Spare Gibbs (part of spelean shunt)
Jumar and 1-inch étrier, plus 9/16-inch mini-étrier
Three extra safety loops, four carabiners
Rigging knife

14

Rappelling

In caving you usually go down before you go up, unlike mountaineering where you begin by going up. Rappelling is the technique used for going down.

On this side of the Atlantic, the decade of the 60s saw a tremendous surge of interest in vertical caving coupled with the development of several new techniques and pieces of specialized vertical equipment. Without doubt, these developments have opened up many new areas of existing caves and led to the discovery of numerous new caves that could not have been explored with earlier techniques.

Today, vertical caving techniques are used by nearly all cavers to some extent, but there still remains a particular breed of vertical cavers who delight in pits ranging in depth from at least 150 feet to more than 1000 feet. Sometimes they are referred to affectionately by other cavers as vertical freaks. However, there is no doubt that the techniques and equipment they have developed have benefited the entire caving fraternity. In particular, the development of new rappelling and prusiking techniques by Alabama, Georgia, and Texas cavers, among others, have changed the character of caving in the U.S., Canada, and Mexico.

Mountaineers and rock climbers originally developed rappelling* as an easy and enjoyable means of getting back down a pitch instead of climbing. Climbing down is harder than climbing up; besides, rappelling is a lot of fun all by itself. Since rock climbing really means climbing *up*, or at least climbing up first, then coming down later, this is the correct order. In caving, however, you're more likely to be going down first, so the order is reversed. It calls for rappelling on the way into the cave and climbing on the way out. But regardless of when you do it, the technique of rappelling is essentially the same.

As is the case with all climbing techniques, you must learn the basics at a practice climb above ground with a group of experienced cavers. They can provide the fine points of technique as well as the advice and encouragement needed. Before attempting any 300-foot pits, a caver should have rappelled extensively in dozens of drops so that the technique is completely second nature.

The Body Rappel. Rappelling can be defined as a method of gliding down a rope safely. You can't do this with your bare hands (or even your hands and feet) for more than a few yards, as anyone who has tried it quickly finds out. So, climbers developed what is now called the hot seat or body rappel (fig. 14–1). This should be learned as a matter of principle by all cavers for use in emergencies (if mechanical devices fail), or for short pitches where it's too much trouble to get rigged up. The body rappel is often done with a doubled rope since it is assumed the drop is short, and the doubled line will be used as a hand line on the way out. A body rappel can be done with a single rope too, but it's even more uncomfortable. The reason for this, as can be seen by the illustration, is that the rope contacts the body directly in three rather sensitive places: the crotch, the right buttock, and the left shoulder. Because of the resulting friction, not too many cavers use the body

---

*Rappelling is called *abseiling* in Britain. Rappel means "retreat" in French. Abseil means "down rope" in German.

rappel, preferring instead mechanical devices attached to a sling or harness.

Rappelling Gear

We discussed seat harnesses in chapter 9 and will review a few points here. The simplest sling is a diaper, but if used it must be backed up with a redundant waist loop. A safer sling is the swami seat. But the most comfortable are the commer-

Fig. 14–1. Body or hot seat rappel. Rope is threaded as shown, between the legs, across the chest, over the left shoulder, and down across the back to the right hand. Every caver should know this technique for emergency use and for short drops (less than 20 feet—6 meters).

cial or homemade 2-inch harnesses. Whatever you wear, be sure that the carabiner you use to clip in the descender is a high-strength, locking type, such as one that meets UIAA tests (4850 pounds or 2200 kilograms).

To rappel into short or medium pits (20- to 60-feet—7- to 20-meters) our personal preference for a rappel device is the MSR Longhorn (fig. 14–2). The CMI, SMC, or Clog Figure–8 Rings are a close second. A rappel rack can also be used but seems a little high-powered for a short drop. We can't in good conscience recommend the popular carabiner/brake bar combination anymore—despite the fact that we have personally used it for hundreds of drops over the years. (The pressure put on the gate, the weakest part of the carabiner, creates an unacceptable hazard in our view.) With a spelean shunt to back it up and provide a resting mode, it would be acceptable, but the other lightweight descenders or the rack are preferable.

The Spelean Shunt. To provide a safety backup for rappel into pits over 60 feet (20 meters), we recommend the spelean shunt. This is a Gibbs ascender with a locking carabiner that serves as a handle to release it after it locks on the line. For a description of the device and its use, see chapter 13.

Rappelling Techniques

To begin the rappel, clip the descender into the locking carabiner attached to your harness. Stay well back from the edge of the drop. Face the anchor point with your back to the drop and the rope on your right side (or left side, if left-handed). Now, reach down, pick up the rope, and place a loop up through the descender. With the Longhorn, you then wrap it around the two horns. With the Figure–8 you must detach the carabiner and run the loop around the body of the descender and clip it back in. With a rack or carabiner/brake bar rig, you snap in the bars as shown in figure 13–7 and 14–3.

This is a good time to check your rig. Start with the locking carabiner. Make sure you remembered to screw it finger-tight. In a recent cave trip to a northern California lava tube with a 60-foot entrance drop, we were at the top directing rappel

Fig. 14–2. Rappelling with doubled 9-millimeter line on an MSR Longhorn/ Figure–8 Ring in the Longhorn configuration. In this instance, the right hand is used above the descender for balance. The left hand is held against the left hip (not behind the hip) for braking. The feet are spread apart for balance. The seat harness is from REI and is connected to the Longhorn with an SMC locking carabiner.

traffic. Eleven people went down. Of that number, we randomly asked three if they had locked their carabiners. None of these three had. We don't know what the probability of the other eight also having forgotten might be, but it points up the need for you to check your own gear and also to remind others to do the same. Next, you should check the descender to be sure it's threaded right, particularly with brake bars in carabiners or on a rack. Watch out for the Suicide Rig with the rope on the wrong side of the bars. A sharp tug upward will usually ferret out this rigging error and should accompany your visual inspection.

Having checked these, you can move over to the edge of the drop. Here you should check again before stepping over the edge. It's quite easy for the rappel line to become loose when you're moving over to the drop and you may lose tension on the bars. During the rappel, the pressure of the rope keeps everything in place. However it's also smart to check the rig several times on the way down, particularly if stops are made on ledges.

Be careful that the rappel rope doesn't touch or run against the seat sling because the friction could fuse and cut through the sling. Also check to be sure that hair, clothing, and electric wires are tucked away and won't get caught in the descender. This happens often with beginners and can be very dangerous.

After inserting the rappel rope into the descender, tuck it against your right hip (but not around in back), grasping it tightly in the right hand (left hip and hand, if you're left-handed). The hand on your hip is the braking hand and must never let go of the rope. If using a rack, you will find that the right hand can stay in front near the descender. Most of the control comes from the left hand which cradles the rack and moves the bars up and down (fig. 14–3). With other descenders, the left hand rides slightly above them on the rope—at chest or head height—and is used for balance, but not control. Downward movement can be stopped quickly by bringing pressure with the hand against the hip or, with a rack, by sliding the bars upward.

To rest or readjust equipment, you need a secure locked position. A Longhorn is locked off as shown in Figure 13–8, a

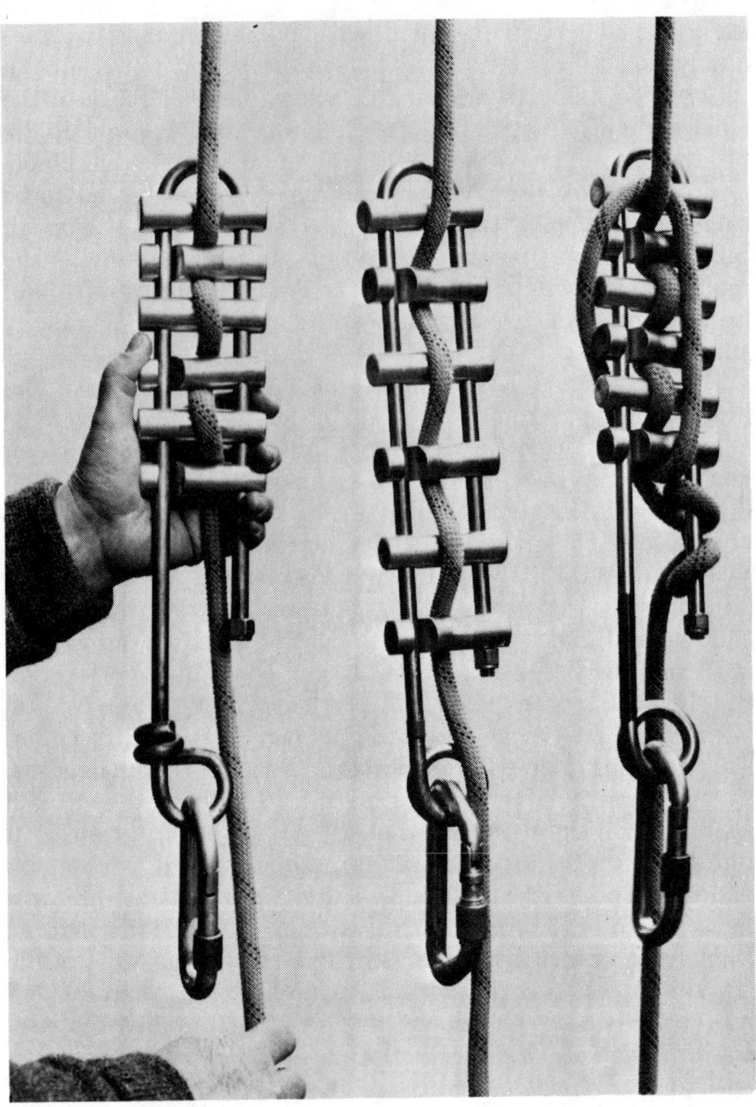

Fig. 14–3. Rappel rack control is provided by the left hand which cradles the rack and presses the bars up to slow your descent. Rack in middle shows bars opened up, as at beginning of descent and for normal movement during descent. Rack at right has been locked off by lifting up the rope and wrapping it between the top bar of the rack and the rope. From there it goes behind the rack and finally is tied off on the open side of the rack with one or two hitches.

rack as shown in Figure 14–3. Another locked position can be achieved by wrapping the rope around one of your legs. On really long drops of over 300 feet (100 meters), the weight of the rope when you're near the top makes any of these locking maneuvers quite difficult—possible, but difficult. A spelean shunt, on the other hand (fig. 13–8), can provide a secure resting position that is easier to engage and disengage no matter how long the drop.

Gloves must be worn on both hands to prevent rope burn. To get more friction, some prefer to run the rope over the shoulder and across the back to the opposite hip. Alternately, the rope can be run around the back to the opposite hip. However, depending on your weight and the length of rope, this may add too much friction and be less comfortable.

There is also a safety problem with the opposite-hip rigging. If you accidentally drop the rope it will tend to return to the other side and may be out of reach of your braking hand. A solution to this problem is the rappeller's bracelet. This is a snug piece of elastic shock cord worn around the wrist of your braking hand with a carabiner snapped into it. The rappel rope is run through this bracelet. Then, if your braking hand drops the line, the bracelet keeps it within easy reach. Thanks to David Brison and an early 1960s Philadelphia grotto newsletter for this idea; we have used it for years.

On drops into pits of unknown depth, put a knot in the end, in case the rope doesn't reach the bottom. The best knot is a figure-of-eight loop which will provide a convenient standing loop if you need to rerig into a prusik to climb back up.

Over the Lip and Bottom Belay. From the novice's standpoint, the really tricky part of rappelling is that first step over the edge of the lip. This is called edge fright and all cavers suffer from it at one time or another. Many cavers say, "I don't mind anything but the first few feet." Conversely, they don't mind ascending except for the *last* few feet. It's interesting that it is exactly the same few feet on each drop!

To help gain confidence, all beginners should be belayed on their first few rappels even though a belay with a separate rope is more trouble than it is worth when rappel technique has been learned properly. Rather than a separate belay, a very effective belay can be run from below by having someone hold the bottom of the rope. In case of an accident, they can stop the descent by simply pulling the rope taut. The natural straightening of the rope increases the tension in the descender and will bring a falling rappeller to a safe stop quite easily. However, the caver below must not stand directly below the rappeller because of the danger of falling rocks dislodged during the descent. This is one of the reasons we recommend gardening of the area at the top of the pit—removing rocks and other debris to out-of-the-way places. Do not, however, throw them down the pit even if no one is down there. It's best to gather them well away from the edge, where they will not roll.

Stepping out over the edge is done as follows: With the rope taut between anchor point and rappel sling, step backwards with your legs spread as far apart as possible for comfort and balance. Then—and this is the hard part—you lean back and literally walk down backwards with your feet firmly planted on the rock face. As long as you are touching the wall there aren't too many problems after you get over the initial edge fright. But often in caves the top of the drop is overhung. After a few feet, you suddenly find yourself some distance from the wall and must change to what is called a free rappel.

What do you do now? Here is where those practice sessions above ground that develop your skill and give you confidence in your equipment really pay off. To do what we're about to suggest is easy and safe if you believe in your gear and in your own ability.

As you start over the edge, lean back at a 45 degree or lower angle (fig. 14–4 and 14–5). Move down slowly to where the wall drops away from you. Then plant your feet firmly against the wall and lean back further and further until the seat of your pants is slightly below your feet. When you first do this, you'll feel like you're hanging out there naked in the cold night air. Just go slowly, and trust your equipment. The next move is to flex your knees and *gently* let go with your feet. You will swing in slightly but only for a foot or so if you have done it right. Do *not* push off hard and pendulum down in a

Fig. 14–4. To negotiate an overhang brace feet firmly and lower your body until your seat is below your feet. Then gently flex your knees and let go with your feet. This puts far less strain on the rope and anchor than a bouncing jump away from the rock.

Fig. 14–5. Going over an overhung lip into a 65-foot (20-meter) pit entrance to a northern California lava tube. Caver is leaning back with feet firmly braced to negotiate the overhang. Note rope pad which caver will lower the rope onto as she descends. Also note that immediate area has been "gardened" of loose rock to prevent knocking rocks into the pit.

big bouncy jump like they do in the movies. It puts huge loads on the rope and anchor and begs for accidents to happen.

At the beginning of a rappel, you may find that you will move so slowly that you have to push the rope through the descender with the right hand. This tendency should be avoided because it removes the right hand from its normal braking position at the right hip. However, if pushing the rope really is necessary, be sure not to drop the line. Return the hand to its braking position as soon as possible.

Keep in mind that an even, steady descent is essential so as not to put undue tension on the rope. As we said before, don't jump or bounce. And don't try to win any speed contests. Forty feet (12 meters) per minute is maximum. When you come to an overhang, the proper technique is as we described above: push off slowly and gently, keeping the legs apart for good balance. According to tests made in Hooper's Well in Alabama, a smooth rappel increases the strain on the rope about 19 to 35 percent. A bouncy rappel between 94 and 169 percent.

In mountain climbing, it's very common to double the rappel rope, pulling it down after the descent has been made. However, in caving the first direction is most often down rather than up. Thus, a single rappel line is used and tends to be left in place for use on the way out for either prusiking or as a belay line for a ladder climb.

During really long rappels (over 300 feet), you may find your legs going to sleep. To keep them awake, move your legs in a bicycling or swinging motion. Alternatively, you can use foot stirrups (such as the sling for a Texas system described in chapter 15) to support your feet and ankles and stand up once in a while.

Changing Over. Suppose you get to the bottom of the line and it's not the bottom of the drop? What do you do? If you've followed our advice so far you will come to a handy figure-of-eight loop in the end of the rope and step into it to take stock of the situation.

Dropping into pits of unknown depth is always risky business. The only way to approach them is to be completely prepared. This means using the spelean shunt or a Jumar to provide an easy resting position and carrying your full vertical pack with you down the drop. If you expect to encounter several such pits you should consider wearing your ascending gear on the way down so you can quickly change over to the other mode.

To make a changeover from rappel to prusik, the first step is to transfer your weight to your seat sling from your descender. If you are wearing a spelean shunt, this will already be attached to your seat sling, in the proper position above the descender. If not, take a safety loop from your bag of tricks and attach it to the line above the descender with a Prusik knot. If you're a Jumar fan, you will probably prefer to attach your right Jumar to the line above the descender. For the moment, it is probably best not to derig the descender.

Next, attach your ascenders to the line, beginning with the bottom one, and stand up. This will allow you to derig the descender and begin ascending. If you are using a Gibbs as the top ascender, the safety loop or spelean shunt will probably ride right above it.

Crossing a Knot. What happens when you have to cross a knot? First of all, we have to assume that the knot isn't going to come as a surprise. The reason a main rope has a knot in it is that it wasn't long enough, so two ropes had to be tied together. This is an unusual enough occurrence that you're sure to have heard about it and are going to be ready for it.

To cross a knot you need to change over to your prusik gear, prusik *down* past the knot, then change back over to rappel again. Obviously, then, you must wear your prusiking gear when rappelling down on a knotted rope. You may not have to attach and reattach all your descenders, but you'll have to at least partially changeover so you can get your weight transferred and retransferred properly and not get hung up in midair.

The procedure differs slightly with Jumar and Gibbs systems and people of different heights. Essentially, what you do is to stop about a body length above the knot. This leaves you room to put on your ascenders and detach your rappel device. Then you slowly *descend* on your ascenders, and one by one, pass them below the knot. Then, you sit in your seat sling and transfer back from prusik to rappel, using the procedure described in chapter 15.

Though it sounds complicated, it really isn't very difficult if you have a spare Jumar, a spelean shunt, or some safety loops. You just have to go through the steps in a certain order. Needless to say, above ground is where you iron out the wrinkles.

Avoid Sliding Sideways. When rappelling on a slope or against the wall, resist the urge to slide or walk sideways when you come to a ledge or similar spot. Sliding sideways can easily dislodge rocks and abrade the rope, negating the purpose of rope pads. If you must move sideways, do it with great caution.

Keeping Clear of the Drop. While you're rappelling, anyone already down should stay well clear of the drop. If you knock anything loose, yell *rock!* to give warning. Falling rocks are a real danger during rappelling and prusiking.

15

Ascending

After rappelling into a cave or pit, getting back up relies on two techniques: ladder climbing and prusiking.

So, there you are at the bottom of this 60-foot drop (20-meters if you're in one of those international pits). What in the world do you do now? Assuming you're not a practitioner of levitation, you can do what other cavers do. Climb a ladder or put on your ascenders and prusik out. Whatever you do, don't try to climb the rope hand over hand. You'll only get a few feet before you fall, and you surely risk injury.

Ladder Climbing

Cable ladders aren't used much anymore for climbing down (at least in North America), because rappelling is easier and more fun. But they are used for climbing up. Just about anyone can learn to climb a ladder on the second or third try. It will take more than that to master it, but the fundamentals are easy.

The first thing you must do is convince yourself that this fragile-looking item will really support your weight. We admit that at first glance it doesn't inspire a lot of confidence with its spindly cables and thin, narrow rungs. But it's compact, strong enough to do its job, and remarkably sturdy. You get 33 feet (10 meters) of pit-climbing capability in a package that's only about 12 by 9 by 6 inches (30 by 23 by 15 millimeters) in size when it's rolled up (plus a belay rope). And its a whole lot cheaper than having everyone buy ascenders if your caves only have one or two short drops.

The trick to cable ladder climbing is to place one foot behind the ladder on every other rung to keep the feet from pushing out from underneath (fig. 15–1). To get started, most cavers face the ladder and place one foot behind the ladder on the bottom rung (let's suppose it's the left). Then, they bring the left hand around behind the ladder at a comfortable height on a rung above the head, and shift the weight up onto the first rung. Next, the right foot is placed on the second rung, this time on the front of the ladder. The right hand goes above the left hand, either on the front or back—whichever is more comfortable—and so on to the top.

Climbing a ladder is strenuous (as any house painter knows), so climb with the legs, not the arms. Walking up stairs is a lot easier than doing pull-ups. Use the arms mainly for balance.

This technique of alternating the feet on the front and back works well when it's hanging free. However, it isn't usually desirable when the ladder is pressed tightly against an over-hang or wall. At this point, the problem is to force the ladder away from the wall, so the hands and feet can get at the rungs (fig. 15–2). One way to do this is to turn the ladder slightly on its side. This takes a bit of strength, but is easy to maintain once done. You can also put both feet on the front side and push the ladder away from the wall with the toes of your boots. It helps to bend the knees and waist more than usual in this mode. With a little practice plus confidence that the ladder isn't going to break if you manhandle it a little bit, you can manage both free and against-the-wall ladder climbs.

Fig. 15–1. Climbing a free hanging ladder. One foot goes on front, the other on rear. Hands can also alternate, or both go on back. Always belay every ladder climb, no matter how short. Ladders test at only 650 pounds. Climber shown here is tied to belay line with a bowline-on-a-coil around her waist.

Fig. 15–2. Climbing when ladder is up against a wall or overhang. *Left:* climber has rotated the ladder 90 degrees. *Right:* the toes of the boots are used to keep the ladder out from the wall.

Belaying Ladder Climbs. Although these methods are easily learned, climbing a ladder—as with most other vertical techniques—is still inherently dangerous, particularly when wet, muddy gloves and fatigue come into the picture. For these reasons, plus the fact that ladders occasionally break, we must caution you to never climb a ladder without a belay no matter how short the pitch (figs. 15–1 and 15–3). It's also possible to fall off if you're tired or it's slippery.

To set up the belay, the first person up a ladder will often climb using a self-belay from a waist or chest sling, tying into the rappel line with either a Prusik knot, or a Gibbs ascender. In this usage, a Gibbs ascender is preferred since it will follow you right up with no effort on your part. On the contrary, the Prusik knot must be loosened and moved up and this requires hanging on to the ladder with only one hand, a tenuous

Fig. 15–3. Climbing a ladder in a New Mexico cave. Note position of boots on front and rear of ladder. Belay rope (1-inch or 25-millimeter tubular webbing) is run through a sling and carabiner rigged at the top of the drop, so it is still a top belay even though the belayer is on the bottom. Belayer is tied into a slab at left rear.

proposition at best. The same is true for a Jumar 79 or CMI-5000, although they're easier to move. Don't use a standard Jumar for this purpose. It is not strong enough to stand the shock-loading of a fall.

If you're the last person up a ladder, it is a good idea to attach the bottom of the ladder to your seat harness or other tie-off point with a short length of rope. This way the ladder will follow you up as you climb, making it easier to unsnag from rocks or overhangs.

Rigging the Ladder. When rigging a ladder be sure to select an anchor point that allows two or three rungs to remain above the lip (fig. 15–4). This makes it far simpler to get off when you reach the top. Surprisingly enough, if the ladder is not rigged in this way, it takes a great deal of strength or an unsafe lunge to make that last three or four feet up over the ledge. The same is true for rigging a belay or prusik line. Rig it well back from the lip of the drop.

When lowering a ladder, let it pay out slowly so it doesn't get snarled on an overhang. It's also wise—if you can do it safely—to watch as it goes down so it doesn't route itself between any overhangs or through any niches that your body can't fit through. It's the job of the first person rappelling down to check for good routing for the ladder, so it will be all set when you are ready to climb back up later. Always ask if the drop is clear, and yell *rope!* before lowering a ladder or rope.

Prusiking

The original technique of prusiking was developed in Austria by Karl Prusik and written up in the *Austrian Alpine Journal* in 1931. It was primarily seen as a means of self-rescue for a climber who had fallen into a crevice. The knot he devised for this purpose still bears his name, as does the general technique of ascending ropes with knots or mechanical ascenders.

The Prusik Knot. Today the Prusik knot is still the knot most commonly used by those who use knots—instead of

Fig. 15-4. When rigging a ladder, leave two or three rungs above edge of drop, making it easier to climb off and derig safely. The same is true of belay and prusik lines. Note rope pad to protect ladder at lip.

mechanical ascenders—even though several other knots have come and gone. While we don't pretend to be expert knot prusikers, we can climb 60 or 70 feet on knots easily, and more if necessary. But if we know ahead of time that the cave has a drop that deep, we—and most other cavers today—will bring along vertical packs and climb with mechanical ascenders. Nevertheless, we firmly believe that all cavers who will have anything at all to do with vertical caves should learn knot prusiking. It's not hard and the equipment needed costs only a few dollars.

The system we are going to describe is certainly not original with us. It's probably one of the oldest. It's a system that you can learn, then use as we do, primarily as an emergency back-up system. We carry it with us in our cave packs in caves without much vertical extent or in new caves where we don't expect to run into pits, but want to be prepared anyway.

Ours is the basic three knot system. Since it doesn't include a seat harness, there is no good resting position. Anyone interested in using knots as a primary system for longer drops will need to attach the upper knot to a seat harness either through a chest sling or not as preferred. See Thrun (1971) for a discussion of the pros and cons of seat/chest rigs.

For a chest loop, we shorten our caver's sling to about 8 feet (2⅔ meters) and tie it in a Figure–8 configuration with a carabiner in front (fig. 9–12). The three Prusik loops are made from ⅜-inch (9-millimeter) Tenstron tied into a loop with a grapevine knot. The loop that attaches to the chest sling is about 22 inches long (55 centimeters). The right or middle foot loop (you can reverse these if you want) is about 64 inches long (160 centimeters). The left foot or lower loop is about 57 inches (143 centimeters). (These lengths are for the finished slings which have been shortened by the length of rope needed to join the ends with a grapevine knot and to form the foot loop by a figure-of-eight knot.) To tie your own slings, remember that the lengths are somewhat critical and must be right for you. Be prepared to fiddle around with them until they're comfortable. Start with about 12 or 13 feet (3⅔ to 4 meters) for each foot, plus about 8 feet (2½ meters) for the chest, for a total of about 34 feet (10⅖ meters). Use ⁵/₁₆- or

Fig. 15–5. Basic three-knot prusik system. See text for description of steps. This system is good for learning how to prusik, for emergency use, or for unexpected pits when you are not carrying regular vertical gear. For serious knot prusiking, a seat sling for resting and comfort are essential to relieve pressure on the chest or upper prusik loop. Note chicken loops of 6-millimeter Perlon cord around ankles.

⅜-inch (6- to 9-millimeter) Tenstron, Perlon cord, or Goldline. We like the Tenstron because it has a hard, scratchy surface and grabs well on kernmantle or laid ropes. If you use a separate chest sling as we do, reduce the size of the upper loop by your chest circumference, some 2½ to 4 feet (¾ to 1¼ meters).

To secure the slings to your feet, a snug figure-of-eight loop is tied in the bottom of the foot slings. A chicken loop of 1-inch tubular webbing is run around the ankle over the slings to prevent them from slipping off and to support your weight if you turn upside down. Instead of ⅜-inch cord at the end of the Prusik slings, some people find foot loops of 1- or 2-inch (25- to 50-millimeters) webbing more comfortable. We use our regular vibram-soled boots and haven't had any problems with thin cord cutting into our feet. If you do use foot webbing, shorten the foot loops about 2 to 3 feet (⅔ to 1 meter), depending on the knots used.

To climb with this system the weight is supported by the foot slings. The chest sling and arms are for balance. Since you are tied into the rope at three points, a separate belay line is not necessary. To begin, you stand astride the rope, raise the chest knot as high as possible, followed by one of the foot knots—the right with this system, but always the one attached to the middle knot and the longer foot sling (fig. 15–5, left, top). Then the weight is shifted onto the right foot (fig. 15–5, left, bottom). Next, the left foot and sling are raised and tucked under the body (fig. 15–5, right). Finally you stand up on both feet, sliding the chest sling as high as possible at the same time to start a new cycle. Raising the slings often requires both hands: one hand to loosen and slide the knot up, the other to hold the rope below the knot tightly, so the first hand can move the knot easier.

This system is fine for free ascents of up to about 25 feet (8 meters). Beyond that the pressure on the chest sling begins to take its toll. Up against a wall, however, you can go 50 or 60 feet (15 to 20 meters) easily without chest problems because you can lean against the wall to relieve pressure (fig. 15–6).

For those who plan to use knots as their primary system, a seat harness is essential. Seat harnesses take some of the

Fig. 15–6. Three knot prusik system used to climb up against a wall. Pressure on the chest is much less, because you can lean on the wall. Note webbing chicken loops around ankles.

pressure off of the chest and provide a rest position for very long ascents. Both seat and chest harnesses are desirable because although the seat harness is excellent for resting, it places the balance a little low and a routing of the slings through a chest harness carabiner is still desirable.

Chicken Loops. Chicken or security loops are mandatory for any vertical system as we have mentioned previously. We have used two different materials, but lately prefer 1-inch (25-millimeter) tubular nylon sewn in loops 6 to 7 inches long (150 to 175 millimeters). We also use 6-millimeter Perlon tied in a loop with a grapevine knot. They should be big enough to fit over the ankle of your boot snugly. Besides holding the ascending loops in place, chicken loops have an important safety function. They keep you attached to the loop and the line if you should turn upside down. Whenever we put boots on, we also slip on the chicken loops, whether it's to be a vertical trip or not, just to keep track of them.

Mechanical Ascender Systems

In the past 15 years, a score of prusiking systems have been devised by enterprising cavers to find the perfect ascending method. Rather than survey them all, we are going to limit ourselves to three that are widely used and have stood the test of time. These are the Texas, the Mitchell, and the Floating-Cam Gibbs or Rope Walker systems.

You will want to study these and try them out for yourself before deciding which is for you. Almost everybody ends up modifying a basic system in some way or another. So please consider what is presented here not as the final word, but as a guide for your own selection.

Texas System. For short pitches of not more than 20 to 60 feet (6 to 18 meters), many people prefer the Texas system (fig. 15–7). Some even use it successfully for much longer drops, but most find it too strenuous beyond 60 feet or so. It requires minimum equipment and is easy to learn. Sling lengths are not as critical as with some other systems, so the Texas is often chosen for group use or training. (Every serious vertical

Fig. 15–7. The Texas system is easy to learn but tiring for drops over 50 or 60 feet (15 or 20 meters). Ascenders are CMI-5000. Note safety features: 7-millimeter Perlon chicken loops on ankles, foot harness attached to seat sling with safety loop, swami-seat harness (instead of diaper sling), locking carabiners used to attach seat sling and to attach foot harness to CMI ascender (don't attach a carabiner directly to a standard Jumar—see figure 13–9). *Left:* shows standing position as caver is raising upper CMI ascender attached to seat sling. *Right:* shows sitting position as she is raising lower (foot) ascender. Note that tension on the rope below the ascender helps to raise it more easily.

caver needs his or her own gear. Sharing equipment may be all right when you're learning, but not after that.)

Basically, the Texas system has only two movements: sit and stand. Although you might think this would be tiring, it has an automatic rest position 50 percent of the time, so you just stay sitting when you want to rest. It does, however, require that you raise yourself completely up from this sitting position each time, so it's more strenuous and less efficient than the Mitchell or Gibbs systems.

Equipment is a seat harness with locking carabiner (see chapter 11), two Jumars (or CMI-5000 or Jumar 79), and a bottom webbing sling for one or both feet. You can also use Prusik knots or Gibbs ascenders, but most people use Jumars (Jumar-type ascenders). The top Jumar is attached to the seat sling carabiner with a loop about 12 inches (30 centimeters) long. A knotted safety loop (chapter 9) would be fine. To add another degree of safety, the short loop of the knotted safety loop or a separate loop should be connected from the seat carabiner to the bottom Jumar. In the system we use, this lower Jumar is attached to the dual foot loop with a carabiner. We prefer a dual foot loop made from our caver's 1-inch (25-millimeter) tubular webbing sling. This is easily tied in the 12-foot caver's sling by doubling it and tying the doubled portion at the top into a doubled figure-of-eight loop for the locking carabiner to attach to the lower Jumar. Then form the sling into an equilateral triangle and tie the bottom two corners with figure-of-eight loops big enough to fit over your boots snugly (see fig. 15–7, right).

Overall, the Texas system is liked because it's simple to rig and easy to learn. It serves well on technical pitches because the hands and feet are relatively free for pushing away from the wall and climbing. Finally, it works well for descending if you run into a problem and have to go back down.

To add a large measure of safety to the Texas system (especially for deeper pits—50 to 150 feet or 15 to 50 meters), a third ascender can be included. Smith (1976) recommends a Gibbs for the third one, positioned above the top ascender (fig. 15–8). It will simply ride there and scarcely be noticed. The best way to attach it to you is via a chest sling which in turn is doubled down to the seat sling.

Mitchell System. Another widely used technique is the Mitchell system. In its basic form, this is a two Jumar system with a chest box (fig. 15–9). The climbing rope and long sling from the right foot to the upper ascender go through separate left and right channels in the box. The motions are very similar to climbing a ladder or Gibbs rope walking. You simply raise the right leg and shove the upper ascender up with the right hand. Then you stand on your right and raise the left pulling up the lower ascender in the same smooth motion. Since you are almost vertical and very close to the line, efficiency is good. Although strenuous for the arms, its simplicity recommends it. It has been used in all kinds of

Fig. 15–8. Texas system with third attachment to the line, a Gibbs ascender, for much improved safety. Note that Gibbs is attached both to the chest harness and to the seat harness (see figure 15–7 for full view of seat harness).

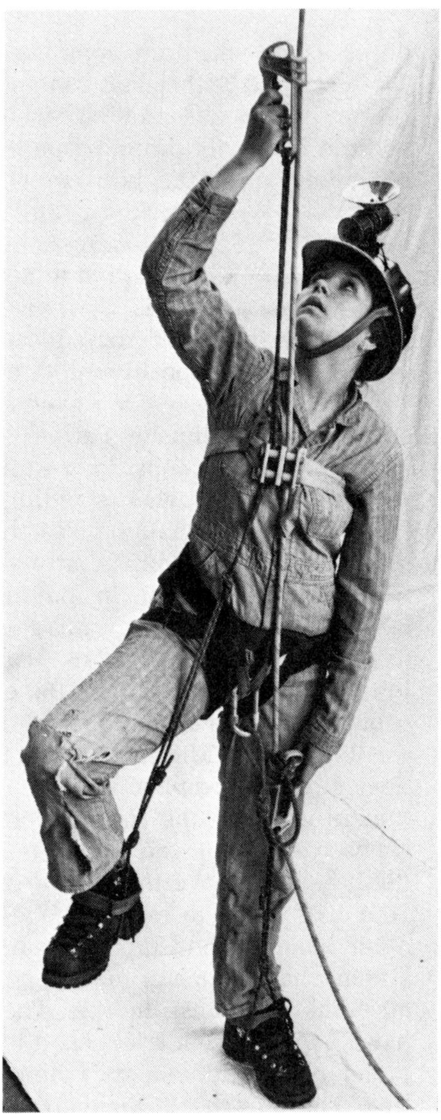

Fig. 15–9. Basic Mitchell system with two Jumar 79 ascenders and a Gossett chest box (which keeps you upright and close to the line, thereby increasing efficiency). Seat harness and short sling from harness to lower ascender adds safety factor. Additional safety can be added by attaching third ascender (Gibbs or Jumar) to seat harness, placing it on the line between the two Jumars at about chest height.

drops—short, medium, long, free, and technical. It and the Gibbs seem to be the main contenders for deep pit honors.

Our rig uses a Gossett box which is easy to open and close without danger of dropping parts. The ropes can be removed separately since the box is in two sections, each latched separately. We often add a third ascender, a Gibbs (again on the advice of Smith) floating between the two Jumars at about chest height and connected to a seat harness. This could also be a Jumar, as in the Cuddington Phase Three mentioned below. The third ascender adds an extra margin of safety and provides a resting position for longer drops.

The Mitchell system is rigged as shown in figure 15–9. The slings are 6-millimeter Perlon cord. The one to the upper ascender should be just long enough to keep the Jumar above the chest harness when standing on both feet (Thrun 1971). The lower sling should place the Jumar as low as you can reach comfortably, to maximize stepping distance. Our slings, for your information in buying your own, are doubled 6-millimeter cord tied with a grapevine knot. The longer upper loop is 62 inches (157 centimeters) long. The shorter, lower one is 27 inches long (69 centimeters). This means you should start with about 20 feet (6 meters) total.

Although the Mitchell system is generally very versatile, it does present a problem when you're up against the wall. The Jumars jam into the rock and are difficult to move. With a Gibbs system, you can simply push away because your hands don't have to move the ascenders. In this situation, probably your best bet is to revert to one-handed operation using the other hand to fend off the wall. Also, at lips, the Mitchell system shares some of the difficulties Gibbs have, in that you are tight up against the line. The solution in both cases is to have a spare ascender attached to a seat harness. This should preferably be a Jumar type, since it is easy to install on the line. You clip the Jumar onto the line above the lip or over-hang. Then the line can be taken out of the box (and the upper ascender cord, too, if you are secure). This done, you can push away from the lip with your hands and muscle on over. It's not quite as easy as it sounds until you've practiced it a few times, but the technique is fundamental to vertical caving.

The extra ascender attached to the seat sling is called the Jumar safety in the Cuddington Phase Three system. Phase Two is essentially the Texas system; Phase One the basic Mitchell system with chest box; and Phase Three, a configuration that you can easily change over to for climbing slopes (fig. 15–10). In this final mode, the sling to the upper ascender and the climbing rope are taken out of the box. Then the Jumar safety is attached to the upper ascender sling cord. This allows you control and safety on slopes.

Fig. 15–10. Cuddington Third Phase for ascending steep slopes. "Safety" Jumar in middle is attached to seat sling and upper (or right-foot) ascender cord. This extra Jumar can also be used very effectively when crossing a lip or overhang.

Floating Gibbs System. For speed in long free drops and good overall performance, we prefer a three Gibbs system with floating knee Gibbs (fig. 15–11). The right foot loop uses a continuous band of 2-inch webbing into which a Gibbs cam has been sewn (fig. 15–12 and 15–13). A buckled chicken loop extends around the boot. The knee Gibbs is attached to the foot with a sling of 1-inch webbing secured by a webbing chicken loop as shown. To tie this, you need about 7 feet (2¼ meters) of 1-inch (25-millimeter) webbing. First, run it through the cam in the knee Gibbs, then tie it in a loop with a secured water knot. Finally, tie a figure-of-eight loop at the bottom big enough for a snug fit on your boot. When tied, the loop will be about 18 inches (½ meter) long. To "float" the Gibbs, a piece of elastic shock cord is attached to the middle Gibbs and the chest harness. This puts continuous upward pressure on the Gibbs cam, so it locks automatically when the left leg is stopped after being raised. Simply tie the cord to the keeper chain of the quick-release pin. In thousands of feet of climbing we've never had a problem. A better place to tie it is in through the hole in the cam *below* the webbing sling. Another method is to attach it to a small, thin, metal plate that is drilled to fit under the head of the quick-release pin.

Despite our success with the 2-inch stirrup for the foot Gibbs, on drops over 300 feet (100 meters) some people have experienced a problem with the foot twisting and a resulting pressure on the ankle. For long drops, an alternate rigging is to float both lower Gibbs. Use a sling as for the left foot, but long enough to position the right Gibbs about hip height or some 12 inches (30 centimeters) above the left Gibbs. Attach shock cord as above to provide the floating action. Use chicken loops on both boots to back up the ascender slings.

Bandage-Wrap Woes. Before we changed to the 2-inch stirrup for the right foot, we used the bandage-wrap of 1-inch tubular webbing that many cavers still use. An incident on an otherwise routine 90-foot ascent convinced my wife that we needed something better. Janet had wound the bandage-wrap around shoe and ankle and back again several times, but apparently hadn't cinched it down really tight. It kept working looser and looser until it finally unravelled and came right

Fig. 15 – 11. Gibbs Rope Walker system with "floating" knee cam. To ascend, caver simply raises left foot and "floating" ascender at knee lifts at the same time. In Figure 15 – 11, lower left, the right foot is raised bringing with it the ascender attached to that foot. Chest ascender follows the body. To rest, as in Figure 15 – 11, right, a Prusik knot safety loop is attached on the line above the top Gibbs and to the seat harness. This loop is also useful for changing over to rappelling, crossing knots, and negotiating overhangs. To increase efficiency on long drops, a Gossett box can replace the top Gibbs to keep you more upright and closer to the line.

Fig. 15–12. Foot loops for Gibbs system. Left foot is attached to floating knee Gibbs via 1-inch (25-millimeter) webbing. Note chicken loop. Right foot has a 2-inch (50-millimeter) loop with Gibbs cam sewn to it.

off, slowly but inexorably sliding down the line to a ledge. Using her two other Gibbs, she descended smartly to a fortunately handy ledge and rerigged her right foot. This time she tied an intermediate knot in the sling just after making the first wrap around the foot and ankle. Thus rerigged, she continued on up without incident, but considerably wiser. We highly recommend this practice of tying an intermediate square knot if you use the bandage wrap rigging as many do.

To tie the bandage wrap, you need about 10 feet (3 meters) of 1-inch (25-millimeter) webbing. Form a bight at the middle and put this through the hole in the Gibbs cam. Pull the bight through the cam hole to form a loop big enough to get the right foot into. Then position the ascender with the cam pointing to the instep and the narrow part of the shell pointing up. Tighten the sling and pivot one strand at the cam *down* around the bottom of the boot, up the opposite side, and across the top. The other strand crosses the first here and you

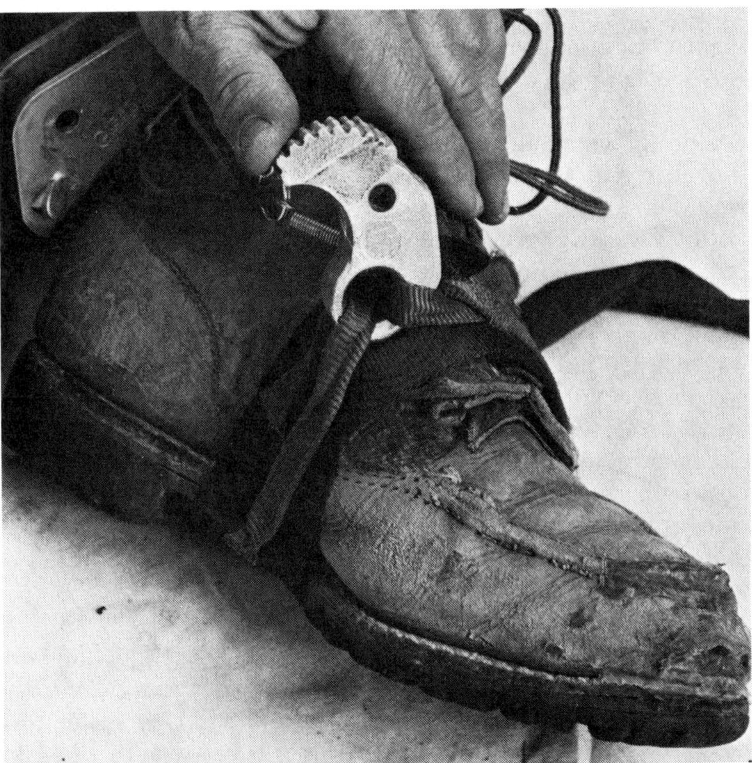

Fig. 15–13. Nine-sixteenths-inch (13-millimeter) webbing in configuration shown is used to sew the Gibbs cam onto the 2-inch (50-millimeter) wide right foot loop. To hold the cam securely and keep it in position, lower webbing on left is U shaped and goes through cam. Upper webbing at right is crossed and also goes through cam. Strap with buckle (not shown) extends around ankle to serve as security (chicken) loop.

tie a square knot at this point. Make sure everything is as tight as you can get it because it's going to carry your full weight. Next, tightly bind the rest of the webbing around your ankle several times and finish off with a square knot.

Incidentally, you can use either foot for the two lower Gibbs. There's nothing magic about our lower Gibbs on the right foot and the floating Gibbs on the left. Suit yourself.

Shoulder or Chest Gibbs. The upper Gibbs is attached to a loop sewn into the chest harness at the shoulder (fig. 15–11). This keeps the body more upright than when it is mounted in the center of the harness, which is the other common location. Advocates of the center mounting point out that it is easier to get up over lips with the center placement. Try both and decide for yourself. If you get this far into ascending, you'll probably end up making your own custom chest sling anyway. For long drops, some prefer to replace the upper Gibbs with a Gossett box. This keeps the body closer to the line and improves efficiency. The safety loop rides above the box, just as it does with the upper Gibbs.

For our system we add a fourth independent tie to the main line via a Prusik safety loop attached to our seat sling. This provides a superior resting position to the more common upper ascender rest. With this separate safety loop, a changeover to rappelling is very easy (see below). Since it is positioned above the top Gibbs, the safety loop Prusik knot rides freely with no binding on the rope. You can forget it's there till you need it. As a final safety feature, chest and seat harnesses are connected with a sling in front and a webbing strap and buckle in the rear.

Now that you've got yourself lashed to the line, how do you get off the ground? It's simple. Just walk up the rope. At the very bottom it will be helpful, as with almost any system, to have someone hold the end of the rope. If you're the last person, you can get a self-start by making a big loop in the rope with your left hand and running it under your left foot. Then, as you ascend, keep the loop tight under your left foot for the first 10 or 15 feet (3 to 5 meters). While ascending, your hands are placed on the rope above your top ascender for balance. If they get tired, you can lower them both or one at a time and still not lose your balance or fall over. To rest, sit down and the Prusik knot safety loop will tighten. You will probably also want to loosen your chest Gibbs to relieve any tension at this point. To begin again, just raise your legs alternately as before. The safety loop will just get picked up by the top Gibbs and carried along without being loosened. If you're using the regular (not the spring-loaded) Gibbs, you may need to kick out. To do this, simply pretend you are riding a bicycle.

To get over a lip, a procedure like that described with the Mitchell system is used. Probably the first thing to do is to remove the chest Gibbs from the line so you can get back away from the wall a bit. Remember, you still have the safety loop and two foot Gibbses in action so you are quite secure. Then, depending on how thick the lip is, you may now be able to walk up the line one or two steps and lean your body over the top. The constraining thing may be the safety loop if the lip is too thick. If so, turn over on your side to free the loop and slide it up further.

This same method will usually work if you have the spare Jumar safety clipped to your seat sling. Attach it to the line over the lip and muscle on over. Once over the lip, be sure to get well back into a secure spot before derigging.

For overhangs that are especially bad, a separate short piece of line or a tail from the main line may prove a godsend. What you do is attach your Jumar safety above the lip on this line and use it to pull yourself over.

Special Techniques

Changing Over. To change from prusik to rappel, the key element is a safe and comfortable resting position so you can thrash around with no danger of falling. We get ours from the safety loop attached above the top Gibbs with a Prusik knot; you can get the same security from a Jumar safety. As with a rappel/prusik changeover, the first thing you do is to shift your weight from ascenders to the seat harness via the safety loop or Jumar safety.

Then attach your rappel device to your seat sling (if it's not already there). To get some slack so you can rig the descender if you're in a Gibbs rig, remove the chest Gibbs from the line and loosen the foot and knee Gibbs but don't remove them from the line yet. If you're in a Mitchell rig, loosen the lower Jumar. Pull up slack and rig in the descender as high as possible below the safety loop or Jumar safety. Then step up on the lower ascender, loosen the safety loop or Jumar safety, and shift your weight onto the descender. Don't remove the safety loop or Jumar safety yet, just leave it on the line for a minute more until you're sure all is well. Transferring your weight to the descender will be easy if you have gotten the descender as high as possible when you rigged it a moment before. If not, sit back down and rig it over again, being sure to get out all upper slack below the safety loop or Jumar. With your weight transferred to the rappel device, you can take the foot and knee Gibbs off the line. Be sure to loosen the Prusik knot or remove the Jumar (or replace it with a spelean shunt if it's a long way back down). Be especially careful not to lock the Prusik or Jumar when you've moving around or you may get trapped in midair.

Crossing Knots. Crossing a knot in the rope while ascending is relatively easy with Jumar systems, but can be a struggle with Gibbs if there is considerable weight of rope below you. With Jumars, you move them one at a time past the knot and continue on. A separate Jumar safety may prove valuable.

With Gibbs, getting the safety loop or Jumar safety over the knot is the first step and isn't too hard. Then you can walk up a bit, remove and reset above the knot your chest Gibbs and probably also your knee Gibbs. The bottom one will be harder because it's down low and the rope below is heavy. It can be done, but it may be a fight. Practice this above ground until you're proficient so you don't get hung up underground. If you are climbing in tandem, as on a really long drop with two on one line at a time, you probably won't be able to loosen the lower Gibbs. In this case the other person on the line below you can prusik up to you, remove your Gibbs, and reattach it for you above the knot.

The sawing action as you gently bounce up a prusik line will damage the rope if it isn't padded correctly. When you come to padded places, be sure to replace the pads carefully so the next person won't damage the rope unknowingly.

When you're waiting down below, take care to stay out of the drop. Many needless injuries have occurred because people have ignored this basic safety rule. Also, when you get up to the top be careful not to dislodge any rocks as you go over the lip. If you do, yell *rock!* Hopefully, you will have gardened the top before rappelling, so this shouldn't be a problem, but be careful anyway.

Emergency Systems. In a pinch, how many ascenders do you need to get up the line? If you have only two ascenders of any type, you can try the Texas-high-kick method (Montgomery 1977). This is very strenuous, but will get you out. One ascender or Prusik knot goes to your seat sling, the other to one foot. If you have enough sling to rig both feet, it's less strenuous.

Start from the sitting position. Slide the upper or seat ascender up as high as you can. Then stand up in the foot loop while simultaneously sliding the seat ascender up. Sit down and begin again. If one of the two ascenders you have is a Gibbs, put it on the seat sling.

If you have only one ascender, what can you do? Montgomery has these thoughts. Put the ascender on the seat sling. Use the rope itself as a foot loop by wrapping it around your foot. Then stand up, raise your seat sling (or let it ride up if it's a Gibbs), and make another foot loop. If you have no ascenders, try taking the end of the rope, attach it back up on itself with a Prusik or helical knot and clip that into your seat sling. Make the end a foot loop as above.

You have no protection with any of these, but in a real emergency they're safer than trying to climb hand-over-hand.

Prusiking Speed. How long will it take you to come up out of a pit with mechanical ascenders? First, let us say again, you shouldn't be trying to win any awards for speed. Going too fast wears the rope unnecessarily because of the sawing action at edges. Typical times for a 61-foot (18-meter) free-fall pit that we clocked recently averaged between 1½ and 3 minutes including negotiating the 4-foot thick lip at the top. This means about 20 to 40 feet per minute (6 to 12 meters per minute) for short drops would be typical. Other data (*Netherworld News* 1971) indicates a speed of about 25 feet per minute (7½ meters per minute) for 200 feet and 20 feet per minute (6 meters per minute) for 400 feet. This means 200 feet took 8 minutes, 400 feet took 20 minutes. These were for average cavers in good condition.

A good method for longer drops is to take a certain number of steps, then rest. Twenty-five to forty steps seems to work well. Take small steps and go at a regular, not a sprint, pace. You'll last longer.

Dangling Your Pack. As we have said, it's always best if everyone carries his or her own pack. An easy way to do this during roped ascents or descents is to let it hang below you, attached to your seat harness with one of your safety loops. Be sure it isn't too heavy, though, or it might pull your harness down.

To help get you and your pack over a tough lip or through a narrow slot here is a technique we find handy. When rigging the drop, hang a tail from the climbing line (or a separate short rope or sling) down the drop so it extends below the lip or the tight spot. Put a figure-of-eight loop in the end of this tail. Then, when you get up to the tail, clip your pack into the loop with a carabiner. After you haul yourself over the lip, simply pull your pack up. You can also use this loop (and one or two more loops, if desired) as a foothold or as a hand line, or you can attach a safety loop or Jumar to the line, if you need an extra assist.

Practicing Prusiking. To practice ascending, you can set up a practice rig with a rescue pulley mounted 15 to 30 feet (5 to 10 meters) above the ground. Select a climbing rope of suitable length, anywhere from 150 to 1200 feet (50 to 400 meters). From the pulley, run the end of the rope down to the climber. On the other side of the pulley, run the rope through a rack or a double carabiner/brake bar rig so that a second person can give tension and assure a steady flow of rope.

Attach the rack to a fixed point (like a tree or a strong wall fixture in a gym) with a sling and carabiner. Be sure the rope is coiled very loosely or set in long, lazy bights on the floor so it won't accidentally get tangled. A third person (or the second person after some practice) is needed to give tension below the climber for the ascenders to grip the rope, and to take up the slack as the climber ascends.

Appendix I

Caving Skills Self-Test

Basic Skills

Knots. Tie the basic caving knots blindfolded or in complete darkness, including back-up overhand knots where required: 1) bowline, 2) bowline-on-a-coil, 3) water knot, 4) grapevine knot, 5) figure-of-eight loop, and 6) Prusik knot.

Carbide Lamp. If using a carbide lamp, extinguish it in total darkness and immediately find and light your secondary source of illumination. Then, determine the cause of the following troubles and correct them. (Another caver may purposely introduce some of these troubles in the lamp or another lamp.) This test assumes you are carrying extra water, carbide, and a spare parts kit at all times in the cave, plus the usual two other sources of light.

• Lamp won't light. No water or carbide, clogged tip, wet felt, bad gasket, loose bottom. Refill the lamp with water and carbide, and put the used carbide in a suitable container for removal from the cave.

• Lamp burns irregularly. Same causes as above. Dismantle lamp and actually replace felt and tip.

- Flame around gasket. Bad gasket or thread seat, loose bottom.
- Flame around tip. Bad or loose tip, bad tip seat.
- Water spurts from tip, bubbles out of water filler cap, or flame is several inches long. Too much water; decrease flow and wait before lighting. Felt may also have been soaked and need replacement.

Electric Lamp. Turn the lamp out. Find and light secondary source of illumination. Then determine the cause and repair the following troubles. It is assumed that you have spare bulbs and batteries at all times as well as two other sources of light.

- No light. Bad bulb, dead batteries, loose connection. Take lamp apart and tighten or replace bulb and batteries.
- Irregular light. Symptoms as above.
- Dim light. Check batteries for corroded or loose connections.
- Cable catches on obstructions. Reroute cable from battery to lamp. Also demonstrate ability to remove lamp from helmet or disconnect cable quickly when it snags in a tight spot.

Crawling. Crawl through a low passage, 18 inches (½ meter) or less in height, 2 feet (⅔ meter) or less in width, and 10 feet (3 meters) or more in length.

Scrambling. In a breakdown area scramble up and down over some good-sized blocks (10 × 10 × 20 feet or 3 × 3 × 7 meters), using walls and ceiling, if available.

Slopes and Slots. Slide downward on a slope (using walls and ceiling if possible), a semi-vertical passage (less than 45 degrees), or a fissure, for at least 10 feet (3 meters) in total depth. (This assumes the landing below has previously been explored and is known to be a safe stopping place.)

Slopes and Slots (up). Similarly, climb, crawl, or chimney back up this or a comparable passage.

Tilted Slots (down). Slide down a tilted slot or fissure of similar dimensions as above, so that you slide not straight down but at an angle.

Tilted Slots (up). Similarly, climb or clamber back through this or a similar slanting passage.

Intermediate and Advanced Skills

Tight Crawling. Crawl through a tight passage 14 inches (350 millimeters) or less in height with at least one S curve that requires turning over or crawling on your side, with one shoulder ahead of you, and pushing hard hat and gear ahead of you.

Verbal Climbing Signals. Demonstrate the proper verbal signals and use them in each test.

Rigging. Find and rig a satisfactory anchor for a belay line.

Static Belaying. Belay a 200-pound (90-kilogram) caver on both an ascent and a descent in a cave, using the sitting hip position. Successfully hold an unannounced fall by both an ascending and a descending climber.

Chimneying Down. Chimney down a vertical or semi-vertical pit (more than 45 degrees), that is wider than 2 feet (⅔ meter) on the average, and at least 15 feet (5 meters) deep. Use a belay if the chimney bells out, is slippery, or is otherwise dangerous.

Chimneying Up. Chimney up the same or a comparable pit.

Traversing. Make a horizontal traverse, while on belay, using three-point rock climbing skills and, if the walls are close together, chimneying.

Free Climbing. Using three-point climbing technique, climb up and down while on belay, a 20- to 30-foot (7- to 10-meter) vertical pit or wall that is too wide for chimneying and too steep for scrambling, using handholds and footholds.

Climbing Calls and Responses. Demonstrate a knowledge of the proper calls.

Conservation Awareness Skills

To check your conservation skills and awareness, there are two additional tests to conduct above ground in full caving gear.

• Make up an obstacle course of chairs and other furniture covered with loose objects that are easily dislodged. Crawl through this course without knocking anything off.

• Walk across a floor densely strewn with easily disturbed objects such as plastic packing material chips or ping pong balls, without touching any of them.

Technical Vertical Skills

Ladder Climbing. Find and rig a satisfactory anchor for a cable ladder.

• Climb *down* and *up* at least a 30-foot cable ladder with a proper static belay from a separate belayer.

• Climb *up* and *down* a 30-foot ladder using a self-belay on a fixed line with a Prusik knot or Gibbs ascender.

Rappelling. Find and rig a satisfactory rappel anchor in a cave.

• Rappel into a tight fissure or pit where you are against the wall most of the way. The drop must be at least 40 to 50 feet.

• Rappel into a medium-width fissure or pit where you have contact and free rappelling. The drop should be at least 40 to 50 feet.

• Rappel into a wide fissure or room where you are mostly free from the wall. Drop must be at least 40 to 50 feet.

• Rappel down into one of these pits, perform a changeover, then ascend back to the top.

• Rappel down a long drop in a cave or outdoors of at least 150 feet and preferably 200 feet or more. Demonstrate your ability to handle the weight of the free hanging rope—from 10 to 30 pounds or more—by adding and removing bars from your rack, locking off and unlocking the rack, and securing and freeing your spelean shunt or other dynamic safety device. (A Prusik knot is not recommended for this purpose because of the difficulty of freeing it under load.)

• Rappel down a line with two knots and successfully pass them both. Then continue on down.

• Rappel down a line to a knot or obstruction. Then transfer to an adjacent line and continue down.

Prusiking. Find and rig a satisfactory anchor in a cave for a prusik line.

• Prusik up the three separate types of drops required for the rappel test (in the same or a different cave).

• Prusik up in one of these drops and perform a changeover to rappel. Then rappel back down.

• Prusik up a line that has two knots and successfully pass them. Continue on up.

• Prusik up to a knot or obstruction, then transfer to an adjacent line and continue up.

• Prusik up a pit at least 150 feet deep of any type, using a three-ascender system and a seat-sling resting position.

Appendix II

Sources of Further Information

Publications, Publishers, and Bookstores

Alpine Karst, 410 East Aspen St., Bozeman, MT 59715.

Association for Mexican Cave Studies, P.O. Box 7672 UT Station, Austin, TX 78712. Their activities newsletter contains accounts of what many call the most interesting caving anywhere.

British Caving, Anne Oldham, Pub., Rhychydwr, Crymmych, Dyfed, SA41 3RB, Great Britain.

The Canadian Caver, P.O. Box 275, McMaster University, Hamilton, Ontario L8P 1JP, Canada.

Cave Research Foundation, 1909 McGavock Pike, Nashville, TN 37216. Publisher of an excellent training manual and maps of Mammoth/Flint Ridge and Carlsbad Caves.

Caves and Caving, British Cave Research Association, 30 Main Road, Westonzoyland, Bridgewater, Somerset, England. A new British caving magazine.

Caving International, P.O. Box 4328, Edmonton, Alberta T6E 4T3, Canada. A new publication documenting caving activities all over the world. Beautiful color photos.

Descent, Bruce Bedford, Ed., 30 Drake Road, Wells, Somerset, England. An independent magazine for British cavers.

Journal of Spelean History, Jack H. Speece, 711 East Atlantic Ave, Altoona, PA 16602.

Mountain Safety Research, 631 South 96 St., Seattle, WA 98108. Publishes a newsletter with test results, news items, and equipment for sale. MSR helmets and ice axes are its best known products.

NSS Bookstore, Cave Avenue, Huntsville, AL 35810. Supplier of caving books, many at a discount, to NSS members.

NSS Bulletin, Cave Avenue, Huntsville, AL 35810. Quarterly scientific and technical journal.

NSS NEWS, Cave Avenue, Huntsville, AL 35810. Monthly news and feature magazine.

Nylon Highway, 319 Kilbourne Ave., Appalachia, VA 24216. Newsletter of the Vertical Section of the NSS.

Off Belay, 15630 SE 124th St., Renton, WA 98055.

Speleobooks, P.O. Box 333, Wilbraham, MA 01095. Large selection of new and used caving books and periodicals.

Summit, P.O. Box 1889, Big Bear Lake, CA 92315.

Equipment Manufacturers and Suppliers

Eastern Mountain Sports, Vose Farm Road, Peterborough, NH 03458. Retail stores in many northeastern cities, plus St. Paul and Denver.

Pathfinder Sports, 5214 E. Pima St., Tucson, AZ 85711. Caving and climbing equipment.

Recreational Equipment Inc., P.O. Box C88125, Seattle, WA 98188. Retail stores on the west coast and Bloomington, MI.

The Speleoshoppe, P.O. Box 8044, Louisville, KY 40208. Very complete stock of caving gear. Fast service, competitive or discounted prices.

Organizations

National Speleological Society, Cave Avenue, Huntsville, AL 35810. The NSS is a nonprofit educational and conservation organization affiliated with the American Association for the Advancement of Science. It has about 5,000 members and over 100 chapters (grottos). Write for membership information and the name of the chapter nearest to you. Please include a self-addressed envelope. NSS publishes a monthly magazine and a quarterly bulletin. It also has an extensive library and operates a bookstore with many publications discounted to members.

British Cave Research Association. Membership: J.R. Woodridge, Assistant Secretary, 9 Chelsea Court, Abdon Ave., Birmingham 29, England. Publications: 30 Main Road, Westonzoyland, Bridgewater, Somerset, England. Issues a monthly bulletin and a quarterly transactions.

Recommended Reading and References

Recommended Reading

Cave Exploration and Famous Cavers

Bedford, B.L. 1975. *Challenge Underground*. Teaneck, NJ: Zephyrus Press. Bedford's adventures and his survey of British caving techniques make for good reading. Recommended.

Boon, J.M. 1977. *Down to a Sunless Sea*. Edmonton: The Stalactite Press, Dept. of Geography, University of Alberta. Personalized accounts of cave diving in Britain, Ireland, Yugoslavia, and Jamaica.

Brucker, R.W., and Watson, R.A. 1976. *The Longest Cave*. New York: Alfred A. Knopf. Must reading for anyone interested in caves. Connecting Mammoth Cave to the caves of the nearby Flint Ridge System took over twenty years and every minute of it is worth reading about.

Casteret, N. 1938. *Ten Years Under the Earth*. London: The Greystone Press. Casteret, a pioneer cave explorer, recounts many of his underground adventures in this fascinating series of books.

————. 1947. *My Caves*. London: J.M. Dent and Sons.

————. 1951. *Cave Men, New and Old.* London: J.M. Dent and Sons.

————. 1954. *The Darkness Under the Earth.* New York: Holt.

————. 1956. *Descent of Pierre Saint Martin.* New York: Philosophical Library.

————. 1962. *More Years Under the Earth.* London: Neville Spearman.

Chevalier, P. 1951/1976. *Subterranean Climbers.* Teaneck, NJ: Zephyrus Press. Twelve years in the world's deepest caves in southeastern France. Reprinted in 1976 with a new introduction by the author.

Conn, H. and J. 1977. *The Jewel Cave Adventure.* Teaneck, NJ: Zephyrus Press. The exciting story of twenty years of discovery in this 50-mile-long cave located in the Black Hills of South Dakota. As much a story of dedication to a monumental task as it is the always interesting unfolding of an intricate maze.

de Joly, R. 1975. *Memoirs of a Speleologist.* Teaneck, NJ: Zephyrus Press. Pioneer French cave explorer, along with Casteret, and inventor of the cable ladder, narrates his lifetime career as a cave explorer.

Folsom, F. 1962. *Exploring American Caves.* New York: Collier. Interesting stories of famous caves, including some information on the formation of caves, cave animals, and techniques. Recommended.

Gurnee, R. and J. 1974. *Discovery at the Rio Camuy.* New York: Crown. Exploration and discovery of a major cave system in Puerto Rico. Fascinating reading.

Gurnee, R.H. 1978. *Discovery of Luray Caverns, Virginia.* Closter, NJ: R.H. Gurnee. One of America's premier show caves, Luray Caverns has a story to equal its beauty. Excellently retold by Russ Gurnee, a lifelong caver and former president of the NSS.

Halliday, W.R., M.D. 1959. *Adventure is Underground.* New York: Harper & Row. Halliday has been described as the "spokesman for speleology" because he was one of the first active cavers to publish his and other cavers' underground adventures. His books are recommended reading for every caver, even though his lofty style and egocentric tone tend to be aggravating to some readers. This, his earlier book, covers western caves and cavers.

————. 1966, 1976. *Depths of the Earth.* New York: Harper & Row. An updated and expanded version of Halliday's survey of United States caves and caving.

Hovey, H.C. 1896, 1970. *Celebrated American Caverns*. New York and London: Johnson Reprint Service. Originally published in 1896 and long out of print, this fascinating survey of 19th century caves is now available in a beautiful new edition.

Judson, D. 1973. *Ghar Parau*. New York: Macmillan. Fascinating story of 1972–73 British expedition to "the big one" in Iran, some 3000 feet deep, in twenty-six small- to medium-sized pitches.

Lawrence, Joe, Jr.; and Brucker, R.W. 1955 and 1975. *The Caves Beyond*. Teaneck, NJ: Zephyrus Press. A very welcome second edition includes a new introduction and the entire text of the original edition. One of the best cave "adventure" books, the one many of us cut our teeth on in the 1950s.

Mercer, H.C. 1896 and 1975. *The Hill Caves of Yucatan*. Teaneck, NJ. Zephyrus Press. Searching for evidence of human antiquity in Central American caverns.

Miller, S. 1942 and 1978. "Why Floyd Collins Couldn't Be Rescued." Louisville Courier-Journal, reprinted in *Journal of Spelean History* 4, no. 4, April/June 1978.

Mohr, C., and Sloane, H.N., eds. 1955. *Celebrated American Caves*. New Brunswick, NJ: Rutgers University Press. Stories of famous caves and cavers.

Sloane, B., Ed. 1977. *Cavers, Caves and Caving*. New Brunswick, NJ: Rutgers University Press. Excellent anthology covering the exploration, history, science, and adventure of caves. Recommended.

Tazieff, H. 1953. *Caves of Adventure*. New York: Viking. Firsthand account of a 2000-foot descent in the Pyrenees.

Waltham, A.C. 1975. *Caves*. New York: Putnam. Beautiful color and black and white pictures with excellent supporting text. Tony is a geologist and active caver. In many instances, he writes from his own experiences. Recommended.

———. 1976. *The World of Caves*. New York: Putnam. Waltham's second book is in an oversize format with many color pictures. Worldwide in scope.

Cave Sciences

Bauer, E. 1971. *The Mysterious World of Caves*. New York: Watts. One of the International Library of Science books for young people. Beautiful color illustrations and authoritative text by a German university professor. Translated from German.

Bögli, A., and Franke, H.W. 1968. *Luminous Darkness*. Berne: Kummerly and Frey. The science of speleology written in lay terms by two eminent Swiss speleologists and beautifully illustrated with their photos—many in color and full page in size—of Höllock in Switzerland and other European caves.

Cullingford, C.H.D., Ed. 1962. *British Caving—An Introduction to Speleology*. 2nd rev. ed. London: Routledge and Kegan Paul. Written by members of the British Cave Research Association. Basic science text oriented to British caves and cavers. Some material on equipment and techniques.

Griffin, D.R. 1958. *Listening in the Dark*. New Haven, CT: Yale University Press. Acoustics and sonar used by bats to avoid bumping into walls and each other.

Mohr, C.E., and Poulson, T. 1966. *The Life of the Cave*. New York: McGraw Hill. Cave life and ecology. A fascinating introduction to the subject. Beautifully illustrated with color pictures.

Moore, G.W., ed. 1960. "Origin of Limestone Caves." (Huntsville, AL: *Bulletin of the National Speleological Society*, 22, no. 1, pp. 1–84). A symposium with discussion.

Moore, G.W., and Sullivan, G.N. 1978. *Speleology, The Study of Caves*. Teaneck, NJ: Zephyrus Press. Revised, second edition of this very readable general text on cave sciences. Highly recommended.

Techniques and Equipment—General

Anderson, J. 1974. *Cave Exploring*. New York: Association Press. Concise treatment, nicely illustrated by the author, but now somewhat dated. For example, her recommendations of brake bar rappels and diaper slings without a back-up waist loop are not in step with current safety practices. In addition, the bowline appears to be tied with the end on the outside of the loop making it only half as strong. Also, two essential knots—the water knot and the grapevine—are omitted. Belaying and knot prussiking are well-documented, but mechanical ascenders and systems, now overwhelmingly preferred to knots, are only mentioned in passing.

Blackshaw, A. 1965, 1977. *Mountaineering: From Hill Walking to*

Alpine Climbing. Harmondsworth, England and New York: Penguin Books. More or less a British equivalent to *Mountaineering: Freedom of the Hills.* Very complete and well-illustrated.

Cullingford, C., ed. 1969. *Manual of Caving Techniques.* London: British Cave Research Group, Routledge and Kegan Paul. Anthology of British techniques. Very complete and authoritative. Vertical techniques are a little out of step with current practices, which rely more on single ropes and less on the ladders that are covered in such detail in this book.

Ferber, P. ed. 1977. *Mountaineering: The Freedom of the Hills.* Seattle: The Mountaineers. Third edition of this comprehensive text covering all aspects of mountain travel including excellent treatment of climbing, belaying, and rappelling. One caution: Tying a sling to the bottom strut of a Jumar as shown in figure 121 (p. 211) is dangerous. It should be run up around the stronger vertical brace as shown in our figure 13–10.

Halliday, W.R., M.D. 1974. *American Caves and Caving.* New York: Harper and Row. This is Bill Halliday's technique book written in the same lofty "spokesman for speleology" style found in his other books. Reasonably comprehensive treatment, with especially good sections on cave medicine and first aid, and a good introduction to cave search and rescue. Vertical sections are generally all right but are now somewhat outdated. Halliday's curious insistence that tennis shoes and manila ropes are suitable and even safe for cave use is certainly outside the mainstream of caving and has frequently been criticized. His very weak conservation and safety messages have also brought him justifiable heat from reviewers and cavers.

Kahrau, W. 1972. *Australian Caves and Caving.* Melbourne: Periwinkle Books. Beautifully illustrated, this is a good short introduction to the caves and cave techniques of the land down under.

Kemsley, W. et al. 1977. *Backpacking Equipment Buyers Guide.* New York: Collier Books. Detailed and very informative equipment reviews from *Backpacker* magazine.

Montgomery, N.R. 1977. *Single Rope Techniques.* Sydney, Australia: Sydney Speleological Society Occasional Paper No. 7. Easily the best book to date on vertical caving. Covers ropes, knots, rigging, descending, and ascending. Our only serious disagreement is his statement that gloves may not be desirable on short rappels. We recommend gloves for all rappels.

References

Safety — chapter 3

American Caving Accidents 1967–1975. Huntsville, Alabama: National Speleological Society. Description and analysis of accidents reported to the NSS.

Bangs, C., M.D. 1979. "Immersion Hypothermia." *Off Belay,* February 1979, p. 26. Details the added dangers of accidentally falling into cold water (below 50 degree F—10 degree C).

Breisch, R.L. 1976. *Physical Hazards in Caves.* Proc. of 1975 National Cave Management Symposium, p. 108, Huntsville, AL: National Speleological Society.

Constantine, D.G., D.V.M. 1967. "Rabies Transmission by Air in Bat Caves." *HEW Public Health Service Pub. No. 1617,* June 1967.

———. 1977. "Bat Rabies Control Policy." *California Department of Health,* March 9, 1977.

Francis, D.F. 1978. "Shock." *Off Belay,* April 1978. Excellent summary article on shock and its treatment as a preventative against hypothermia.

Lathrop, T.G., M.D. 1972. *Hypothermia, Killer of the Unprepared.* Portland: Mazamas.

Martin, E. 1976. "Hypothermia, a Killer For All Seasons." *Wilderness Camping,* November 1976.

Reddell, J.R. 1974. "Biological Hazards of Mexican Cave Exploration." Austin, TX: *Association for Mexican Cave Studies,* 4, no. 4. Describes preexposure rabies vaccine, among other things.

Stein, J.M. 1976. Hypothermia. Proc. of 1975 National Cave Management Symposium, p. 114, Huntsville, AL: National Speleological Society.

Wilkerson, J.A., M.D. 1975. *Medicine for Mountaineering.* Seattle: The Mountaineers.

Personal Equipment and Techniques — chapters 6, 7, 10, 11

Eastern Mountain Sports Catalog. 1979–80. (EMS, Peterborough, New Hampshire). Issued two or three times yearly. Retail stores in many Northeastern cities, St. Paul, and Denver. Catalog has useful equipment specifications and shows the range of selection.

Recreational Equipment Inc. Catalog. 1979–80. REI, Seattle, WA. Retail stores in Seattle, Portland, Berkeley, Los Angeles, and Bloomington, MN. Catalog includes equipment specifications and other useful data.

Baz-Dresch, J. 1978. "Flexane and Cave Boots." *NSS News,* June 1978, p. 130.

Davison, D. 1978. "Preventing Wheat Lamp Acid Spillage." *NSS News,* June 1978, p. 132.

Karmizki, K. and Toth, W. 1978. "Wet Suits—Under (Ground) Wear." *Alpine Karst,* Summer 1978, p. 58.

McCullock, T.E. 1978. "Vapor Barrier Reconsidered." *Off Belay,* December 1978, p. 26. Discussion of the value of wool as a protection against wet conditions.

Padgett, A. 1977. "Head Protection for Cavers." *Nylon Highway #6,* March 1977.

Strudwick, R. "Selecting a Battery" and "Maintenance of Nickel Cadmium Batteries." Papers delivered at 1972 NSS Convention White Salmon, Washington. Reprinted in *Huntsville Grotto Newsletter,* Vol. 14, November 1972.

Ropes, Slings, and Knots chapters 8, 9

Borwick, G.R., 1974. "Mountaineering Ropes." *Off Belay,* June 1974.

Clapp, R.D. and Weber H., 1975. "Sunlight and Climbing Ropes." *Off Belay,* August 1975.

Cullingford, C., ed. 1969. *Manual of Caving Techniques.* London: Cave Research Group: Routledge and Kegan Paul. Safety factor of ropes 12:1 for personnel, 5:1 for gear and general use.

Environmental Degradation of Ropes: Product Bulletin R-5. Auburn, New York: The Cordage Group, Columbia Rope Co. (manufacturers of Goldline). A product report on nylon unaffected by "organic" solvents, but softened by phenolic compounds, soluble in concentrated formic acid, and destroyed by strong mineral acids.

Irving, J., 1968. *Knots and Splices.* London: Routledge and Kegan Paul.

Isenhart, K. 1974. "Care and Feeding of Nylon Ropes." *Nylon Highway,* February 1974.

"Life of Climbing Ropes." *MSR Newsletter,* Reprints 1–6, p. RR-17. Chemicals that damage ropes are acids such as battery, sulfuric, hydrochloric, or nitric, lye (caustic soda), and household bleaches.

Magnussen, C. 1972. "How Strong is a Stitched Splice in Nylon Webbing?" *Off Belay*, October 1972; and NSS *News* May 1975.

Robbins, R. 1979. "Climbing Rope Myths." *Summit*, February/March, 1979.

Wheelock, W. 1967. *Ropes, Knots, and Slings for Climbers*. Glendale, CA: La Siesta Press.

Vertical Equipment and Anchors — chapters 12 and 13

Davison, D. 1975. "Beyond the Seventh Tooth." Nylon Highway, May 1975. Detecting wear on Gibbs ascenders.

———. 1976. "Rappel Racks." NSS *News*, November 1976.

———. 1976. "Safety Rappel Cam." NSS *News*, August 1976, p. 140.

———. 1977. "Cracked Jumar Frame." NSS *News*, April 1977. Crack resulting from tying to thin bottom frame instead of thicker upright frame. See our figure 13–10.

———. 1977. "Super Rack." NSS *News*, May 1977.

———. 1979. "Test Results: Mailon Rapide Link." NSS *News*, April 1979.

Hansen, D.S. 1977. "Load Equalizing Anchors." *Off Belay*, December 1977, p. 36.

Isenhart, K. 1974. "The Super Rack." *Nylon Highway*, February 1974.

———. 1976. "Bolts." *Nylon Highway*, January 1976.

———. 1977. "The Super Rack Proven Safe." NSS *News*, May 1977.

Toomer, W.B. and Welch, B.R. 1978. "The Spelean Shunt Technique." *Nylon Highway*, May 1978.

Wallock, O. 1978. "A Dropped Carabiner—How Safe?" *Off Belay*, October 1978, p. 21.

Wilts, C. 1956. "Expansion Anchors in Climbing." From *Belaying the Leader*, San Francisco: Sierra Club.

Vertical Techniques — chapters 14 and 15

Aleith, R.C. 1975. *Bergsteigen: Basic Rock Climbing*. New York: Scribner. Well written and illustrated text covering all aspects of rock climbing. Somewhat more comprehensive than Robbins.

Baumgartner, P., 1974. "UIAA Belaying Report" *Off Belay*, October 1974, p. 15.

Leonard, R.M. and Wexler, A., et al. 1946 and 1956. *Belaying the Leader*. San Francisco: The Sierra Club. Although the title article first appeared in 1946, it and the other material added later are still well worth reading. However, dynamic belaying by letting the rope run for a few feet through the hands of the belayer before braking (as Leonard and Wexler recommend) was really more suited to the older manila ropes. Modern nylon ropes provide an "automatic" dynamic belay by their built-in stretch characteristics.

Livesey, P. 1978. Rock Climbing. Seattle: The Mountaineers. Excellent beginners volume by a well known British climber and climbing instructor.

Mendenhall, R. and J. 1969. *Beginners Guide to Rock and Mountain Climbing*. Harrisburg, PA: Stackpole. Step-by-step instructions for the beginning rock climber, including snow and ice terrain in addition to rock and mountain techniques.

Owens, G., 1975. "Ascending Safety." *Off Belay*, August 1975. A vertical caver writes about prusiking for rock climbers.

Padgett, A. and K. 1974. "A Guide to Rappelling." *Nylon Highway*, December 1974.

"Prusik Safety Knot Accident and Analysis." *Tech Troglodyte* (Virginia Polytechnic Institute, Blacksburg, VA) Vol. 3, no. 1, Fall, 1964; Vol. 3, No. 2, Winter, 1964.

Robbins, R. 1971. *Basic Rockcraft*. Glendale, CA: La Siesta Press. Perhaps the best introduction to rock climbing by one of the Yosemite "big wall" climbers. A must for all serious cavers.

————. 1973. *Advanced Rockcraft*. Glendale, CA: La Siesta Press. Companion to the above, another must book. However, avoid tying to bottom brace of a Jumar as shown on page 45. See our figure 13–10 for safer method.

"The Ropewalker" *Netherworld News* 19(1): 30–32. (reprinted in the 1971 *Speleodigest*, p. 321.) Early description and climbing speeds of Gibbs ascending systems.

Smith, B. 1976. "Attach Three for Safety." *Nylon Highway*, January 1976. Discussion of high degree of safety afforded by a third point of attachment to prusiking line.

Smutek, R, 1976. "The Questionable Prusik 'Safety.'" *Off-Belay*, December 1976.

Thrun, R. 1971. *Prusiking*. Huntsville, AL: National Speleological Society. Detailed descriptions of knot and mechanical ascender systems, now a little dated, but still a must for vertical cavers.

Glossary

ANCHOR. A secure point (rock projection, breakdown block, tree, expansion bolt) to which a caving rope, ladder, or belayer can be safely attached. A secondary or back up anchor is suggested unless physically impossible.

ARAGONITE. A less common form of calcium carbonate found in caves (the more common is calcite), usually in the form of needle-like crystals.

BACON OR BACON RIND. Speleothem made up of a thin sheet of calcite with alternating bands of color. The brown or darker bands are usually caused by iron oxide.

BASALT. A common type of lava, in which lava tubes form.

BEDDING PLANE. The surface or boundary that divides two adjacent beds of sedimentary rock (such as limestone).

BELAY. A method of protecting a climber in case of a fall. A rope is tied around the first caver (the climber) or to a harness on the first caver, so that the second caver (the belayer), who is securely anchored, can stop a fall. In Britain, this is sometimes known as safetying or life lining.

BELAY-IS-ON. The call used by the belayer to tell the climber that the belayer is ready to belay and the climber is now protected.

BELAY-IS-OFF. After a climber has reached a safe spot, and has called off-belay, the belayer relaxes and indicates protection has ended by answering *belay is off*.

BINER. Colloquial for carabiner. The British slang term is krab.

BLOWING CAVE. A cave that has large air currents moving in or out for extended periods. Changes in barometric pressure are believed to be the cause.

BOXWORK. Honeycomb-like speleothem of calcite projecting from a cave wall or ceiling.

BOWLINE. A knot used to form a nonslipping loop; one of the basic knots any caver should know. *See* knots.

BREAKDOWN. Large piles of rocks and boulders that have fallen from the ceiling or walls at an earlier time in the cave's geologic history.

CABLE LADDER. *See* ladder.

CALCITE. The most common cave mineral, a crystalline form of calcium carbonate.

CANYON HOPPING. *See* straddling.

CARABINER. An oval-shaped, aluminum-alloy or steel link with a spring-loaded gate in one side, used in climbing and rappelling. Sometimes equipped with a locking sleeve and called a locking carabiner (or, in Britain, a screwgate carabiner). Spelled karabiner in Britain. Slang terms are *biner* in America, *krab* in Britain.

CARBIDE LAMP. A miner's lamp used by cavers. Acetylene gas produced by mixing water with carbide is ignited and burns at a jet positioned in a reflector.

CARBONIC ACID. A weak acid made from carbon dioxide and rain or soil water that slowly dissolves limestone to form caves.

CAVE. A natural void beneath the earth, usually made up of several rooms and passages.

CAVE FORMATION. *See* speleothem.

CAVE ICE. Year round ice formed in some caves, especially lava tubes.

CAVE SPRING. *See* resurgence.

CHIMNEY. 1: A vertical or near-vertical shaft, either tubular or simply where two walls come close together; 2: climbing up or down such a shaft by means of pressure on both surfaces by back and feet.

CLEAR-OF-THE-DROP? A question shouted down a drop before lowering a rope or ladder.

CLIMBING. Caving movement used in pits, fissures, and cave walls; involves three points of contact and other classic rock climbing techniques. Also, the call *climbing* is used by a climber to indicate that a climb has actually begun so the belayer can pay out or take in the belay rope.

CLIMBING CALLS. Signals used between cavers during climbing, and to a smaller extent during technical rope work (rappelling and prusiking), such as *belay-is-on, climbing, tension,* and so forth. The ones listed here are only suggested. Many local variations are in common use.

COLUMN. A speleothem formed where a hanging stalactite and a rising stalagmite have grown together.

CORKSCREW PASSAGE. A twisting passage, often a tight crawlway or fissure, either horizontal or vertical.

rack. Today, cavers usually rappel into a pit, then come out by prusiking, or in short drops, by a ladder.

RAPPEL RACK. A multi-carabiner descending device, primarily for medium and long drops.

READY-ON-BELAY. A climber uses this call to tell the belayer that he or she is tied into the belay rope. Often shortened to on-belay. The belayer answers, when ready, with belay-is-on.

READY-TO-CLIMB. Call used by climber after belayer has indicated that belay-is-on and climber is protected.

RESURGENCE. Point where a cave stream reappears on the surface.

ROCK. Shout this loud and clear the instant you dislodge anything down a drop or pit.

ROPE. Before lowering a rope (or ladder), ask if the drop is clear, then shout rope!

RIMSTONE. A crusty calcite deposit at the edge of a lake or series of pools.

RUNNER. A sling used to attach a rope or ladder to an anchor.

SAFETY. See belay.

SCRAMBLE. A half-crawling, half-climbing movement used to negotiate steep or muddy slopes.

SEA CAVE. A void or cavity in rock along a shore caused by wave action.

SEAT HARNESS. Used for rappelling, prusiking, and belays. Usually made of 2-inch (50-millimeter) webbing with a waistband and separate leg loops. The best (and safest) are sewn at all joints.

SHELTER CAVE. A cavity in any kind of rock offering shelter from the weather.

SINK. A depression, often 30 to 100 feet or more across, caused by collapse of a cave passage below the surface of the ground.

SLACK. Call used by a climber to have the belay rope loosened somewhat.

SLOVENIAN KARST. Area around Postonja in northern Yugoslavia, the so-called "Mother Karst," where many of the original scientific studies of cave development were done.

SNAPLINK. See carabiner.

SLING. Short (8- to 20-foot, 3- to 6-meter) piece of flat nylon material (or 7- to 9-millimeter Perlon cord), used to attach ropes and ladders to anchors, or to attach safety lines, rappelling devices, and ascenders to cavers.

SODA STRAW. A thin, hollow form of stalactite from which water drips and deposits calcite at the tip.

SOLUTION TUBE. Type of passage developed by dissolving action. Usually of nearly tubular proportions.

SQUEEZE. An extremely tight passage. Also squeezeway.

SPELEOGENESIS. The origin and development of caves.

SPELEOTHEM. Generic name for cave deposits of calcite, aragonite a[nd]

CREVICE. A narrow opening or fissure in the floor of a cave, often 10 to 50 feet or more deep; also a high, narrow passage.

DEAD CAVE. A cave in which the speleothems have stopped growing because water is no longer seeping into the cave.

DIAPER SLING. A common, but unsafe, harness for rappelling usually made of 1-inch nylon webbing. A separate, redundant waist loop can add the necessary safety factor in case the diaper might break and unwind.

DIG. An attempt to break into a cave or a new area of a known cave by excavation, and in some cases blasting.

DOLOMITE. A sedimentary rock similar to but less common than limestone in which caves can occur.

DOMEPIT. A large, dome-shaped cavity above a room or passage, created by solution, not breakdown.

DRAPERY. A thin, curtain-shaped speleothem caused by a sheet of dripping water rather than a single series of drops.

DRIPSTONE. Any of several calcite deposits caused by dripping water, including stalactites, stalagmites, and flowstone.

DROP. A descending slope, pitch, or pit.

DUCKUNDER. A place in a stream passage or lake room where the ceiling comes down into the water causing a caver to duck under for a few feet. Extremely hazardous and not for beginners.

EXPANSION BOLT. A type of anchor for ropes and ladders. It is placed into a hole drilled into limestone and expands as it is driven in. Typically, a ⅜-inch (9-millimeter) bolt has a working load (25 percent of test load) of about 1550 pound (700 kilograms).

EXPOSURE. See hypothermia.

FALLING! An emergency cry for help from climber to belayer.

FALSE FLOOR. A thin floor made of calcite or lava under which dirt or gravel has been worked away.

FIGURE-OF-EIGHT KNOT. A versatile knot with several forms. Has become almost as popular as the bowline for modern nylon ropes. It is the recommended knot for tying a loop in the middle of the rope as well as several other applications.

FILL. Clay, mud, rock, or other material found on the floor of a cave.

FISSURE. A narrow crack, break, or fracture. Fissures (and crevices) are usually negotiated by chimneying or traversing movements.

FREE OR FREE CLIMBING. Term used by rock climbers to signify climbing without artificial aids such as slings (runners), wedges, nuts, or pitons. However, rock climbers are normally belayed on all but the simplest climbs, whether free or aided by hardware.

FLOWSTONE. A coating of calcite deposited by flowing water.

FLUTE, STREAM. Scallop-like ripples in a cave wall caused by stream action.

FORMATION. See speleothem.

GIBBS ASCENDER. A device used for prusiking up a rope, in a technique called rope walking.

GRAPEVINE KNOT. The recommended knot for tying Perlon slings together. Also commonly called the double fisherman's knot.

GROTTO. A small room or chamber opening off of a larger one. Also, a local chapter of the National Speleological Society.

GUANO. In cave terminology, bat dung. A very rich fertilizer.

GYPSUM. A sedimentary rock (primarily calcium sulphate), which is softer and more soluble than limestone. Sizable caves can occur in gypsum.

GYPSUM FLOWERS AND HAIR. Varieties of delicate gypsum speleothems, often of great beauty.

HARNESS. See seat harness.

HAND LINE. A short (10 to 30-foot—3 to 10-meter) fixed rope (tied at the top) used for climbing or scrambling on steep pitches when holds are scarce.

HAWSER ROPE. British term for laid or three-strand rope.

HELECTITE. A beautiful, twisting speleothem that seems to grow in defiance of the laws of gravity.

HOLD, HAND OR FOOT. Small ledge, knob, or crevice that can provide assistance in climbing, scrambling, or chimneying.

HYDROLOGY. Scientific study of underground and surface water.

HYPOTHERMIA. A dangerous condition caused by wet and cold where body heat is being lost rapidly. Lack of food can accelerate the effects. Can kill if not checked. Sometimes known as exposure.

ICE CAVE. A type of cave, usually in lava, which contains ice all year.

JOINT. A crack, usually formed at right angles to the bedding plane in limestone.

JUMAR ASCENDER. A device for prusiking up a rope.

JUNCTION. A place where two or more passages come together.

KARST. Terrain with many sinkholes, disappearing streams, underground drainage, and caves. See Slovenian karst.

KARABINER. British spelling of carabiner.

KERNMANTEL. The most common type of nylon climbing rope. Made of a core (kern) of straight, twisted, or braided nylon filament covered by an outer sheath (mantel) of braided nylon. Laid or three-stranded rope (called hawser in Britain) is the other, less common type.

KEYHOLE. A keyhole shaped passage, usually tight.

KNOTS. The basic caving knots recommended are: bowline, figure-of-eight, grapevine, Prusik, and water knot.

KRAB. British slang term for carabiner.

LADDER. Caving ladders, made of aircraft cable and aluminum rungs, are used for climbing out of 10- to 30-foot (3- to 10-meter) pits. Deeper pits are more commonly prusiked now.

LAID ROPE. Made of three main strands of continuous filament nylon. N[ow] less common than kernmantel ropes, but Goldline mountain-laid rope[s are] still widely used by American cavers.

LAVA TUBE. A type of cave formed in lava as it cools. Often nearly circu[lar] in cross section.

LEAD. A side passage, often small or obscure, hopefully leading to more cav[e].

LIVE CAVE. A cave with speleothems still being developed by water.

LIMESTONE. A rock composed primarily of calcium carbonate and readi[ly] dissolved by carbonic acid. Most caves are formed in limestone.

LOST RIVER. A stream that runs underground for some of its length.

MARBLE. Limestone later subjected to heat and pressure. Many caves occ[ur] in marble.

MOON MILK. Whitish, puttylike form of flowstone.

MOVE. During a climb, an individual movement or step progressing to t[he] next position.

NUT, CLIMBING. See wedge.

ON-BELAY. See ready-on-belay.

OFF-BELAY. A climber uses this call to tell the belayer that a safe positi[on] has been reached. Belayer will usually answer belay-is-off.

OFF-ROPE. Call or shout up or down the drop indicating the rope is free [for] the next person to use. Climber has now untied or unfastened person[al] equipment from the rope.

PERLON ACCESSORY CORD. 4- to 8-millimeter kernmantel rope for slin[gs]. Perlon is the European generic term for nylon.

PINCH-OUT. In caver talk, a passage that tapers down and becomes too sm[all] to penetrate.

PIT. A more or less tubular hole. Also loosely applied to crevices and fissur[es]. A number of caves have pit entrances resulting from breakdown, do[me] pit solution, or stream action.

PITCH. A steep ascent or descent. A long climb is frequently divided i[nto] several pitches.

PITON. Used in rock climbing (but rarely in caving), a flat spikelike dev[ice] with a carabiner eye in one end that is driven into a crack in the ro[ck]. Also called pins or, in Britain, pegs.

PRUSIK KNOT. A basic caving knot used primarily for climbing up a fix[ed] rope. Easily moved upward, but when weight or tension is applied[,] holds fast.

PRUSIKING. Method of climbing out of a pit, crevice, or fissure using Pru[sik] knots or mechanical ascenders on a fixed rope with slings attached to [feet] and chest. Used for pits from 25 to 1000 feet or more.

RAPPELLING. Method of safely sliding down a fixed rope using for exampl[e] Figure—8 or Longhorn descender, carabiners with brake bars, or a rap[pel] gypsum. Includes stalactites, stalagmites, columns, drapery, flowstone, rimstone, gypsum flowers, helectites, and others caused by deposition.

SPELUNKER. A term used to describe a caver. Not generally favored by cavers or used by them.

STALACTITE. A hanging speleothem formed by calcite in dripping water.

STALAGMITE. A calcite deposit built upward from the floor by dripping water.

STRADDLING. Bridging across a narrow canyon or pit with arms and legs on opposite walls.

SWALLET OR SWALLOW HOLE. The point where a stream disappears in karst country.

SWAMI SEAT. An excellent seat harness, tied with knots, rather than sewn, to provide separate waist and leg loops. Safer than an unsecured diaper sling or unsewn Texas seat.

TALUS CAVE. An underground cavity formed by falling rock or where soil has been washed away between large boulders.

TAPE. British term for webbing.

TENSION. Climbing call used when climber wants the belay rope tighter.

TEXAS SEAT SLING. An easily adjusted seat harness often made from 2-inch (50-millimeter) nylon webbing. Leg loops are formed by metal clips. Although comfortable, it lacks sewn joints, so could unravel if it broke (as can a diaper sling).

TROGLODYTE. An animal, including the human, who lives in a cave.

TRAVERTINE. A course type of flowstone, formed by calcite in water flowing over a surface.

TUBE. *See* solution tube and lava tube.

UP ROPE. Climbing call to indicate rope is ready to be pulled up.

WALK-IN CAVE. A cave with a large entrance, often, but not always, with large, walking passages inside.

WATER KNOT. The recommended knot for tying webbing into a loop. Also called webbing knot and tape knot.

WATER TABLE. Top or highest level of underground water in a given area. Below this level, cavities and voids may be flooded.

WEBBING. Tubular nylon, usually the 1-inch (25-millimeter) size, used for slings and runners. Called tape in Britain.

WEDGE, CLIMBING. A new type of easy-to-place and easy-to-remove rope anchor used by rock climbers and only rarely by cavers. Most have a hole to attach a rope or sling. Also called a climbing nut or chock.

WILD CAVE. An undeveloped cave in its natural state, in contrast to a commercial cave where lighting and paths have been added.

WINDOW. A hole in the ceiling of a lava tube passage, usually from bubbling or pressure of the lava. In a limestone cave, usually from breakdown.

CREVICE. A narrow opening or fissure in the floor of a cave, often 10 to 50 feet or more deep; also a high, narrow passage.

DEAD CAVE. A cave in which the speleothems have stopped growing because water is no longer seeping into the cave.

DIAPER SLING. A common, but unsafe, harness for rappelling usually made of 1-inch nylon webbing. A separate, redundant waist loop can add the necessary safety factor in case the diaper might break and unwind.

DIG. An attempt to break into a cave or a new area of a known cave by excavation, and in some cases blasting.

DOLOMITE. A sedimentary rock similar to but less common than limestone in which caves can occur.

DOMEPIT. A large, dome-shaped cavity above a room or passage, created by solution, not breakdown.

DRAPERY. A thin, curtain-shaped speleothem caused by a sheet of dripping water rather than a single series of drops.

DRIPSTONE. Any of several calcite deposits caused by dripping water, including stalactites, stalagmites, and flowstone.

DROP. A descending slope, pitch, or pit.

DUCKUNDER. A place in a stream passage or lake room where the ceiling comes down into the water causing a caver to duck under for a few feet. Extremely hazardous and not for beginners.

EXPANSION BOLT. A type of anchor for ropes and ladders. It is placed into a hole drilled into limestone and expands as it is driven in. Typically, a ⅜-inch (9-millimeter) bolt has a working load (25 percent of test load) of about 1550 pound (700 kilograms).

EXPOSURE. *See* hypothermia.

FALLING! An emergency cry for help from climber to belayer.

FALSE FLOOR. A thin floor made of calcite or lava under which dirt or gravel has been worked away.

FIGURE-OF-EIGHT KNOT. A versatile knot with several forms. Has become almost as popular as the bowline for modern nylon ropes. It is the recommended knot for tying a loop in the middle of the rope as well as several other applications.

FILL. Clay, mud, rock, or other material found on the floor of a cave.

FISSURE. A narrow crack, break, or fracture. Fissures (and crevices) are usually negotiated by chimneying or traversing movements.

FREE OR FREE CLIMBING. Term used by rock climbers to signify climbing without artificial aids such as slings (runners), wedges, nuts, or pitons. However, rock climbers are normally belayed on all but the simplest climbs, whether free or aided by hardware.

FLOWSTONE. A coating of calcite deposited by flowing water.

FLUTE, STREAM. Scallop-like ripples in a cave wall caused by stream action.

FORMATION. *See* speleothem.

GIBBS ASCENDER. A device used for prusiking up a rope, in a technique called rope walking.

GRAPEVINE KNOT. The recommended knot for tying Perlon slings together. Also commonly called the double fisherman's knot.

GROTTO. A small room or chamber opening off of a larger one. Also, a local chapter of the National Speleological Society.

GUANO. In cave terminology, bat dung. A very rich fertilizer.

GYPSUM. A sedimentary rock (primarily calcium sulphate), which is softer and more soluble than limestone. Sizable caves can occur in gypsum.

GYPSUM FLOWERS AND HAIR. Varieties of delicate gypsum speleothems, often of great beauty.

HARNESS. *See* seat harness.

HAND LINE. A short (10 to 30-foot—3 to 10-meter) fixed rope (tied at the top) used for climbing or scrambling on steep pitches when holds are scarce.

HAWSER ROPE. British term for laid or three-strand rope.

HELECTITE. A beautiful, twisting speleothem that seems to grow in defiance of the laws of gravity.

HOLD, HAND OR FOOT. Small ledge, knob, or crevice that can provide assistance in climbing, scrambling, or chimneying.

HYDROLOGY. Scientific study of underground and surface water.

HYPOTHERMIA. A dangerous condition caused by wet and cold where body heat is being lost rapidly. Lack of food can accelerate the effects. Can kill if not checked. Sometimes known as exposure.

ICE CAVE. A type of cave, usually in lava, which contains ice all year.

JOINT. A crack, usually formed at right angles to the bedding plane in limestone.

JUMAR ASCENDER. A device for prusiking up a rope.

JUNCTION. A place where two or more passages come together.

KARST. Terrain with many sinkholes, disappearing streams, underground drainage, and caves. *See* Slovenian karst.

KARABINER. British spelling of carabiner.

KERNMANTEL. The most common type of nylon climbing rope. Made of a core (kern) of straight, twisted, or braided nylon filament covered by an outer sheath (mantel) of braided nylon. Laid or three-stranded rope (called hawser in Britain) is the other, less common type.

KEYHOLE. A keyhole shaped passage, usually tight.

KNOTS. The basic caving knots recommended are: bowline, figure-of-eight, grapevine, Prusik, and water knot.

KRAB. British slang term for carabiner.

LADDER. Caving ladders, made of aircraft cable and aluminum rungs, are used for climbing out of 10- to 30-foot (3- to 10-meter) pits. Deeper pits are more commonly prusiked now.

LAID ROPE. Made of three main strands of continuous filament nylon. Now less common than kernmantel ropes, but Goldline mountain-laid rope is still widely used by American cavers.

LAVA TUBE. A type of cave formed in lava as it cools. Often nearly circular in cross section.

LEAD. A side passage, often small or obscure, hopefully leading to more cave.

LIVE CAVE. A cave with speleothems still being developed by water.

LIMESTONE. A rock composed primarily of calcium carbonate and readily dissolved by carbonic acid. Most caves are formed in limestone.

LOST RIVER. A stream that runs underground for some of its length.

MARBLE. Limestone later subjected to heat and pressure. Many caves occur in marble.

MOON MILK. Whitish, puttylike form of flowstone.

MOVE. During a climb, an individual movement or step progressing to the next position.

NUT, CLIMBING. *See* wedge.

ON-BELAY. *See* ready-on-belay.

OFF-BELAY. A climber uses this call to tell the belayer that a safe position has been reached. Belayer will usually answer *belay-is-off.*

OFF-ROPE. Call or shout up or down the drop indicating the rope is free for the next person to use. Climber has now untied or unfastened person or equipment from the rope.

PERLON ACCESSORY CORD. 4- to 8-millimeter kernmantel rope for slings. Perlon is the European generic term for nylon.

PINCH-OUT. In caver talk, a passage that tapers down and becomes too small to penetrate.

PIT. A more or less tubular hole. Also loosely applied to crevices and fissures. A number of caves have pit entrances resulting from breakdown, dome pit solution, or stream action.

PITCH. A steep ascent or descent. A long climb is frequently divided into several pitches.

PITON. Used in rock climbing (but rarely in caving), a flat spikelike device with a carabiner eye in one end that is driven into a crack in the rock. Also called pins or, in Britain, pegs.

PRUSIK KNOT. A basic caving knot used primarily for climbing up a fixed rope. Easily moved upward, but when weight or tension is applied, it holds fast.

PRUSIKING. Method of climbing out of a pit, crevice, or fissure using Prusik knots or mechanical ascenders on a fixed rope with slings attached to feet and chest. Used for pits from 25 to 1000 feet or more.

RAPPELLING. Method of safely sliding down a fixed rope using for example a Figure–8 or Longhorn descender, carabiners with brake bars, or a rappel rack. Today, cavers usually rappel into a pit, then come out by prusiking, or in short drops, by a ladder.

RAPPEL RACK. A multi-carabiner descending device, primarily for medium and long drops.

READY-ON-BELAY. A climber uses this call to tell the belayer that he or she is tied into the belay rope. Often shortened to *on-belay.* The belayer answers, when ready, with *belay-is-on.*

READY-TO-CLIMB. Call used by climber after belayer has indicated that belay-is-on and climber is protected.

RESURGENCE. Point where a cave stream reappears on the surface.

ROCK. Shout this loud and clear the instant you dislodge *anything* down a drop or pit.

ROPE. Before lowering a rope (or ladder), ask if the drop is clear, then shout *rope!*

RIMSTONE. A crusty calcite deposit at the edge of a lake or series of pools.

RUNNER. A sling used to attach a rope or ladder to an anchor.

SAFETY. *See* belay.

SCRAMBLE. A half-crawling, half-climbing movement used to negotiate steep or muddy slopes.

SEA CAVE. A void or cavity in rock along a shore caused by wave action.

SEAT HARNESS. Used for rappelling, prusiking, and belays. Usually made of 2-inch (50-millimeter) webbing with a waistband and separate leg loops. The best (and safest) are sewn at all joints.

SHELTER CAVE. A cavity in any kind of rock offering shelter from the weather.

SINK. A depression, often 30 to 100 feet or more across, caused by collapse of a cave passage below the surface of the ground.

SLACK. Call used by a climber to have the belay rope loosened somewhat.

SLOVENIAN KARST. Area around Postonja in northern Yugoslavia, the so-called "Mother Karst," where many of the original scientific studies of cave development were done.

SNAPLINK. *See* carabiner.

SLING. Short (8- to 20-foot, 3- to 6-meter) piece of flat nylon material (or 7- to 9-millimeter Perlon cord), used to attach ropes and ladders to anchors, or to attach safety lines, rappelling devices, and ascenders to cavers.

SODA STRAW. A thin, hollow form of stalactite from which water drips and deposits calcite at the tip.

SOLUTION TUBE. Type of passage developed by dissolving action. Usually of nearly tubular proportions.

SQUEEZE. An extremely tight passage. Also squeezeway.

SPELEOGENESIS. The origin and development of caves.

SPELEOTHEM. Generic name for cave deposits of calcite, aragonite and gypsum. Includes stalactites, stalagmites, columns, drapery, flowstone, rimstone, gypsum flowers, helectites, and others caused by deposition.

SPELUNKER. A term used to describe a caver. Not generally favored by cavers or used by them.

STALACTITE. A hanging speleothem formed by calcite in dripping water.

STALAGMITE. A calcite deposit built upward from the floor by dripping water.

STRADDLING. Bridging across a narrow canyon or pit with arms and legs on opposite walls.

SWALLET OR SWALLOW HOLE. The point where a stream disappears in karst country.

SWAMI SEAT. An excellent seat harness, tied with knots, rather than sewn, to provide separate waist and leg loops. Safer than an unsecured diaper sling or unsewn Texas seat.

TALUS CAVE. An underground cavity formed by falling rock or where soil has been washed away between large boulders.

TAPE. British term for webbing.

TENSION. Climbing call used when climber wants the belay rope tighter.

TEXAS SEAT SLING. An easily adjusted seat harness often made from 2-inch (50-millimeter) nylon webbing. Leg loops are formed by metal clips. Although comfortable, it lacks sewn joints, so could unravel if it broke (as can a diaper sling).

TROGLODYTE. An animal, including the human, who lives in a cave.

TRAVERTINE. A course type of flowstone, formed by calcite in water flowing over a surface.

TUBE. *See* solution tube and lava tube.

UP ROPE. Climbing call to indicate rope is ready to be pulled up.

WALK-IN CAVE. A cave with a large entrance, often, but not always, with large, walking passages inside.

WATER KNOT. The recommended knot for tying webbing into a loop. Also called webbing knot and tape knot.

WATER TABLE. Top or highest level of underground water in a given area. Below this level, cavities and voids may be flooded.

WEBBING. Tubular nylon, usually the 1-inch (25-millimeter) size, used for slings and runners. Called tape in Britain.

WEDGE, CLIMBING. A new type of easy-to-place and easy-to-remove rope anchor used by rock climbers and only rarely by cavers. Most have a hole to attach a rope or sling. Also called a climbing nut or chock.

WILD CAVE. An undeveloped cave in its natural state, in contrast to a commercial cave where lighting and paths have been added.

WINDOW. A hole in the ceiling of a lava tube passage, usually from bubbling or pressure of the lava. In a limestone cave, usually from breakdown.

About the Author

David R. McClurg is an avid caver and a resident of Mountain View, California. Active in the National Speleological Society since 1958, Mr. McClurg has held several offices in that organization, including administrative vice president, director, and chairman of the Program and Activities Committee. Currently, Mr. McClurg is chairman of the NSS Public Relations Committee. He has traveled widely through Europe, including a 1975 caving trip to Yugoslavia. *Exploring Caves: A Guide to the Underground Wilderness* represents a substantial revision of his 1973 work, *Amateur's Guide to Caves and Caving* (Stackpole Books).